MEMOIR

A History

ALSO BY BEN YAGODA

When You Catch an Adjective, Kill It:
The Parts of Speech, for Better and/or Worse

The Sound on the Page: Style and Voice in Writing

About Town: The New Yorker *and the World It Made*

Will Rogers: A Biography

The Art of Fact: A Historical Anthology of Literary Journalism (coeditor)

All in a Lifetime: An Autobiography (with Ruth Westheimer)

MEMOIR

A History

BEN YAGODA

RIVERHEAD BOOKS

a member of Penguin Group (USA) Inc.

New York 2009

RIVERHEAD BOOKS
Published by the Penguin Group
Penguin Group (USA) Inc., 375 Hudson Street, New York, New York 10014, USA • Penguin
Group (Canada), 90 Eglinton Avenue East, Suite 700, Toronto, Ontario M4P 2Y3, Canada
(a division of Pearson Penguin Canada Inc.) • Penguin Books Ltd, 80 Strand, London WC2R 0RL,
England • Penguin Ireland, 25 St Stephen's Green, Dublin 2, Ireland (a division of Penguin Books
Ltd) • Penguin Group (Australia), 250 Camberwell Road, Camberwell, Victoria 3124, Australia
(a division of Pearson Australia Group Pty Ltd) • Penguin Books India Pvt Ltd, 11 Community
Centre, Panchsheel Park, New Delhi–110 017, India • Penguin Group (NZ), 67 Apollo Drive,
Rosedale, North Shore 0632, New Zealand (a division of Pearson New Zealand Ltd) • Penguin
Books (South Africa) (Pty) Ltd, 24 Sturdee Avenue, Rosebank, Johannesburg 2196, South Africa

Penguin Books Ltd, Registered Offices: 80 Strand, London WC2R 0RL, England

The author gratefully acknowledges permission to quote from *An Arsonist's Guide to Writers' Homes in
New England* by Brock Clarke. © 2007 Brock Clarke. Reprinted by permission of Algonquin Books
of Chapel Hill. All rights reserved.

Library of Congress Cataloging-in-Publication Data

Yagoda, Ben.
Memoir : a history / Ben Yagoda.
p.   cm.
Includes index.
ISBN 978-1-59448-886-3
1. Autobiography.   I. Title.
CT25.Y34   2009   2009030859
809'.93592—dc22

Printed in the United States of America
10 9 8 7 6 5 4 3 2 1

Book design by Susan Walsh

While the author has made every effort to provide accurate telephone numbers and Internet addresses
at the time of publication, neither the publisher nor the author assumes any responsibility for errors,
or for changes that occur after publication. Further, the publisher does not have any control over
and does not assume any responsibility for author or third-party websites or their content.

To Gigi

CONTENTS

MEMOIR

A History

BY WAY OF DEFINITION

IN THIS BOOK I USE THE WORDS "memoir" and "autobiography"—
and, on occasion, "memoirs"—to mean more or less the same thing: a
book understood by its author, its publisher, and its readers to be a factual
account of the author's life. (The one clear difference is that while
"autobiography" or "memoirs" usually cover the full span of that life,
"memoir" has been used by books that cover the entirety *or* some portion
of it.) Therefore, the following autobiographical works are not considered: diaries, collections of letters, autobiographical novels, and, for the
most part, any unpublished text.

My interchanging of the terms may seem odd, since in (very) recent
years, the years of *This Boy's Life* and *The Liars' Club* and *Running with
Scissors*, "memoir" has acquired a distinctive sense. A brief stroll through
the history of the words may clarify things. "Autobiography" is unambiguous. It was first used in 1809 and within a couple of decades acquired
its current meaning: a biography of a person written *by* that person. (A

fuller account of the origin of the word is in chapter 3.) "Memoirs" and "memoir," both of which are derived from the French *mémoire*, or "memory," are more complicated. The plural form was and is synonymous with "autobiography"; the *Oxford English Dictionary* cites William Wycherley, who in 1678 referred to "a volume entire to give the world your memoirs, or life at large." "Memoirs" is still in use and is often chosen by statesmen and other eminences—or, as a result, is used ironically, as in Albert Nock's *Memoirs of a Superfluous Man* (1943) and Bernard Wolfe's *Memoirs of a Not Altogether Shy Pornographer* (1972).

Roy Pascal, in his 1960 book *Design and Truth in Autobiography*, succinctly laid out the traditional contrast between autobiography and *s*-less memoir: "In the autobiography proper, attention is focused on the self, in the memoir or reminiscence on others." A well-known, fairly recent example of the latter would be A. E. Hotchner's 1966 *Papa Hemingway: A Personal Memoir*, in which Hotchner is a supporting player and Hemingway the star. That distinction still held sway as late as 1984, when another scholar, Richard Coe, observed that while in an autobiography "it is the writer himself who is the center of interest," in a memoir "the writer is, as a *character*, essentially negative, or at least neutral."

In France, at least, there was also a distinction among the forms in their respective requirements for accuracy and truthfulness. In 1876, Louis-Gustave Vapereau wrote in the *Dictionnaire universel des littératures*: "Autobiography leaves a lot of room to fantasy, and the one who is writing is not at all obliged to be exact about the facts, as in memoirs."

The twenty-first-century memoir, of course, is 180 degrees different. Attention is resolutely focused on the self, and a certain leeway or looseness with the facts is expected. (The gross liberties or outright fabrications perpetrated by James Frey and many other recent fraudulent memoirists are another matter, and will be considered at length in the pages that follow.)

Writing in his 1996 memoir *Palimpsest*, Gore Vidal reversed Vapereau's classifications: "A memoir is how one remembers one's own life, while an autobiography is history, requiring research, dates, facts, double-checked." Another recent memoirist, Nancy Miller, was hardly going out on a limb in describing her possible strategies for writing about an event in her past: "I could write down what I remembered; or I could craft a memoir. One *might* be the truth; the other, a good story. . . . When I sit down to reconstruct my past, I call on memory, but when memory fails, I let language lead. . . . As a writer, the answer to the question of what 'really' happened is literary—or at least textual. I will know it when I write it. When I write it, the truth will lie in the writing. But the writing may not be the truth; it may only look like it. To me." Among other things, this book will try to explain how and why the change took place.

My main approach in seeking the answers to these and other questions is not thematic, theoretical, generic, psychological, moral, or aesthetic, but historical. That is, Rousseau's *Confessions* makes sense only if the earlier tradition of spiritual autobiography is considered, and Frank Conroy's *Stop-Time* makes sense only in the context of Rousseau's *Confessions*. A historical frame of mind is helpful, as well, in corralling the tens of thousands of autobiographies that have been written since the dawn of time into a manageable, useful, and readable narrative. There is no room to consider every memoir, a majority of memoirs, or even a majority of *great* memoirs. (And that is why such exceptional works as Vladimir Nabokov's *Speak, Memory*, Mary McCarthy's *Memories of a Catholic Girlhood*, and Saul Friedlander's *When Memory Comes*, among many others, won't be discussed here.) Pride of place goes to books that memorably or notably did a significant thing first, and thus changed the way the genre was conceived.

Chapter 1

MEMOIR ~~NATION~~ UNIVERSE

As mankind "matures," as it becomes more possible to be frank in the scrutiny of the self and others and in the publication of one's findings, biography and autobiography will take the place of fiction for the investigation and discussion of character.

—H. G. WELLS, *Experiment in Autobiography*, 1934

I moved on to the memoir section. After browsing for a while, I knew why it had to be so big: who knew there was so much truth to be told, so many lessons to teach and learn? Who knew that there were so many people with so many necessary things to say about themselves? I flipped through the sexual abuse memoirs, sexual conquest memoirs, sexual inadequacy memoirs, alternative sexual memoirs, remorseful hedonist rock star memoirs, twelve-step memoirs, memoirs about reading (A Reading Life: Book by Book). *There were five memoirs by one author, a woman who had written a memoir about her troubled relationship with her famous fiction-writer father; a memoir about her troubled relationship with her children; a memoir about her troubled relationship with the bottle; and finally a memoir about her more loving relationship with herself. There were several memoirs about the difficulty of writing memoirs, and even a handful of how-to-write-memoir memoirs:* A Memoirist's Guide to Writing Your Memoir *and the like. All of this made me feel better about myself, and I was grateful to the books for teaching me—without my even having to read them—that there were people in the world more desperate, more self-absorbed, more boring than I was.*

—BROCK CLARKE, *An Arsonist's Guide to Writers' Homes in New England: A Novel,* 2007

I probably, especially had some scorn for memoirs that were about the worst thing that ever happened to you. Then something really, really bad happened to me, and I realized that I needed to write about it.

—ELIZABETH McCRACKEN, author of
An Exact Replica of a Figment of My Imagination: A Memoir,
National Public Radio interview, January 2009

DOG MEMOIRS WERE THE RAGE. It started with the mind-boggling success of John Grogan's 2005 book *Marley & Me: Life and Love with the World's Worst Dog.* That spurred memoirs devoted to Lava, Gus, Bob, Orson, Bodo, Sadie, Merle, Sprite, and two separate dogs named Beau (masters: Anna Quindlen and Mark Doty). Perhaps sensing that the genre was close to exhaustion, Grand Central Publishing paid a reported $1.25 million for the right to publish a book about a rescued cat who lived for nineteen years in a library in a small town in Iowa. (This was actually the second library memoir of the year, following *Free for All: Oddballs, Geeks, and Gangstas in the Public Library,* by Don Borchert.) It was a good business move: *Dewey: The Small-Town Library Cat Who Touched the World* shot to the top of the bestseller lists. There followed memoirs devoted to the authors' relationships with an owl (*Wesley the Owl*) and a parrot (*Alex & Me*). But Marley wasn't done yet. Hollywood's version of his story was the number-one movie of Christmas 2008, and John Grogan himself produced three separate Marley texts for kids—*Bad Dog, Marley!* and *Marley: A Dog Like No Other* and *A Very Marley Christmas*.

As the first decade of the third millennium shambled to its conclusion, canine chronicles were just the tip of the autobiographical iceberg. Even after James Frey got exposed for making up large swaths of his book *A Million Little Pieces: A Memoir*, was dressed down on television by Oprah Winfrey, and was followed by a seemingly endless stream of memoir scandals, the genre seemed to be getting stronger. According to Nielsen BookScan, which tracks about 70 percent of U.S. book sales, total sales in the categories of Personal Memoirs, Childhood Memoirs, and Parental Memoirs increased more than 400 percent between 2004 and 2008. You certainly could not avoid memoir by turning on Oprah's television show. Early in 2007, she chose Sidney Poitier's autobiography, *The Measure of a Man*, for an Oprah's Book Club Selection; the title went on to sell 558,000 copies for the year. One of Oprah's previous selections, Elie Wiesel's venerable Holocaust memoir, *Night*, continued to sell well—so well, in fact, that after a run of eighty consecutive weeks (bringing the total sales figure to some ten million copies), *The New York Times* summarily and rather unsportingly dropped the book from its bestseller list. A member of the *Times Book Review* staff explained to the newspaper's public editor, Clark Hoyt, "The editorial spirit of the list is to track the sales of new books. . . . We simply cannot track such books [as *Night*] indefinitely."

Nor could you escape memoirs by visiting a Starbucks. The second choice for the coffee chain's own book program was Ishmael Beah's *A Long Way Gone: Memoirs of a Boy Soldier*, which sold 116,000 copies in Starbucks stores, and a total of 458,000 for the year. The coffee chain went on to anoint more memoirs, including *The House at Sugar Beach*, American journalist Helene Cooper's reminiscences of her Liberian girlhood; *Crazy for the Storm: A Memoir of Survival*, by Norman Ollestad; *Happens Every Day: An All-Too-True Story*, by Isabel Gillies; and *Beautiful Boy: A Father's Journey Through His Son's Addiction*, by David Sheff. This was not to be confused with *Tweak: Growing Up on Methamphetamines*, written by Nic Sheff, son of David, which went on sale in the same month as his father's book. Or with *Memoirs of a Beautiful Boy*, in which, according to its publisher, "Robert Leleux describes his East Texas boyhood and coming of age under the tutelage of his eccentric, bewigged, flamboyant, and knowing mother." That book could not fail to bring to mind Sean Wilsey, whose 2005 memoir, *Oh the Glory of It All*, focused on *his* eccentric mother, Pat Montandon. Two years later Montandon released her own memoir, *Oh the Hell of It All*, which imitated not only the title but the cover art and design of her son's book. Susanna Sonnenberg, Lee Montgomery, and Mary Gordon also wrote memoirs about their unconventional moms, Gordon's being a companion piece to her 1996 memoir about her troubled dad. Bernard Cooper, Lucinda Franks, Dinah Lenney, and Leslie Garis published memoirs about their difficult relationships with their fathers, and Joan Wickersham one about coming to terms with her father's suicide, but probably the most conflicted father of the moment, memoir division, was Anatole Broyard, the late book critic of *The New York Times*, who had neglected in his own two memoirs, *Kafka Was the Rage* and *Intoxicated by My Illness*, to mention the facts that he was raised by mixed-race parents who were considered (by themselves and the world at large) to be black and that he had spent his adult life passing as white. This task fell to Broyard's daughter, Bliss, who published a memoir that detailed the complicated family history of race and deception. (Not surprisingly, it fell to Bliss Broyard to write a *Times* review of David

Matthews's memoir about growing up with an African-American father and a schizophrenic Jewish mother.) Outselling all of these books, of course, were sportscaster Jim Nantz's and the late Tim Russert's memoirs about their extremely warm and fuzzy relationships with their fathers.

As ubiquitous as memoirs seem in the United States, they are—if there are degrees of ubiquity—even more so in Britain, accounting for seven of the top ten bestselling nonfiction hardcovers in both 2007 and 2008. Almost all successful U.K. memoirs fall into two categories. The first is the "misery memoir": an account, usually by a noncelebrity, of childhood abuse or otherwise painful or difficult circumstances. The genre actually originated in the United States with such works as Dave Pelzer's *A Child Called "It"* and its many sequels, Augusten Burroughs's *Running with Scissors*, and Jeannette Walls's *The Glass Castle*, but has struck a big and highly sensitive nerve in the U.K. over the past decade. The genre has colonized substantial real estate in bookstores, with scores and scores of books, each one with a white or off-white or pale pastel cover containing a staged photograph of a little boy or girl (usually a model rather than the author when young) looking sad. British misery memoirs tend to have brief titles, like *Sickened, Damaged, The Little Prisoner, Broken Wings, Ugly*, and *Beyond Ugly*, except when they consist of complete sentences, as in the similarly titled *Don't Ever Tell; Don't Tell Mummy; Tell Me Why, Mummy; Ma, He Sold Me for a Few Cigarettes;* and *Mum, Can You Lend Me Twenty Quid?*, a memoir by a middle-class teacher whose teenage sons became heroin addicts.

The second category is the life story of a mid-level radio disk jockey, television presenter, athlete, or comedian, or their WAGs, i.e., wives and girlfriends. Thus the top British nonfiction book of 2007 was *On the Edge*, by TV personality Richard Hammond, and number one in 2008 was *At*

My Mother's Knee . . . and Other Low Joints: The Autobiography,[*] by Paul O'Grady, a comedian, followed by the memoirs of Dawn French (comedian), Julie Walters (actress), Michael Parkinson (chat-show host), Alan Carr (comedian), Cliff Richard (singer), and Fern Britton (daytime TV presenter).

While it's true that a number of North American A- or at least B+ listers put out memoirs as the decade neared its end—including not only Sidney Poitier but also Barbara Walters, William Shatner, Carrie Fisher, Quincy Jones, Ted Turner, Hugh Hefner, Christopher Plummer, Tony Curtis, Robert Wagner, and Michael Phelps, whose book was written, typeset, bound, and on the shelves within four months after he was handed his final Olympic gold medal—the continent's readers also were graced with many life stories of the less notable. I shudder to think what a Brit would make of an American bookstore shelf groaning with the autobiographies of Tori Spelling, her mom Candy Spelling, game-show hosts Bob Barker and Tom Bergeron, Howard Stern sidekick Artie Lange, George Hamilton, Madonna's brother, Oprah Winfrey's cousin, teenage singer-actress Miley Cyrus,[†] fifteen-minutes-of-famester Joe the Plumber, *American Idol* loser Sanjaya Malakar, and 1970s and 1980s TV personalities Valerie Bertinelli, Maureen "Marcia Brady" McCormick, Marie Osmond, Cloris Leachman, and Jodie Sweetin (*Full House*), who penned a redemptive memoir about her recovery from methamphetamine addiction.

U.S. memoirs are less dominant on the bestseller lists than their U.K.

[*]British celebrity memoirs are often titled or subtitled *The* (as opposed to *An*) *Autobiography*, the definite article conveying the obligatory nature of such a person's writing such a book.

[†]At sixteen, Cyrus became the second-youngest person to publish an autobiography (by my informal tally), trailing only 1970s child actor Mason Reese, who put one out at age nine. In 2009 came word of an autobiography by *Slumdog Millionaire* star Rubina Ali, nine as well.

counterparts, but they make up for this in breadth. The American memoir is so capacious that it cannot be contained by just one category; this is the time of a million little subgenres. Even more popular than celebrity, misery, canine, methamphetamine, and eccentric-mother memoirs is the one memorably dubbed (by Sarah Goldstein) "shtick lit": that is to say, books perpetrated by people who undertook an unusual project with the express purpose of writing about it. The progenitor was arguably Henry David Thoreau, who in 1845 decided to live in a cabin he built near Walden Pond and document the experience in prose. (Fun fact: Thoreau actually spent two years in the cabin but collapsed them into one for the book, an early example of "the year of" memoir.) There have been numerous examples over the years, including Nellie Bly's *Ten Days in a Mad-House* (1887), for which she pretended to be insane; Jack London's *The People of the Abyss* (1903), for which he pretended to be poor; John Howard Griffin's *Black Like Me* (1961), for which he pretended to be black; George Plimpton's *Paper Lion* (1966), for which he pretended to be a professional football player; and Norah Vincent's *Self-Made Man: One Woman's Journey into Manhood and Back* (2006), for which she pretended to be a man. As these examples suggest, the projects undertaken for such books have tended to grow ever more stuntlike over time. The trend was certainly borne out by the flowering of shtick lit at decade's end. The book that got the most attention—probably because of the excellent photo opportunity of a man wearing a robe and carrying a staff on Manhattan sidewalks—was *The Year of Living Biblically: One Man's Humble Attempt to Follow the Bible as Literally as Possible*, by A. J. Jacobs, who had previously published *The Know-It-All: One's Man's Humble Quest to Become the Smartest Person in the World*, a memoir of his attempt to read the entire *Encyclopædia Britannica*. (Jacobs's works partook of both popular titular conventions for such volumes: a play on the book and movie title *The Year of Living Dangerously* and a subtitle commencing "One Man's/One Woman's . . .") About as derivative as could be was a 2008 tome titled *Reading the OED [Oxford English Dictionary]: One Man, One Year, 21,730 Pages.*

Many of these books had the element of a quest, notably Elizabeth Gilbert's *Eat, Pray, Love*, in which she described her efforts at transcendence by, well, eating, praying, and loving in exotic locales; Nielsen Book-Scan has counted more than four million copies sold. There was also *Dishwasher: One Man's Quest to Wash Dishes in All Fifty States; Nine Ways to Cross a River*, in which the author, Akiko Busch, describes swimming across, yes, nine rivers; *The Geography of Bliss: One Grump's Search for the Happiest Places in the World; Cabin Pressure: One Man's Desperate Attempt to Recapture His Youth as a Camp Counselor*; and books that recounted the authors' attempts to master the games of bridge and pocket billiards. Others documented a period of time (usually a Thoreauvian year) spent under self-imposed limitations or other behavioral requirement. Thus *Animal, Vegetable, Miracle: A Year of Food Life* was about the effort of Barbara Kingsolver and her family to eat only home-grown or local food for a year. It was joined by:

- *A Year Without "Made in China": One Family's True Life Adventure in the Global Economy*
- *Plenty: One Man, One Woman, and a Raucous Year of Eating Locally*
- *Not Buying It: My Year Without Shopping*
- *The Big Turnoff: Confessions of a TV-Addicted Mom Trying to Raise a TV-Free Kid*
- *Helping Me Help Myself: One Skeptic, Ten Self-Help Gurus, and a Year on the Brink of the Comfort Zone*

Norah Vincent's return to the genre brought it, full circle, back to Nellie Bly: *Voluntary Madness: My Year Lost and Found in the Loony Bin*. Julie Powell had a progression that in its typicalness was somehow archetypal: several years earlier she created a blog devoted to her attempt to spend a year cooking recipes only from Julia Child's *Mastering the Art of French Cooking*. Then she published a memoir based on the blog— *Julie & Julia: 365 Days, 524 Recipes, 1 Tiny Apartment Kitchen*. Powell then wrote another memoir, about her experience learning to be a butcher, which was scheduled to be published to coincide with the release of Nora Ephron's movie adaptation of *Julie* [Amy Adams] *& Julia* [Meryl Streep]. Powell's second book inevitably recalls Bill Buford's memoir of working with chef Mario Batali, *Heat*. Child's own memoir, *My Life in France*, was posthumously published in 2006; this was followed by a memoir from her editor, Judith Jones, and one from Child's chef and TV producer. There was also a memoir by cookbook author Marcella Hazan, the fourth memoir by food editor and writer Ruth Reichl, and a food-related memoir by Maya Angelou. That was Angelou's eighth memoir overall since *I Know Why the Caged Bird Sings* appeared in 1969. That may or may not be a record, depending on how one classifies the books Shirley MacLaine has written chronicling her past, present, and future lives, the eleventh of which came out in 2007.

Other popular autobiographical subgenres emerged for reasons similar, presumably, to the simultaneous discovery of calculus by Newton and Leibniz. Something was in the air. How else could one explain the popularity of the dad memoir (being, as opposed to possessing, one), seen in books titled *Alternadad: The True Story of One Family's Struggle to Raise a Cool Kid in America*; *Dadditude: How a Real Man Became a Real Dad*; *Dinner with Dad: How I Found My Way Back to the Family Table*; *Backcast: Fatherhood, Fly-fishing and a River Journey Through the Heart of Alaska*;

China Ghosts: My Daughter's Journey to America, My Passage to Father-hood; and *Punk Rock Dad: No Rules, Just Real Life?* Similarly, it would be hard to come up with a reason for the sudden explosion of autobiographies about autistic spectrum disorders. It just seemed to happen, with books about raising autistic children by Jenny McCarthy, Cathleen Lewis, Charlotte Moore, and Rupert Isaacson, one by Karl Taro Greenfeld about having an autistic brother, and memoirs about life with autism or Asperger's by Daniel Tammet, husband and wife Jerry and Mary Newport, and John Elder Robison, the brother of *Running with Scissors'* Augusten Burroughs. Burroughs himself published his fourth memoir, about his father, in 2008; later that year, his *mother*, Margaret Robison, signed a contract to write a memoir of her own. Both of these were part of the trend of memoirs by successful memoirists' relatives, as were the memoirs written by Frank McCourt's brothers Malachy and Alphie.

Not that autobiographical one-offs have not been plenty plentiful. They've included memoirs about dissecting a cadaver, growing up in an immigrant Vietnamese family in Michigan, being a waitress at a fancy Manhattan restaurant, being a fan of the New York Giants football team and being a fan of the rock group Guided by Voices (those are two separate books by two separate authors), being a deaf Peace Corps volunteer in Africa, spending from 1950 and 1952 at the polio rehabilitation hospital established by Franklin Roosevelt in Warm Springs, Georgia, building public schools in rural Pakistan and Afghanistan, being twins separated at birth and finding each other half a lifetime later, being kidnapped and held for ransom one night in 1998, being a brain scientist who suffered a stroke, being (as the memoir's title put it) a "mean little deaf queer," being the brother of a well-known author who committed suicide, being the addicted and troubled brother of a moderately well known deceased writer-editor, and being the son of that writer-editor's boss, not to mention a

sufferer of agoraphobia, claustrophobia, and elevator, tunnel, bridge, fly-
ing, and parking lot phobia. (The authors are, respectively, Christine
Montross, Bich Minh Nguyen, Phoebe Damrosch, Roger Director, John
Sellers, Josh Swiller, Susan Richards Shreve, Greg Mortenson, Elyse
Schein and Paula Bernstein, Stanley Alpert, Jill Bolte Taylor, Terry Gal-
loway, Christopher Lukas, Steve Geng, and Allen Shawn.)

On the other hand, many memoirs were in keeping with very old
traditions. The first autobiography ever written, according to some
counts, was Saint Augustine's *Confessions*. Since then, noteworthy spiri-
tual autobiographies have been written by Saint Teresa of Ávila, Jonathan
Edwards, John Henry Cardinal Newman, and, in our own time, Denise
Jackson (who is the wife of country music singer Alan Jackson but is referring to God in the title of her book, *It's All About Him*), football coach
Tony Dungy, former boxer George Foreman, screenwriter Joe Eszterhas,
Christian singer Amy Grant, and Britney Spears's mother, Lynne Spears.[*]
The most successful spiritual memoir of the moment was by a preacher
who says he was hit by a truck, saw heaven, and came back to life. The
story of that experience, *Ninety Minutes in Heaven*, had sold more than 1.4
million copies as of the middle of 2009, according to BookScan. Other
spiritual memoirs were *Easter Everywhere*, about growing up as the daugh-

---

[*]Mrs. Spears was putting the finishing touches on her book, to be called *Pop Culture Mom: A Real Story of Fame and Family in a Tabloid World*, when word came out that her other daughter, Jamie Lynn, sixteen and the star of a wholesome Disney Channel television series, was pregnant. Her publisher, Thomas Nelson Inc., which specializes in Christian fare, issued a press release with the heading "LYNNE SPEARS' BOOK IS NOT A PARENTING HOW-TO/Contrary to Media Reports, *Pop Culture Mom* Is a Memoir—and a Warning." In the release, the president of the company was quoted as saying, "We believe in redemption. Therefore, we are standing with Lynne and her family during this difficult time. Though the book has been delayed, we believe God is at work. The story is still being written, and we are confident in His ability to turn ashes into beauty (Isaiah 61:3)." The book was eventually published, with a different title—*Through the Storm*—and without cataclysmic consequences. Early in 2009, rumors swirled that Britney Spears had signed up to write a memoir of her own. Press accounts rarely noted that this would actually be her second memoir, the first having been published when she was eighteen.

ter of a Lutheran minister; *The Water Will Hold You*, about a skeptic who learns to pray; and *Leaving Church*, about an Episcopal priest who takes over a country church, only to find that her fantasy of running a rural parish is unrealistic. Two books by women who escaped polygamous marriages in fundamentalist Mormon sects were sort of antireligious memoirs, as was Shalom Auslander's *Foreskin's Lament: A Memoir*, a painfully funny (or funnily painful) account of his disaffection with the Orthodox Jewish religion in which he was raised. Tagline: "That's so god." On the other hand, Antony Flew published *There Is a God: How the World's Most Notorious Atheist Changed His Mind*. Mary Karr, author of the neo-memoir classic *The Liars' Club* and its sequel, *Cherry*, told *The New York Times*, "I'm working on my third memoir, *Lit*, which concerns my journey from blackbelt sinner and lifelong agnostic to unlikely Catholic (maybe not the Pope's favorite, but still an on-my-knees spouter of praise and beggar for favors)." Brian Welch (a.k.a. Head), the former lead guitarist of the rock group Korn, also published his autobiography. In an interview with *Newsweek*, Welch explained his motivation: "I would love people to know God; I want people to know what I've found. It's really personal. It's, like, real. God is not some mean old man in the sky. He's not far away, he's near. He's with us on Earth; he opens your life."

The rock-star memoir was abundant in the late 2000s—oddly so, given the widespread belief that rock fans are not the most enthusiastic readers. Besides Head's opus, there were entries by Eric Clapton, Ronnie Wood of the Rolling Stones, Slash of Guns N' Roses, Nikki Sixx of Mötley Crüe, AC/DC's Brian Johnson, Eminem, and veteran producer Joe Boyd. In the rock-star muse subcategory, Pattie Boyd (who was married to both Clapton and George Harrison), Catherine James (who dated and/or married Jackson Browne, Bob Dylan, and other luminaries), and Johnny Cash's first wife, Vivian, all told their stories. So did Lance Bass, formerly of the boy band 'N Sync, who has since come out as gay. "I've been asked too many times to write a book by the fans," Bass commented. "And it was very, I don't know, like, therapeutic, writing this book. Because the whole time, with 'NSync especially, it went by just so fast, it was like a blur. There was a lot of different things that I didn't realize were going on." Chuck Panozzo, the gay bass player for the '70s rock band Styx, put forth a memoir as well. (Other famous or semifamous gay memoirists were actors Farley Granger and Rupert Everett; Mike Jones, the male escort who outed preacher Ted Haggard; John Amaechi, the first NBA player to publicly acknowledge his homosexuality; and Renée Richards, born Richard Raskind, who had briefly played on the women's tennis tour after a sex-change operation and written her first autobiography back in 1986.) Looking toward the future, Keith Richards of the Rolling Stones signed a $7.3 million deal to write a memoir. Much of the discussion centered on how much of his past Richards could and would remember. The publisher of Little, Brown did not meet with the guitarist but read a ten-page excerpt, and said, "Seeing what was on the page allayed any concerns." The text, he continued, "had a clarity and vividness which I envy."

Even more and even more unaccountably numerous than rock-star memoirs were ones by politicians, and Richards's fee was in keeping with what heavy-hitting statesmen have been getting. The all-time record is generally agreed to be the $10 million Bill Clinton received for *My Life*, and for a time second place was held by former Federal Reserve Board chairman Alan Greenspan, who got $8.5 million for *The Age of Turbulence*, published in 2007. He was nudged into third by Tony Blair, the former prime minister of Britain, who agreed to write his autobiography for a reported advance of around $9 million. (Spookily, the same week as the announcement, Simon & Schuster published *The Ghost* by Robert Harris, a thriller about a Blair-like former British prime minister who sells his memoirs for $10 million.) Senator Edward Kennedy announced the sale of his own book the following month but couldn't quite match the advance: his reported figure was $8 million. Fetching even more modest prices were such Bush administration figures as Karl Rove, Condoleezza Rice, Donald Rumsfeld, Laura Bush, Dick Cheney, and the former president himself, all of whom inked pacts shortly before or after the administration got out of Dodge.

Autobiographies were also issued by a long list of not-quite-as-eminent political figures, including Supreme Court Justice Clarence Thomas, Speaker of the House Nancy Pelosi, venerable speechwriter and adviser Ted Sorensen, former CIA chief George Tenet, Elizabeth Edwards (wife of John), Democratic operatives Robert Shrum and Terry McAuliffe, and former congressman Tom DeLay. During the 2008 presidential campaign, old autobiographies by candidates Barack Obama, Hillary Clinton, Rudolph Giuliani, and John McCain were dusted off; when it was over, losing vice presidential candidate Sarah Palin signed a memoir deal. There were a couple of intriguing pairs of dueling political memoirs. How did Dina Matos McGreevey respond to *The Confession*, the memoir of her ex-husband, former New Jersey governor Jim McGreevey? With her own memoir, of course. When the book was announced, Mrs. McGreevey said in a statement, "I've had a lot of requests for interviews and appearances, but thought it best for my daughter and myself to stay out of the public maelstrom." That would seem to be a (reasonable) reason *not* to write a memoir. Her reasons for going ahead and writing one anyway came across as a tiny bit sketchy: "But two years have passed and still I am the subject of much speculation as to the nature of my relationship with my husband. Enough is enough." Meanwhile, Valerie Plame

Wilson's *Fair Game: My Life as a Spy, My Betrayal by the White House* could be purchased as a matched set with *The Prince of Darkness: 50 Years Reporting in Washington*, by Robert Novak, the columnist who blew her cover. (In a publishing first, Plame's book arrived in stores with substantial portions redacted, or blacked out, by her former employer, the CIA. Some of the redactions were puzzling. An article in *The New York Times* quoted a line in which she describes her first CIA training class: "It looked like I was the [BLACK INK] by far." Logic, and eyeballing the width of the splotch, tells me the word the vigilant censors have kept from me has got to be "youngest.")

The eminent authors Robert Stone, Julian Barnes, Alexander Waugh, Günter Grass, Bill Bryson, Lisa Alther, Paule Marshall, Reynolds Price, Donald Hall, and Larry McMurtry wrote books about their lives, but that was about it for that venerable genre, the literary memoir. One big reason for the paucity, it seems clear, is the current expectation that ambitious writers issue forth a memoir or memoirs *early* in their careers, possibly before even producing a novel or collection of poetry. Bryson, whose book focused on his childhood in 1950s Des Moines and sold less well in the United States than in Britain, his adopted home, was also part of another, even smaller group—memoirs by quote-unquote normal, reasonably content people. Mildred Armstrong Kalish and Harry Bernstein (respectively, an Iowan in her eighties and a ninety-six-year-old native of northern England currently living in New Jersey and working on volume two of his memoirs) had the temerity to come out with thoughtful and beautifully written books about their nontraumatic childhoods long, long ago.

All the memoirs I've mentioned have one thing in common: they were evaluated, accepted, physically produced, and marketed by a publishing house. This apparatus was capable of putting into print many hundreds if not thousands of memoirs a year. But that still left legions of unpublished aspiring memoirists, and subsidiary enterprises sprang up to serve their needs. For some years, as Brock Clarke's narrator observes, how-to-do-it memoir-writing guides have been almost as plentiful as memoirs themselves. Moreover, every community college and writers' workshop in the land offered well-attended memoir-writing classes. And for anyone who didn't want to leave the comfort of home, there were websites like memoirsbyme.com ("A site dedicated to delivering the message that Everyone has a story to tell and telling those stories!") or writemymemoirs.com, which claimed that its "FREE, innovative software helps you write one memoir or event at a time. It then helps keep you on track by dividing life's memoirs into sections, so it's easier to remember key moments and ideas, and then put together your autobiography." Better-heeled aspirants could engage the services of modernmemoirs.com, which, for a fee (not specified on the site), will interview them, transcribe and edit the interviews, and bind the end product into a book. (This is clearly a full-service organization. The website points out, for example, "Other family members often want to review the manuscript. Modern Memoirs supports the family in working through possible differences of opinion.")

Modern Memoirs notes, "Our books are usually hard covered, with pages folded into signatures and sewn together in a process known as Smythe-sewing." But that seemed quaintly old-school at a time when hundreds of thousands of personal (as opposed to political or topical) bloggers—their ranks growing daily—displayed an urge, or need, to put their lives before the world. In this they resembled traditional memoirists. In truth, blogs, in their free-form dailyness and openness to random details, bear a closer resemblance to journals or diaries than to memoirs, which require a certain Wordsworthian recollected-in-tranquillity element, as well as endorsement by a gatekeeping publisher. An online magazine called *Smith* (www.smithmag.net) tried to combine the two models, offering a rich and sometimes bewildering assortment of short memoirs, some of them solicited, approved, and edited (as in a traditional publishing operation), some of them merely submitted and automatically published (as in an online forum). The most successful of its many projects was "Six-Word Memoirs," which inspired tens of thousands of entries, the best of them collected in a book with a six-word memoir for a title: *Not Quite What I Was Planning*. It included some entries by well-known memoirists—"Me see world! Me write stories!" (Elizabeth Gilbert), "He wore dresses. This caused messes" (Josh Kilmer-Purcell), Mario Batali ("Brought it to a boil, often"), Joan Rivers ("Liars, hysterectomy didn't improve sex life!"), and "Eight thousand orgasms. Only one baby" (Neal Pollack)—as well as the winner of a nationwide contest, Abigail Moorhouse, whose life was summed up by "Barrister, barista, what's the diff, Mom?" The book was so successful that it spawned a sequel, *Six-Word Memoirs on Love & Heartbreak*. Another online micro-memoir project that led (at current count) to four books was PostSecret (postsecret.blogspot .com), in which people are invited to mail a postcard containing an anonymous secret or secret confession. The results are irresistible, in part because of the emotional and thematic range typified by the following entries. One: "When I see someone with something cute, I tell them I have something just like it and ask where they got theirs from. Then I go and actually get it." Two: "Today I realized I could no longer remember what you were like when you still loved me." As of 2009, the site had been visited more than 210 million times.

The brilliance of memoirs, short and long, did not really matter: all of them were eclipsed by smoke from the seemingly endless series of bombshells over fraudulent lives. The run started in January 2006, with two separate detonations. One of them, about James Frey and *A Million Little Pieces*, was universally reported and discussed, undoubtedly because Frey had been Oprah-anointed. The other one flew under the radar. It had to do with an individual known as Nasdijj, who in 2000 published *The Blood Runs Like a River Through My Dreams: A Memoir*. It was praised in the *Times Book Review* because it "reminds us that brave and engaging writers lurk in the most forgotten corners of society." The scholarly journal *Studies in American Indian Literatures* was equally enthusiastic and offered this description:

> Nasdijj (Athabaskan for "to become again") has lived in many worlds: the world of mixed race (Navajo and Caucasian), fetal alcohol syndrome (his mother drank heavily while pregnant), migrant camps (he was the child of migrant workers), homeless (living for a while in his truck and a tent), the Tenderloin District of San Francisco (at the request of two Sioux mothers, he goes to find their sons who have become heroin addicts and male prostitutes), and American Indian reservations (living on the Navajo Reservation in Arizona).

In 2002, Nasdijj responded to a survey in which prominent writers were asked to describe their literary lineage: "My literary lineage is Athabaskan. I hear Changing Woman in my head. I listen to trees, rocks, deserts, crows, and the tongues of wind. I am Navajo and the European things you relate so closely to often simply seem alien and remote. I do not know them. What I know is the poetry of peyote, the songs of drums, and the dancing of the boy twins, Tobajishinchini and Neyaniinezghanii— Child Born for Water and Monster Slayer. They are warriors who sing everything I put on paper."

His second book, *The Boy and the Dog Are Sleeping*, was one of five winners of the 2004 PEN/Beyond Margins Award for writers of color. He published yet another memoir, *Geronimo's Bones*. Then a writer for *LA Weekly*, following up on the suspicions of Native American writers Irvin Morris and Sherman Alexie, published an article revealing that "Nasdijj" was actually Timothy Barrus, a white North Carolina man whose literary output under his own name consisted of works of gay fiction and erotica.

A Million Little Pieces was originally published in 2003. It got some respectful reviews and some dismissive ones, and showed up on the *Times* nonfiction bestseller list for a total of one week, in sixteenth and last place. But in the fall of 2005, Oprah struck. After a period in which she chose for her book club only classic literature, like *East of Eden* and *Anna Karenina*, she returned to contemporary works, and made Frey's memoir her first selection. "I'm going bold, people, bold, bold, bold," she told her audience. "It's bold. It's bold and it's great. It's kept me up nights. It's great, great, great, great. I promise, I promise, I promise." The book shot to the top of the bestseller list and stayed there for fifteen consecutive weeks.

Then, early in 2006, the Smoking Gun website published an extensive investigation demonstrating that in the book, Frey "wholly fabricated or wildly embellished details of his purported criminal career, jail terms, and status as an outlaw 'wanted in three states.'" Oprah defended Frey on *Larry King Live*. Then she invited him again onto her show and hung him out to dry. "I feel that you betrayed millions of readers," she said. *A Million Little Pieces* and its sequel, another memoir called *My Friend Leonard*, kept selling, even as various lawsuits were filed against Frey and his publisher, Random House. By late 2007, these had been combined into one action and settled. A federal judge announced that the 1,729 readers who had come forward to say they had bought the book with an expectation that it was factual would be reimbursed for the purchase price—a total of $27,348. Another $783,000 was paid out in legal fees. And Random House agreed to include a warning in the book that not all portions of it may be accurate. A lawyer for the plaintiffs noted that Frey had received a total of more than $4.4 million in royalties. It was not clear whether the payments would come out of his deep pockets or Random House's.

The doubts raised about Frey spread to other writers and other books. In August 2007, a settlement of an undisclosed amount was reached in the $2 million defamation lawsuit filed against the author Augusten Burroughs by the Turcotte family, who were depicted (under another name) in his memoir *Running with Scissors*. According to an Associated Press account, "Events in the book which the suit claimed were false include the Turcottes' condoning sexual affairs between children and adults, Turcotte's wife eating dog food and the family using an electroshock machine it stored under the stairs. The lawsuit claims the book also falsely portrays a home in unbelievable squalor." In an article about the case for *Vanity Fair*, journalist H. G. Bissinger said that in interviews with the six Turcotte children, they stated that what was kept under the stairs was not an electroshock machine but, rather, an old Electrolux vacuum cleaner with a missing wheel. Burroughs would speak to Bissinger only generally, saying: "This is my story. It's not my mother's story and it's not the family's story, and they may remember things differently and they may choose to not remember certain things, but I will never forget what happened to me, ever, and I have the scars from it and I wanted to rip those scars off of me." The financial terms of the settlement were not revealed, but Burroughs and the publisher, St. Martin's Press, publicly agreed to call the volume a "book" instead of a "memoir" in the author's note (although the word "memoir" will still appear on the cover and elsewhere), and to change the acknowledgments in future editions to say that the Turcotte family's memories of events he describes are "different from my own," and to express regret for "any unintentional harm" to them. In a statement, the family said, "We have always maintained the book is fictionalized and defamatory. This settlement is the most powerful vindication of those sentiments that we can imagine." In his own statement, Burroughs called the settlement "not only a personal victory but a victory for all memoirists. I still maintain that the book is an entirely accurate memoir, and that it was not fictionalized or sensationalized in any way."

Even when they weren't aired in lawsuits or courtrooms, Frey-like issues kept popping up. *The Australian* and *The Village Voice* raised doubts about the accuracy of episodes in the critically lauded Starbucks selection *A Long Way Gone*, by Ishmael Beah. (The author stuck to his guns.) In an article for *The New Republic*, Alex Heard conducted a factual investigation into the work of David Sedaris, and found numerous examples of gross exaggerations and outright fabrications. It was an odd exercise. True, Sedaris's books and articles were about the events and relationships of his life—and that was a big reason why people wanted to read them—but wasn't Sedaris a humorist, in the tradition of James Thurber and Mark Twain, where substantial exaggeration was not only permitted but required? Heard anticipated the objection. There would be no problem, he said, if Sedaris's publishers hadn't classified his books as nonfiction, the Library of Congress hadn't categorized them as such, and *The New York Times* hadn't listed them on its *nonfiction* bestseller list. The call-number argument made a certain amount of sense, but it seemed somehow limited and limiting.

And then, just as it seemed that any possible deception in a memoir had been exposed, came three more autobiographical bombshells. Misha

Defonseca, the Belgian-born author of the 1997 Holocaust memoir *Misha,* which told of how she trekked across Europe as a small girl, living part of the time with wolves, confessed that she had actually spent the war safely in Brussels and that she is not even Jewish. (In a statement she said, "Ever since I remember, I felt Jewish.") The next revelation came less than a week later, and had to do with the acclaimed new memoir *Love and Consequences* ("human and deeply affecting"—*The New York Times*), author Margaret B. Jones's story of growing up in South Central Los Angeles, a half-white, half–Native American girl living in an African-American foster home and running drugs for the Bloods. "Margaret B. Jones" was revealed to be Margaret Seltzer, a one-hundred-percent Caucasian woman who grew up with her biological family in well-to-do Sherman Oaks, California.

Would it ever stop? No. In December 2008, *The New Republic* trained its eye on another Holocaust tale, a forthcoming memoir by a concentration camp survivor named Herman Rosenblat. It told of how, when he was at Buchenwald, a little girl had thrown him apples over the fence. He met the girl years later, on a blind date in New York. She became his wife. Before becoming a memoir, Rosenblat's heartwarming story was featured in the Chicken Soup for the Soul series, as the basis for a children's book, and, naturally, on *The Oprah Winfrey Show.* But *The New Republic* presented a compelling collection of circumstantial evidence suggesting that the story was hooey. Days later, Rosenblat acknowledged that the apple-tossing little girl was indeed a complete fiction.

The larger point that was emerging was that the stories in memoirs weren't just stories. They were commodities, containing within them impossibly tangled issues of ownership, propriety, and truth. As if in recognition of this conundrum, new hybrid forms began to appear. Dave

Eggers, who had written one of the most popular, influential, and smart recent memoirs, *A Heartbreaking Work of Staggering Genius*, was collaborating on a book with Valentino Achak Deng, one of the "lost boys" of Sudan—young refugee victims of the civil wars of recent decades—when it became clear that some of Valentino's memories were too cloudy to be included in a book shelved in the Memoir section of the library. So the two decided that Eggers would take Valentino's voice and the stories he had shared with him, add material that Eggers extrapolated from further research and his own imagination, and publish the result as a novel. *New York Times* reporter David Carr took a different tack. He wanted to write a memoir about his Freyesque past as a crack addict but felt hampered by the fact that he could remember almost none of it. So he embarked on his own story as if it involved someone else—interviewing everyone concerned, poring over court records and old clippings—and emerged with an "investigative memoir" called *The Night of the Gun*. Former New York Yankees manager Joe Torre—collaborating with sportswriter Tom Verducci and following in the footsteps of Julius Caesar, Pope Pius II, and Henry Adams—published a memoir in the third person.

Probably the most bizarre hybrid was a memoir in the conditional mood—O. J. Simpson's *If I Did It* (*If I Had Done It* would have shown better grammar, but that's neither here nor there)—in which he recounts the manner in which he *would* have killed his wife, if he had done so, which he didn't, or so he seems to be saying. The book was to have been published by Judith Regan at HarperCollins, who had made her name in the 1980s and 1990s acquiring and editing outrageous celebrity autobiographies by the likes of Drew Barrymore, Kathie Lee Gifford, Howard Stern, Rush Limbaugh, wrestlers Mick Foley and The Rock, steroidal baseball player Jose Canseco, and porn actress Jenna Jameson. In 2007, her *New York Times* bestsellers included autobiographies by guitarist Brian "Head" Welch and tennis player James Blake, one of the PostSecret collections, and her biggest-selling book of all, Neil Strauss's *The Game*, a memoir about "penetrating the secret world of pickup artists." The announcement of *If I Did It*, late in 2006, prompted widespread public outcries, and Regan's employer, Rupert Murdoch's News Corporation, canceled publication. (It was later picked up by a small press and sold more than 100,000 copies, with the proceeds benefiting the family of Ron Goldman, Simpson's other murder victim.) A few weeks later, word came out that ReganBooks was going to publish *7: The Mickey Mantle Novel*, Peter Golenbock's "inventive memoir" (as he described it in an author's note) of the late baseball player, narrated in an attempt to replicate the ballplayer's voice. Mantle himself had been a superstar autobiographer: he participated in the writing—or at least approved the publication—of six separate memoirs, many of them covering the same episodes; after his death, his widow and sons published two more. But none of them included a sex scene between Mantle and Marilyn Monroe, as Golenbock's book did, for the simple reason that such a coupling never occurred.*

Autobiographically speaking, there has never been a time like it. Memoir has become the central form of the culture: not only the way stories are told, but the way arguments are put forth, products and properties marketed, ideas floated, acts justified, reputations constructed or salvaged.

---

*Late in 2006, News Corporation fired Regan and canceled publication of *7*, which was picked up and published by Lyons Books. The following year, Regan filed a $100 million lawsuit against News Corporation. It alleged that she was smeared, defamed, and fired in part because corporation executives were trying to protect former New York City mayor and then presidential candidate Rudolph Giuliani, about whom they believed Regan, the onetime lover of Giuliani's police commissioner Bernard Kerik (and publisher of his autobiography), had damaging information. The terms were undisclosed when the suit was settled in January 2008, presumably guaranteeing that the damaging information would remain forever undisclosed.

The sheer volume of memoirs is unprecedented; the way the books were trailed by an unceasing stream of contention, doubt, hype, and accusations is distressing. Yet every single one of the books, and every piece of the debate about them, had a historical precedent. How did we come to this pass? The only way to answer that question is to go back a couple of thousand years and tell the story from the beginning.

Chapter 2

BEFORE MEMOIR: CHRONICLES AND CONFESSIONS

IT IS A WESTERN, OR POSSIBLY HUMAN, trait to want to tell others about one's experiences, and people have done so in their various ways since time immemorial. Until quite recently, these narratives disappeared into the air the moment they were spoken—or in rare cases a little bit after that—with the death of the last person to whom they were repeated. The advent of the written word afforded a means of preservation and with it a motivation for lengthier and more formal presentations. Elements of autobiography can be found in both the Old Testament (especially the Psalms, often taken to be written by David, and some of the Prophets) and the New (Paul's testimony in Acts). There is evidence of a Roman autobiographical tradition, already waning by the time of Tacitus, who observed that in "our fathers' times . . . many men counted it not presumption, but self-respect, to narrate their own lives."

Virtually none of these texts has survived. An exception is the *Commentaries* of Julius Caesar, notably a series of seven about the Gallic War, written in roughly 50 BCE, in which he recounts the nine years he spent battling local armies. Anticipating Henry Adams and Norman Mailer, he referred to himself in the third person; the scholar T. P. Wiseman suggests that was because each of the commentaries was designed as a dispatch to be read aloud to groups of Romans eager to hear the news from the front. In plain style, he described his actions and calculations and the triumphs of his forces. Here he is in the midst of a long campaign against Pompey, his former ally and now bitter enemy:

> Caesar, being uneasy about the retreat of his soldiers, ordered hurdles to be carried to the further side of the hill, and to be placed opposite to the enemy, and behind them a trench of a moderate breadth to be sunk by his soldiers under shelter of the hurdles: and the ground to be made as difficult as possible. He himself disposed slingers in convenient places to cover our men in their retreat. These things being completed, he ordered his legions to file off. Pompey's men insultingly and boldly pursued and chased us, levelling the hurdles that were thrown up in the front of our works, in order to pass over the trench.

Autobiography reemerged in Christian Europe, where it took on a religious rationale: a means of public conversion, apology, redemption, confession, or justification. The inescapable example—indeed, one of the most remarkable autobiographies of all time—is *The Confessions of Saint Augustine*, written in the fifth century. It stands like a lone literary skyscraper in a vast flat medieval landscape. Often addressing God directly, Augustine chronicles his spiritual path starting from his childhood in what is now Algeria. The emphasis is on his sins: grave ones, fleshly ones, and quite familiar juvenile ones: "A pear tree there was near our vineyard, laden with fruit, tempting neither for color nor taste. To shake and rob this, some lewd young fellows of us went, late one night (having according to our pestilent custom prolonged our sports in the streets till then), and took huge loads, not for our eating, but to fling to the very hogs, having only tasted them. And this, but to do what we liked only, because it was misliked." Along the way we get telling and colorful details of life in North Africa and Milan; Augustine, when he puts his mind to it, is a terrific storyteller. But the procession is always toward the moment when, in a moment of despair, a reading of the letters of Paul inspires him to renounce the flesh and take up a life of chastity. For the first time but by no means the last (see the *Autobiography* of John Stuart Mill), the reading of someone *else's* personal narrative constitutes a memoir's emotional climax. Augustine hears a disembodied child's voice chanting:

> "Take up and read; Take up and read." Instantly, my countenance altered. . . . So checking the torrent of my tears, I arose; interpreting it to be no other than a command from God to open the book, and read the first chapter I should find. . . . I seized, opened, and in silence read that section on which my eyes first fell: Not in rioting and drunkenness, not in chambering and wantonness, not in strife and envying; but put ye on the Lord Jesus Christ, and make not provision for the flesh, in concupiscence. No further would I read; nor needed I: for instantly at the end of the sentence, by a light of serenity infused into my heart, all the darkness of doubt vanished away.

Probably the oldest post-Augustine memoirs date from the twelfth century and were written by French monks. One of them, Peter Abelard's *Historia calamitatum* (*The Story of My Misfortunes*), remains a compelling cautionary tale and, in its depiction of mental and physical hurt, anticipates today's misery memoirs. It is addressed to an unnamed correspondent, and its purpose, Abelard writes, is consolation: "In comparing your sorrows with mine, you may discover that yours are in truth nought, or at the most but of small account, and so shall you come to bear them more easily." The claim is credible, as Abelard describes the revenge taken upon him for his famous love affair with Heloise: her uncle and some henchmen "cut off those parts of my body with which I had done that which was the cause of their sorrow." Ouch. He adds that when word of this assault spread, his fellow citizens "tortured me with their intolerable lamentations and outcries, so that I suffered more intensely from their compassion than from the pain of my wound. In truth I felt the disgrace more than the hurt to my body, and was more afflicted with shame than with pain."

The honor of being the first English autobiography is usually given to *The Book of Margery Kempe*, which was written in the 1430s and is in the Augustinian tradition of a spiritual chronicle. An introductory note explains that Margery, an illiterate Norfolk wife and mother, dictated her story to one unnamed man, and that it was transcribed by another; in the text, she is referred to in the third person, often as "this creature." Despite the layers of mediation, the book, once it's rendered into modern English, is vivid and in parts—as in the descriptions of Margery's mystical visions, which were often accompanied by "boisterous" crying spells—gripping. One night she is lured from her bed by the strains of beautiful music: "This melody was so sweet that it surpassed all the melody that ever might be heard in this world, without any comparison." From that point on she refused to talk about worldly things, saying only, "It is full merry in heaven." Not surprisingly, this irked her neighbors. We're told, as well, that the thought of sex—"the debt of matrimony"—became "so abominable to her that she had rather, she thought, eat or drink the ooze, the muck in the channel, than to consent to any fleshly communing." It took three or four years of negotiations (during which she bore the last three of their fourteen children), but finally her husband agreed to a mutual vow of chastity.

Pope Pius II's *Commentaries*, completed in 1463, adopted from his ancestral countryman Caesar both a title and a usually-third-person-singular-sometimes-first-person-plural approach. In his preface, Pius—known as Aeneas Sylvius until his elevation to the papacy—explains that the main purpose of the work is to prevent himself from acquiring the crummy reputation of the typical pope, "whom almost all men abuse while he lives among them but praise when he is dead. We ourselves have seen Martin V, Eugenius IV, Nicholas V, and Calixtus III condemned by the populace while they lived and extolled to the skies when they were dead." That sort of candor comes through as refreshing at the outset, but it sours a bit when one begins to grasp his tendency—common to so many politicians and chief executives—to make himself the hero of every story. At one point, he recounts the rumor (false, it would turn out) that he was one of a number of newly created cardinals.

> Many came to congratulate him as he lay sick with the gout and when he heard the news, he said, "If this news is true, it will generally be known within two hours. Meantime I shall be prepared for either result. I shall not be shaken by fear nor deluded by vain hope." On the other hand Juan, Bishop of Zamora, when he was greeted in the same way, said, "At last I have attained that which I have been anxiously awaiting for thirty-nine years!" and after making a present to the messenger, he knelt before the image of the Blessed Virgin and gave thanks to her and to her Son, because they had at last answered his prayer. So different are the natures of men! Some are ready to believe what they desire and others what they fear.

Soon after, he is indeed made cardinal, and when Pope Calixtus III dies, he participates in the election of a successor. His account of horse trading and skulduggery in this process is probably unprecedented in its candor; certainly, no American president has dished such dirt. He is a strong candidate but has to deal with various dirty tricks, including the attempt of his rival, the Presbyter of Rouen, to cheat him out of a vote. When Pius is ultimately selected, his comment is predictable: "There was no one who did not rejoice. You might have seen not men only but the very animals and the buildings of the city exulting."

Pius's profession notwithstanding, the *Commentaries* don't properly belong to the tradition of religious autobiography; rather, they are a product of Renaissance humanism and the mirror it held up to the self. (The development of glass mirrors at the end of the fifteenth and beginning of the sixteenth centuries has been cited as a key factor in the Renaissance emphasis on the self; mirrors certainly made possible the newly popular genre of the artist's self-portrait, a form of visual autobiography.) Dante, Petrarch, Montaigne, Erasmus, Shakespeare, John Donne, and virtually all other important Renaissance writers reflected on themselves in such forms as diaries, personal essays, literal self-portraits in poetry (most extensively in Dante's *La vita nuova*, briefly in lyric poems by the thousand), and veiled ones in fiction or drama. A small but significant number of Renaissance men and women attempted proper autobiographies. In his authoritative book *The Flight of Icarus: Artisan Autobiography in Early Modern Europe*, James S. Amelang cites works from Germany (Johann Butzbach's account of this "youth as a wandering weaver and apprentice tailor," written in 1506), Spain (Luis de Carvajal, "a migrant peddler, shepherd, merchant's clerk, teacher and commercial jack of all trades," who in 1594 wrote a narrative of his return to the Jewish faith of his ancestors), and France (Ambroise Paré, a royal surgeon who published his *Apology* and *Journeys in Diverse Places* in 1585). Also worth a mention are two books by military men, Martin du Bellay of France (1559) and Sir Francis Vere of England (1602), both called *Commentaries* and both modeled on Caesar's work, down to the third-person style.

But the two most notable Renaissance autobiographies were written by Italians: the Florentine goldsmith and sculptor Benvenuto Cellini, born in 1500, and the Milanese physician and mathematician Girolamo Cardano (sometimes known as Jérome Cardan), born a year later. Cardano's *The Book of My Life*, which he embarked on in 1570, a year before his death, is deservedly lesser known, though it has, by virtue of its strangeness, an arresting quality. He begins, as did Pope Pius and as would many subsequent memoirists, with his rationale: "None, of all ends which man may attain, seems more pleasing, none more worthy than recognition of the truth." He quickly adds—in a flourish that will also be familiar to readers of modern autobiography—"No word, I am ready to affirm, has been added to give savor of vainglory, or for the sake of mere embellishment." But Cardano's project inevitably has something of the vainglorious to it: his unshakable conviction, with something close to the narcissism of a contemporary pop star, that nothing about himself is uninteresting. This would include, in the words of the title of his fourth chapter, his "Stature and Appearance":

> I am a man of medium height; my feet are short, wide near the toes, and rather too high at the heels, so that I can scarcely find well-fitting shoes; it is usually necessary to have them made to order. My chest is somewhat narrow and my arms slender. The thickly fashioned right hand has dangling fingers, so that chiromantists [that is, palm readers] have declared me a rustic; it embarrasses them to know the truth. The line of life upon my palm is short, while the line called Saturn's is extended and deep. My left

hand, on the contrary, is truly beautiful with long, tapering, well-formed fingers and shining nails.

The Life of Benvenuto Cellini is the first autobiography that feels utterly modern, starting with *his* rationale, which he offers up in the second paragraph: "No matter what sort he is, everyone who has to his credit what are or what really seem great achievements, if he cares for truth and goodness, ought to write the story of his life in his own hand." (He adds, "But no one should venture on such a splendid undertaking before he is over forty." As the examples of Miley Cyrus and hundreds of other youthful memoirists attest, this is not a modern notion.)

Cellini started out writing the book in his own hand, he tells us, "but it took up too much of my time and seemed utterly pointless." Then he enlisted a sickly fourteen-year-old boy with a lot of time on his hands to take dictation; Cellini talked as he went about his work in his studio, "with the result that I quite enjoyed doing this." (You can see the same logorrheic effect when a modern CEO gets his hands on an amanuensis or a tape recorder.) The method is certainly relevant to the 225,000-plus-word length of the memoir: much more a series of rollicking yarns than an Augustinian confession. In fact, the lack of almost any manner of reflection in the book is startling; it takes place almost entirely on the surface of events, as perhaps one should expect from a sculptor. Fortunately, Cellini knows how to spin a yarn and is generous with the details of his dealings with popes and Medicis, the making of his works, his relationships with almost all the important artists of his day, his whoring, his enduring of the venereal diseases that resulted, and, strikingly, the many times he punched, stabbed, or killed other individuals.

In this period, relatively few Catholics composed religious autobiographies; the exceptions, such as the Englishwoman Julian of Norwich, the

Spanish mystic Saint Teresa of Ávila, and the founder of the Jesuit order Saint Ignatius of Loyola, did so because the spirit compelled them to. In contrast, Protestant spiritual autobiographies are legion—especially so among members of denominations in the Calvinist tradition, particularly the Puritan strain. John Calvin directed believers to look inward and, naturally, to find fault with what they saw: "We cannot aspire to Him in earnest until we have begun to be displeased with ourselves." This sorry record of sins should be confessed directly to God—not to priests, as the Catholics would have it. But Calvin left a loophole: if a believer "is so agonized and afflicted by a sense of his sins that he cannot obtain relief without the help of others," he can seek out such help and share his tale of wickedness with others. Then there was the matter of salvation. Since good works or sacraments could not be held up as signs or proof of this state, a believer was led (in the words of Paul Delany, in his book *British Autobiography in the Seventeenth Century*) "to embark on a complicated, even devious process of rationalization which always seemed to culminate in a semimystical assurance that *he*, at least, was enrolled among the elect." Publishing an account of the process would announce it to the world, obviously something to be desired. More nobly, it would help others on their own journeys.

This notion was advanced by a key English interpreter of Calvinism, William Perkins (1558–1602), whose extremely popular book *The Golden Chain* laid out a sort of schedule of personal salvation that, in the words of historian D. Bruce Hindmarsh, "would provide the structure of countless autobiographies in the seventeenth century and beyond." Addressing his readers, Perkins counseled, "If . . . thou desirest seriously eternal life, first take a narrow examination of thy selfe and the course of thy life by the square of God's law."

Puritan autobiographical texts—now commonly referred to as "conversion narratives"—started to appear in the very early 1600s. But the genre didn't truly blossom until the middle of the century, when the English Civil War led to the relaxation of censorship, relatively cheap printing became available for the first time, and a hundred dissenting sects sprang to life: the familiar Presbyterians, Baptists, and Quakers, plus splinter groups with names that sounded like British Invasion rock bands—the Diggers, the Ranters, and the Seekers. There was a sense among believers that Christ's return to earth was imminent, which was all the more reason for as many of them as possible to tell their stories in print. And by doing so, these farriers, tailors, farmers, tinkers, and itinerant preachers opened up the memoir to a wide array of social classes.

The sect that produced the most memoirs was the Society of Friends, better known as the Quakers. Scores of members followed the model of their founder, George Fox, in keeping a journal of their travels to prayer meetings, their keeping of the faith, and their observations of the sins of the world. Following Fox, who observed, "When I came to eleven years of age, I knew pureness and righteousness; for while I was a child I was taught how to walk to be kept pure," Quaker memoirs tend to have a holier-than-thee quality, not exactly an enticement for the modern reader.

The *Confessions* of Richard Norwood, written in 1639–1640, are neither sanctimonious nor bland. They begin with the declaration "Jesus Christ came into the world to save sinners of whom I am chief." Norwood enumerates the missteps of his youth, notably when, at the age of fifteen, "I acted the part of a woman in a stage-play. I was so much affected with that practice that had not the Lord prevented it I should have chosen it above any other course of life." (This would have been about 1605, the very zenith of the Elizabethan theater.) Later he goes to sea to fight in the Dutch wars, and flirts with Catholicism, guilt over which was mixed up with sexual shame: he says he was afflicted "with that nightly disease which we call the mare, which afterwards increased upon me very grievously that I was scarce any night free from it, and seldom it left me without nocturnal pollutions; besides, whilst it was upon me I had horrible dreams and visions." Helped by his reading of none other than Saint Augustine's *Confessions*, Norwood gradually finds his way to deliverance via Presbyterianism, and closed out his life in prosperity as one of the pioneers of the island of Bermuda.

The autobiographical works that proliferated in the 1650s and 1660s, many in the form of pamphlets, were more raucous yet. You can get a taste of a 1660 work called *The Lost Sheep Found*—and the striking egocentrism that was beginning to distinguish the genre—from (a portion of) its subtitle: "The Prodigal returned to his Fathers house, after many a sad and weary Journey through many Religious Countreys, Where now, notwithstanding all his former Transgressions, and breach of his Fathers Commands, he is received in an eternal Favor, and all the righteous and wicked Sons that he hath left behinde, reserved for eternal misery. . . . Written by Laur. Claxton, the onely true converted Messenger of Christ Jesus, Creator of Heaven and Earth." Clarkson—as his name is usually rendered—describes in his book a truly impressive spiritual journey. Born into the Church of England, he in turn aligned himself with the Presbyterians, the Independents, the Antinomians, and the Anabaptists, as a member of which he was arrested for baptizing "six Sisters one night naked." He reports the judge stating, "Nay further, it is reported, that which of them you liked best, you lay with them in the water." He replied: "Surely your experience teacheth you the contrary, that nature hath small desire to copulation in water, at which they laughed." The laughter was inauspicious; Clarkson and his wife were sent to jail. Upon his release he aligned himself with yet another sect, the Seekers, and became a traveling evangelist. In one town, he relates, using his typical anything-goes spelling, he encountered "a maid of pretty knowledge, who with my Doctrine was affected, and I affected to lye with her, so that night prevailed, and satisfied my lust, afterwards the mayd was highly in love with me." He offered an ingenious rationalization for this behavior: "No man could be free'd from sin, till he had acted that so called sin." Next he joined the Ranters, with whom he further refined his hubba-hubba doctrine: "Till you can lie with all women as one woman, and not judge it sin, you can do nothing but sin. . . . I being as they said, *Captain of the Rant*, I had most of the principal women came to my lodging for knowledge, which then was called The Head-Quarters." His next allegiance (after another brief jail term) was with necromancy and "magyck." His inevitable disillusionment with this creed led to a global loss of faith:

> I really believed no Moses, Prophets, Christ, or Apostles, nor no resurrection at all: for I understood that which was life in man, went into that infinite Bulk and Bigness, so called God, as a drop into the Ocean, and the body rotted into the grave.

But this kind of blatant atheism was not really tenable in seventeenth-century England, and Clarkson ends his book by returning to the Christian fold and becoming a Muggletonian. The strangeness of this sect's Harry Potteresque name, taken from its founder, Lodowick Muggleton, is matched by the strangeness of the doctrine. Muggleton's own memoir, *The Acts of the Witnesses of the Spirit,* published in 1699, a year after his death at the age of eighty-nine, explains that in about 1650, when he was going through a spiritual crisis, his cousin and fellow tailor John Reeve "said unto me, that God had given him a Commission, and that he had given Lodowick Muggleton to be his Mouth." This knowledge was sufficient for them to form a sect, whose eventual doctrine included the claims that Muggleton and Reeve were the two "witnesses of the spirit" mentioned in the Book of Revelation; that God had a human body between five and six feet tall and lived in heaven, which was about six miles above the earth; and that the stars and moon were much the same size as they appeared from the ground. It is not surprising that Muggleton (Reeve died in 1658) should have been tried and convicted for blasphemy on several occasions; locked up in the pillory, he writes, "I was maul'd by the People, some cast Dirt, and Mud out of the Kennel at me, others rotten Eggs, and Turnips, and others cast Stones at me, some Stones weighed a Pound; and out of the Windows at the Exchange, they cast down Fire Brands." He concludes by looking forward to the Last Judgment, when he and Reeve will "judge all those wicked despisers and persecutors of us when we were upon Earth."

Amid the silliness, this capacious genre produced one classic: John Bunyan's *Grace Abounding to the Chief of Sinners*, written in 1666, while Bunyan was in prison for the crime of preaching his Baptist faith. (He would also compose *The Pilgrim's Progress* while behind bars.) To counter any criticism of his self-absorption, Bunyan's Preface cites numerous biblical exhortations calling on people to remember and share their experiences, and also Paul's habit of recounting his conversion. Before settling down to his story, he calls on his readers to join in the fun: "Remember your terrours of conscience, and fear of death and hell: remember also your tears and prayers to God; yea, how you sighed under every hedge for mercy."

As to why he has resisted the temptations to write an expansive narrative, and to indulge in a high and highly adorned literary style, it is simply, he says, because "I dare not: God did not play in convincing of me; the Devil did not play in tempting of me; neither did I play when I sunk as into a bottomless pit, when the pangs of hell caught hold upon me: wherefore I may not play in my relating of them, but be plain and simple, and lay down the thing as it was: He that liketh it, let him receive it, and he that does not, let him produce a better."

The style may be plain, in Bunyan's lights, but it is nonetheless informed by a depth of feeling that makes it hard to resist, as when, upon being sent to prison, he likens the forced separation from his wife and children to "the pulling the flesh from the bones." He also has the attention to particulars and specifics you find in almost all good writers. Even the obligatory recitation of juvenile sins has a freshness to it: "Until I came to the state of marriage, I was the very ringleader of all the Youth that kept me company, into all manner of vice and ungodliness." It has to be pointed out, however, that Bunyan's sins, as he portrays them, are decidedly on the mild end of the spectrum. The main problem seems to be "that I had but few Equals . . . both for cursing, swearing, lying and blaspheming the holy Name of God." He also indulged in bell ringing and in dancing on the church green. The offense that he describes in greatest detail was playing, on a Sunday, a game called Cat, or Tipcat. (A contemporary scholar describes this as "placing a six-inch oval-shaped piece of wood [the cat] on a spot on the ground [the hole], knocking it with a bat so that it jumped up, and then striking it in mid-air.") During one game, he writes,

> having struck it one blow from the hole; just as I was about to strike it the second time, a voice did suddenly dart from Heaven into my Soul, which said, *Wilt thou leave thy sins, and go to Heaven? or have thy sins, and go to Hell?* At this I was put to an exceeding maze; wherefore leaving my Cat upon the ground, I looked up to Heaven, and was as if I had with the eyes of my understanding, seen the Lord Jesus looking down upon me, as being very hotly displeased with me.

This vision leads to a temporary repentance, but that is followed by backsliding and painful visions and fantasies, most unbearably the suspicion that he had committed "the unpardonable sin" of blaspheming against the Holy Spirit. The pattern repeats itself until finally, walking one day in a field, Bunyan reports that "suddenly this sentence fell upon my Soul, *Thy righteousness is in Heaven*; and methought withal, I saw with the eyes of my Soul, Jesus Christ at God's right hand." Not long afterward, he is called to the ministry; and that vocation, at least until he was sent to jail for it, allowed him a forum to describe his burdens and demons. Presumably writing his autobiography and other texts provided him a similar kind of comfort: "I can truly say, and that without dissembling, that when I have been to preach, I have gone full of guilt and terror, even to the pulpit door, and there it hath been taken off, and I have been at liberty in my mind until I have done my work; and then immediately, even before I could get down the pulpit stairs, I have been as bad as I was before."

The spiritual autobiography as practiced by Bunyan and so many others in the seventeenth century laid the groundwork for the greatest literary invention of the eighteenth: the novel. Born in 1660 and raised in a family of dissenters, Daniel Defoe was so driven to express himself on such an array of topics that, at a certain point, he found that one voice wasn't enough for his purposes. So he established the practice of literary ventriloquism. In 1717, he published a supposed memoir by a man who had supposedly helped negotiate the peace for France, *Minutes of the Negotiations of Monsr. Mesnager at the Court of England, towards the Close of the Last Reign*. The following year came *A Continuation of Letters Written by a Turkish Spy at Paris* and *Memoirs of Majr. Alexander Ramkins*. He topped them a year later with a book titled *The Life and Strange Surprizing Adventures of Robinson Crusoe, of York, Mariner*. There was an even longer subtitle and then the words "Written by Himself." An unsigned preface, though brief, addresses both of the two questions all autobiographers in all times, explicitly or implicitly, must face. First, a rationale: "If ever the Story of a private Man's Adventures in the World were worth making Publick, and were acceptable when Publish'd, the Editor of this Account thinks this will be so." And second, veracity:

> The Editor believes the thing to be a just History of Fact; neither is there any Appearance of Fiction in it: And however thinks, because all such things are dispatch'd, that the Improvement of it, as well to the Diversion, as to the Instruction of the Reader, will be the same; and as such, he thinks, without farther comment to the World, he does them a great Service in the Publication.

Over the next eight years, Defoe published about a half-dozen novels (the authorship of some is disputed), all in the form of autobiographies. In the most famous of these, *The Fortunes and Misfortunes of the Famous Moll Flanders* (1722), Defoe expands on the framing device he used in *Crusoe*, an anonymous introduction that explains the provenance of the text. Here it's part of an intricate Chinese box. In the novel, "Moll Flanders" is a pseudonym, and the "editor" realizes this may make readers doubt the veracity of the tale: "The world is so taken up of late with novels and romances, that it will be hard for a private history to be taken for genuine, where the names and other circumstances of the person are concealed." He also allows that "the style of the famous lady we here speak of is a little altered," and that he has excised "some of the vicious part of her life." But some edgy material is retained, for reasons familiar to all bad-girl-turned-good memoirs, past and present: "To give the history of a wicked life repented of, necessarily requires that the wicked part should be make as wicked as the real history of it will bear, to illustrate and give a beauty to the penitent part, which is certainly the best and brightest, if related with equal spirit and life."

It is worth pausing here, because Defoe, and in particular *Robinson Crusoe*, represent such a critical moment in the history of books. It was a moment when the technology of printing and rising literacy rates made it possible, for the first time, for someone to make a living as a writer of prose. And Defoe was the quintessential professional author. Before the turn of the seventeenth century, people wrote books in order to praise God, to justify or promote themselves, or for myriad other personal reasons. But afterward, they could, and did, write for profit.

The age of Defoe is also a turning point in the history of attitudes toward truth. Previously, those few citizens who *could* read tended not to think of literature in terms of categories; they would, for many reasons, view the way we divide and classify libraries, bookstores, book prizes, and bestseller lists as peculiar. True, some texts, such as Cervantes' *Don Quixote* and Sir Thomas Malory's romance *Le Morte d'Arthur*, were clearly fictional, but more often narrative texts were seen as occupying an indeterminate middle ground. Works as diverse as the Bible itself, spiritual autobiographies like *Grace Abounding*, and explorers' reports of their travels were all presented as true, and depended for their authority and power on being accepted as such. Yet the truth was of a general quality; it wouldn't have occurred to anyone that every detail happened precisely as described.

Defoe shook everything up. While some readers realized *Crusoe* was fiction, others believed it to be true. The evidence for that is a pamphlet produced by the prominent author Charles Gildon. *Robinson Crusoe Examin'd and Criticis'd* explicitly called Defoe a liar—and thus was the first recorded instance of an attack on a fake memoir. But Defoe wasn't trying to deceive anyone. He merely recognized, and was one of the first

BEN YAGODA

authors to exploit, the fact that human beings respond powerfully to narratives that are (or make credible claims to be) true. The philosopher David Hume may have had him in mind when he observed in 1740, in *A Treatise of Human Nature*, that if two people read the same book, but one thought of it as a "romance" and the other as "a true history," they would react to it very differently:

> The latter has a more lively conception of all the incidents. He enters deeper into the concerns of the persons: represents to himself their actions, and characters, and friendships, and enmities: he even goes so far as to form a notion of their features, and air, and person. While the former, who gives no credit to the testimony of the author, has a more faint and languid conception of all these particulars; and except on account of the style and ingenuity of the composition, can receive little entertainment from it.

Defoe died in 1731 but had a profound influence on the novelists who emerged in the 1740s: Henry Fielding, Tobias Smollett, Laurence Sterne, Samuel Richardson, and John Cleland (author of *Fanny Hill, or, Memoirs of a Woman of Pleasure*, often called the first erotic novel in English, published in 1749). All followed his lead in writing fictional books in autobiographical form—and by this point, readers understood that the people and events in novels were fictional. Defoe also had an impact on autobiography itself. Remarkably, his books appeared to inspire *real* people to write and publish their stories. In *The History and Remarkable Life of the Truly Honourable Colonel Jacque*, one of his incredible trio of 1722 novels (along with *Moll Flanders* and *A Journal of the Plague Year*), Defoe has the narrator observe: "Perhaps, when I wrote these things down, I did not foresee that the Writings of our own Stories would be so much the

Fashion in *England*, or so agreeable to others to read." Colley Cibber, the famous actor, playwright, theater manager, and poet laureate, put out his memoirs in 1740. The narrator of Fielding's *Joseph Andrews*, published two years later, says Cibber's book "was written by the great person himself, who lived the life he hath recorded, and is by many thought to have lived such a life only in order to write it."

Also mirrored in actual autobiographies was the diversity of Defoe's narrators, in class, gender, and propriety. A late-eighteenth-century autobiographer, James Lackington, lamented how "many dreadful offenders against law and justice" wrote and published accounts of their lives and conversions. Real-life female counterparts to Defoe's Moll Flanders and Richardson's Pamela and Clarissa emerged as well, notably the trio of "scandalous memoirists" who wrote at mid-century: Charlotte Clarke (who was Colley Cibber's daughter), Laetitia Pilkington, and Constantia Phillips. These women used their books to defend themselves, settle scores, and achieve a measure of liberation. Pilkington's husband had accused her of adultery and divorced her. She tried to support herself and her son by writing poetry, to no avail, then settled on autobiography. She writes, dripping with irony, that had her "loving Husband . . . but permitted me to what Nature certainly intended for me, a harmless household Dove, in all human Probability I should have remained contented with my humble situation, and, instead of using a Pen, been employed with a Needle, to work for the little ones we might, by this time, have had." Pilkington conceived a three-volume work and in the first frankly set out her a plan of literary blackmail: "If any married Man, who has ever attacked me, does not subscribe to my *Memoirs*, I will without the last Ceremony, insert their Names, be their Rank ever so high, or their Profession ever so holy."

. . .

WHILE SECULAR AUTOBIOGRAPHY was booming in England, the New World remained devoted to the spiritual variety. Since many of the colonies that would become the United States were populated by Puritans or Quakers, it follows that a lot of colonists should have gone in for the genre. New England Puritans wrote personal narratives from the get-go, because unlike their counterparts across the Atlantic, they were required, as a condition for church membership, to give an account of their experience of grace. Because they are simply conforming to an expected and accepted pattern, these early accounts by the "visible saints" blend together, even when their authors are such notables as Edward Taylor, Anne Bradstreet, Thomas Shepard, and both Increase and Cotton Mather. By the middle of the eighteenth century, Puritan-based doctrines had changed in unexpected ways, notably Jonathan Edwards's spearheading of revivalism and the Great Awakening, but the "Personal Narrative" Edwards composed in the 1740s, while sometimes sublime in its style and ardor, still conformed to the classical structure: a back-and-forth dance between doubt and faith.

The many American Quakers who followed George Fox by writing pious journals and other kinds of memoirs were also generally generic. The notable exception is *Some Account of the Fore Part of the Life of Elizabeth Ashbridge*, the first words of which are: "My Life being attended with many uncommon Occurences, some of which I through disobedience brought upon myself, and others I believe were for my Good, I therefore thought proper to make some remarks. . . ." Who could resist reading on? Ashbridge does not disappoint. Born in 1713 in Cheshire, England, she eloped at the age of fourteen as a result of a "foolish passion," saw her miserly husband die just five months later, was kidnapped by a trafficker in indentured servants, escaped, and boarded a ship to

America, on which she prevented a mutiny and ended up signing herself into indentured servitude anyway. In New York she is bought by an abusive master who "would not suffer me to have Clothes to be Decent in, having to go barefoot in his Service in the Snowey Weather & the Meanest drudgery." She trains herself as a seamstress and eventually buys her freedom, marries for a second time, adopts the Quaker faith (to the dismay of her abusive husband, Mr. Sullivan), and becomes a preacher. Sullivan keeps trying to shake her of her faith; once, in a Philadelphia tavern, he insists that she violate it by dancing with him:

> I trembling desired to be Excused; but he Insisted on it, and knowing his Temper to be exceeding Cholerick, durst not say much. . . . He then pluck'd me around the Room till Tears affected my Eyes, at sight whereof the Musician Stopt and said, "I'll play no more, Let your wife alone," of which I was Glad.

Sullivan ultimately sees the light and becomes a Quaker himself, but this works out badly for him: one day "he got in Drunk, & Enlisted him Self " in the English army. Ordered to take up arms, he refuses on religious principle, is badly beaten, and dies nine months later of his injuries. (Ashbridge's account ends here, in 1741, but I am pleased to say that five years later she entered into her first happy marriage, to an affluent Quaker, and she fruitfully spread the word until her death in 1755.)

While the spiritual autobiographies themselves were mostly bland and predictable, they had a major and long-lasting impact. If you look closely enough, you can find their influence in the majority of American memoirs. And they continue to be as powerful a model as ever, with traces in such diverse works as *The Autobiography of Malcolm X*, Jimmy Carter's *Living Faith* (one of eight memoirs by the former president, who rivals Maya

Angelou and Shirley MacLaine in productiveness), Augusten Burroughs's
Running with Scissors, and James Frey's *A Million Little Pieces*: books that
follow an account of the author's wayward past (and the more wayward
the better), his or her discovery of some sort of secular or sacred light,
and then, finally, sweet redemption.

In the seventeenth century, the conversion narrative laid the groundwork for what the critic Annette Kolodny has called "the single narrative
form indigenous to the New World," the "captivity narrative." Given that
European arrivals in the Americas were in various ways encroaching on
the people already living there, it isn't a shock that on occasion the natives
should have taken them prisoner. One recent estimate is that from the first
explorers' arrival through the nineteenth century, this happened more
than ten thousand times. With some frequency, those who returned to tell
the tale actually did tell the tale, in print. The first instance was the work of
a German privateer, Hans Staden, who in the 1550s was captured in what
is now Brazil by members of the Tupinambá tribe. He eventually was
freed, and published *True History and Description of the Man-eaters Who
Dwell in the New World Called America*. Illustrated with many woodcuts—
the first widely disseminated images of Native Americans—the book
became a European bestseller and went through some seventy-six editions.
The "Man-eaters" were the key element, no doubt; Staden emphasized
the tribe's cannibalistic practices, and the numerous occasions on which
he narrowly escaped being eaten.

North America was where the genre flourished, however, starting
about a century later. In 1676, a Massachusetts settler named Mary Rowlandson was captured by a band of Narragansett Indians during a raid on
the town of Lancaster. They held her for about three months, when she
was ransomed. She composed and published an account of her experience.
She certainly didn't waste any time in cutting to the chase. Her opening

lines anticipate the scores of narratives that followed, and the hundreds and hundreds of movies:

> On the tenth of February 1675, came the Indians with great numbers upon Lancaster: Their first coming was about sun-rising; hearing the noise of some guns, we looked out; several houses were burning, and the smoke ascending to heaven. There were five persons taken in one house, the father, the mother, and a sucking child, they knocked on the head; the other two they took and carried away alive. There were two others, who being out of their garrison upon some occasion were set upon; one was knocked on the head, the other escaped: another there was who running along was shot and wounded, and fell down; he begged of them his life, promising them money (as they told me), but they would not hearken to him but knocked him in the head, and stripped him naked, and split open his bowels.

For Rowlandson and other Puritans, the captivity experience not only fit snugly into an established template of spiritual autobiography, but also gave it some nifty new widgets. In Cotton Mather's words, the Indians' *"religion* was the most explicit sort of *devil-worship"*; being among them was often compared, literally and figuratively, to being in hell. It was sometimes seen as a punishment: John Williams called the experience "the most Lively and Awful sense of Divine Rebukes, which the Holy God has seen meet in Spotless Sovereignty to dispense to me, my Family and People, in delivering us into the hands of those that Hated us." It was almost always seen as a trial and a test. Some captives, like Hannah Dustan, experienced religious conversion in the wilderness: "In my Affliction God made his Word Comfortable to me." And for almost all, returning home from it was seen as a sign of divine favor. Why else should Rowlandson have titled her book *The Sovereignty & Goodness of God, together, with*

Faithfulness of His Promises Displayed, or John Williams his 1707 work *The Redeemed Captive, Returning to Zion?*

Combining ripping narratives with didactic agendas, these works struck a resounding chord with the public. On its publication in 1682, Rowlandson's book was second in popularity only to the Bible, according to one scholar. Frank Luther Mott, the preeminent historian of American publishing, lists it and eighteenth-century captivity narratives by Williams, Jonathan Dickinson, and Mary Jemison as among the greatest all-time bestsellers. Another historian, Richard VanDerBeets, writes, "First editions are rare today because they were quite literally read to pieces."

As the genre progressed, the image of Indians displayed in it underwent changes. For the Puritan Rowlandson, everything her captors did, whether kind or cruel, was a manifestation and proof of God's glory. Subsequent works, doing their part toward constructing an exculpatory national myth, tended to portray natives as savages whose actions were bad in and of themselves. The title of an 1823 text gives the general idea: *A Narrative of the Sufferings of Massy Harbison from Indian Barbarity . . . with an Infant at Her Breast.*

The longer a writer stayed with natives, the more measured and sympathetic the approach tended to be. Mary Jemison, a fifteen-year-old Pennsylvania girl, was taken into captivity in 1758. She married two Seneca men, Sheninjee, who died after three years of marriage, and Hiokatoo, with whom she lived for fifty years. She chose to remain with her captors for all of her very long life, even when given the opportunity to leave. She explained, "With them was my home; my family was there, and there I had many friends to whom I was warmly attached." The quotation is from *A Narrative of the Life of Mrs. Mary Jemison*, a result of three days she spent in 1823, when she was about eighty, collaborating with a white writer named James Everett Seaver. The book became one of the biggest bestsellers of the 1820s, rivaling the works of James Fenimore Cooper, which also, of course, featured captivity by Indians. A comparable story was that of John Tanner, who was captured in Kentucky by Shawnee Indians in 1790, when he was nine. He subsequently was sold to the Ojibwa; over time he lost his knowledge of English, acquired a wife, and became a thoroughly assimilated member of the tribe. Tanner subsequently journeyed back to white culture, was reunited with his mother and sisters, worked as a guide and interpreter, and in 1830 published *A Narrative of the Captivity and Adventures of John Tanner (U.S. Interpreter at the Saut de Ste. Marie) During Thirty Years Residence Among the Indians in the Interior of North America*. While not a commercial success on the scale of Jemison's book, Tanner's offered contemporary readers a remarkably detailed look at Native American life, including a one-hundred-page anthropological account of the language, customs, and beliefs he had observed.

Captivity narratives flourished through the nineteenth century and expanded their reach: their elements could be seen in scores of novels, and in African-American slave narratives, which were, after all, composed by people who were taken captive and forced to live in another culture, and later in such cinematic westerns as *The Searchers* and *Little Big Man*. Today, vivid traces of the genre can be seen in a wide range of autobiographies by white Americans held against their will by scary, usually darker-skinned people: Patty Hearst's account of her time with the Symbionese Liberation Army; the 1977 *Midnight Express*, about a young American held under brutal conditions in a Turkish prison; Terry Anderson's *Den of Lions*, about being held hostage in Lebanon in the 1980s; and Betty Mahmoody's phenomenally successful *Not Without My Daughter*, which tells of her virtual imprisonment by her Iranian husband and eventual escape. Today, there is a burgeoning subgenre of memoirs written by Westerners held in Southeast Asian jails; they have such titles as *Forget*

You Had a Daughter: Doing Time in the "Bangkok Hilton"; *4,000 Days: My Life and Survival in a Bangkok Prison*; and *Escape: The True Story of the Only Westerner Ever to Break out of Thailand's Bangkok Hilton*. The UFO abduction tale is certainly a related narrative form, and it can't be a coincidence that the aliens featured in them usually have (in addition to, as offered by Wikipedia, a "bulbous, hairless head supported by a thin neck, which is dominated by large . . . lidless eyes") gray skin.

Chapter 3

THESE AUTOBIOGRAPHICAL
TIMES OF OURS

ON SATURDAY, NOVEMBER 24, 1759, in the weekly essay he published under the byline "The Idler," Samuel Johnson noted that of "the various forms of narrative writing," biography was "most eagerly read, and most easily applied to the purposes of life." However, he went on, the genre had a distinct limitation: it most commonly related to the victories and defeats of statesmen and generals, which were of little relevance to the common man. "As gold which he cannot spend will make no man rich, so knowledge which he cannot apply will make no man wise," he observed.

Far better and more valuable are works in which "the writer tells his own story." Such books "tell not how any man became great, but how he was made happy; not how he lost the favour of his prince, but how he became discontented with himself." Autobiographies—Johnson did not use the word, as it would not be coined for another four decades—had another advantage: they were dependably accurate and truthful. That claim is of course ironic to anyone with knowledge of subsequent developments, but even in its day Johnson's logic may have seemed sophistic and his understanding of human psychology somewhat limited:

> The writer of his own life has at least the first qualification of an historian, the knowledge of the truth. . . . Certainty of knowledge not only excludes mistake, but fortifies veracity. . . . That which is fully known cannot be falsified but with reluctance of understanding, and alarm of conscience. But he that speaks of himself has no motive to falsehood or partiality except self-love, by which all have so often been betrayed, that all are on the watch against its artifices. He that writes an apology for a single action, to confute an accusation, or recommend himself to favour, is indeed always to be suspected of favouring his own cause; but he that sits down calmly and voluntarily to review his life for the admonition of posterity, or to amuse himself, and leaves this account unpublished, may be commonly presumed to tell truth, since falsehood cannot appease his own mind, and fame will not be heard beneath the tomb.

Rather incredibly, at the very moment those words were appearing, a Swiss philosopher was developing a strikingly similar rationale for embarking on the greatest memoir of all time. Among other distinctions, Jean-Jacques Rousseau's *The Confessions* was the first autobiography to contain an account of its own beginnings: "For some strange reason," Rousseau writes, in a passage referring to the years 1759–1760, his publisher "had been urging me for some time to write my memoirs." The request seemed strange simply because not much had happened to him. However, he felt that such a book could "become interesting through the frankness which I was capable of devoting to the task; and I decided to make it a work unique in its unparalleled truthfulness." He began work on it in 1764, when he was fifty-two, and finished it about six years later.

Rousseau's varied influences included Saint Augustine's *Confessions*, the title of which he would ultimately borrow (with the key difference being that Rousseau's confessions were directed not to God or to a priest but to his fellow men); *Robinson Crusoe*; such French first-person novels as Alain-René Lesage's *Gil Blas* and *Confessions of the Count of* ***, by Rousseau's friend Charles Duclos; and the French court memoir tradition, which by the middle of the eighteenth century was more considerably developed than the English one. But no influence can account for the originality and singularity of his book. One of its most distinctive qualities, as I've suggested, is self-consciousness. In Rousseau's original preface (subsequently replaced by one reflecting the low-grade paranoia he developed in the course of working on *The Confessions*), he laid out a thorough rationale, starting with the observation that human beings do not understand one another because they (wrongly) assume other people are just like them. "I have decided to encourage my readers into taking a step forward in their knowledge of men," he writes, by allowing them to know "one other person, and that other person will be me."

"No one can write a man's life except himself," Rousseau goes on, echoing Johnson. Unlike Johnson, he rejects every previous self-portrait on the grounds of falseness. The autobiographer typically "presents himself as he wants to be seen, not at all as how he is. The sincerest of people are at best truthful in what they say, but they lie by their reticence, and what they suppress changes so much what they pretend to reveal that in telling only part of the truth, they tell none of it."

Not Rousseau: "I will speak the truth, I will do so unreservedly; I will tell everything; the good, the bad, everything, in short. . . . The reader has only to take me at my word and begin to read; he will not get far before seeing that I mean to keep it."

Indeed. Within a dozen pages, he is confessing that at the age of eight, he was sexually aroused when spanked by the wife of the minister with whom he was boarding. The experience, he goes on to say, led him to a lifelong masochistic predilection and, attendant to this, sexual frustration:

> The taste I had acquired as a child, instead of disappearing, became so identified with other pleasures that I was never able to dissociate it from the desires aroused through the senses; and this vagary, in conjunction with my natural timidity, has always inhibited me in my approaches to women, because I dare not tell them everything. . . . And so I have spent my life coveting but never declaring myself to the women I loved most. Never daring to reveal my proclivities, I have at least kept them amused with relationships that allowed my mind to dwell on them. To lie at the feet of an imperious woman, to be obliged to beg for her forgiveness, these were sweet pleasures, and the more my inflamed imagination roused my blood, the more I played the bashful lover.

Such passages—and others, in which he describes his masturbatory practices—caused a great scandal when Rousseau read them to some private gatherings in Paris in 1771. (They so shocked one of his listeners that she petitioned the police to stop the readings.) However, as he wisely says, "It is not what is criminal that is the hardest to reveal, but what is laughable or shameful." The most deservedly famous passage of the book consists of his most painful confession, and it's far more mundane than a taste for being whacked on the posterior. It involves an incident that took place when he was sixteen and working in a household in Turin. At one point he stole a small old ribbon that had inexplicably tempted him. Its absence was noted, he was discovered with it, and he mendaciously said that Marion, the young cook, had given it to him. In a public inquiry, he repeated the charge, to which the girl "said nothing, then threw me a glance which would have disarmed the devil himself, but which my barbarous heart resisted." She denied, Rousseau persisted, and though they were both dismissed from the household, "the presumption was in my favor," and he notes that such an imputation to her reputation would have made life quite difficult for her. At the time of his writing, forty years had passed since the event, but, he tells us,

> at times I am so troubled by this cruel memory, and so distressed, that I lie sleepless in my bed, imagining the poor girl advancing towards me to reproach me for my crime as though I had committed it only yesterday. . . . I have never been able to bring myself to unburden my heart of this confession by entrusting it to a friend. . . . The most that I have been able to do has been to confess my responsibility for an atrocious deed, without ever saying of what exactly it consisted. The burden, then, has lain unalleviated on my conscience until this very day; and I can safely say that the desire to be in some measure relieved of it has greatly contributed to the decision I have taken to write these confessions.

Stung by the reception to his public readings, Rousseau decided that *The Confessions* would be published posthumously. It appeared in France in 1782 and in its first English translation the following year. Predictably, the book attracted a few brickbats, one early review calling it "an incredible tissue of puerility, folly and extravagance." The initial English reviewers tended to be bemused by Rousseau's audacious frankness. The critic James Treadwell quotes writers who described Rousseau as "an aggregate of contradictions," "that most irreconcilable . . . of all human characters," and a combination of "eccentricities so singular and so opposite," and the book as "a mad confession . . . of mad faults" (this from Edmund Burke) and "a dwelling with pleasure on what never ought to have been recollected, at least never ought to have been written." But *The Confessions* very quickly began to assume the shape of a classic; more specifically, it altered the understanding of autobiography. At least four principles embodied in the book are so commonplace among contemporary memoirists as to go without saying, but were revolutionary at the time: a belief in total frankness and honesty; an emphasis on the inner life of the mind and emotions rather than on the external one of action; a significant attention to childhood and youth; and a recognition that mundane matters, like a lie about a ribbon, could be as earthshaking as a grand battle, maybe even more so. As Stendhal would observe, "The empire of the ridiculous has shrunk today, and that is the work of Jean-Jacques Rousseau."

At the start, even as the book set a towering example, its lessons were difficult to follow. David Hume—with whom Rousseau had a notoriously stormy relationship—allotted only a few pages to *My Own Life* in 1776: "It is difficult," he explained, "for a man to speak long of himself without vanity; therefore, I shall be short." Writing in 1789, the historian Edward Gibbon was more ambivalent. In his opening pages he claims, "I have exposed my private feelings, as I shall always do, without scruple or reserve." But later on he is more demure, writing, for example: "The discovery of a sixth sense [i.e., love], the first consciousness of manhood, is a very interesting moment of our lives, but it less properly belongs to the memoirs of an individual, than to the natural history of the species." Thomas Jefferson embarked on what he called his "memoranda and . . . recollections," and dropped it when he was halfway done.

But soon the Enlightenment gave way to Romanticism, and *The Con-*

fessions was an essential text for the movement. Rousseau's example struck an especially resonant chord in Germany, where the philosopher Johann Gottfried Herder championed autobiography as a "window to the soul" and called for the publication of an anthology to which people would contribute "confessions about themselves." That led to two separate collections: Johann Georg Müller's *Confessions of Notable Men* (six volumes, 1791–1810) and David Christoph Seybold's *Self-Biographies of Famous Men* (two volumes, 1796, 1799). In 1811, the quintessential Romantic writer Johann Wolfgang von Goethe—who had invented the autobiographical novel in 1774, with *The Sorrows of Young Werther*—published the first volume of his memoirs, *Out of My Life: Poetry and Truth*, thus establishing the literary memoir as a genre. Stendhal's *The Life of Henry Brulard* (1834) was another key early example, noteworthy in dealing exclusively with his childhood.

The memoir movement created more and earlier excitement on the Continent than across the Channel, as Madame de Staël noted in 1800: "There is nothing at all in England of memoirs, of confessions, of narratives of self made by oneself; the pride of English character refuses to this genre details and opinions: but the eloquence of writers in prose often loses through too severe an abnegation all that seems to come from personal affections."

But England quickly caught up. Just a year before Madame de Staël wrote those words, William Wordsworth embarked on a contemplative record of his intellectual, emotional, and spiritual development that followed Rousseau in its underlying assumptions and approach but was groundbreaking in at least two ways. First, where the unspoken understanding had always been that one composed one's memoirs in the reflective calm of maturity or old age (recall that Cellini trusted no autobiographer under forty), Wordsworth, a mere twenty-nine years old when he started, had the idea that a good time to write about youth *was* youth. Second, he told his story in a poem, eventually accumulating ten thousand lines of blank verse. Wordsworth fiddled with the work throughout his long life, and the poem would not be published until after his death, in 1850, when his widow gave it the title *The Prelude*.

Autobiography was in the air. In his influential essay "On a Man's Writing Memoirs of Himself "—it appeared in twenty editions between 1805 and 1856—the Reverend John Foster recommended that *everybody* get Wordsworthian: "endeavoring not so much to enumerate the mere facts and events of life, as to discriminate the successive states of the mind, and so trace the progress of what might be called the character." Anticipating modern memoir therapy, Foster referred mainly to people writing these memoirs for the value of the exercise and their own eyes only. He acknowledges, toward the end of the essay, that there have arisen a considerable "number of historians of their own lives, who magnanimously throw the complete cargo, both of their vanities and their vices, before the whole public." Rousseau escapes his wrath: "If we could . . . pardon the kind of ingenuousness which he has displayed, it would certainly be in the disclosure of a mind so wonderfully singular as his." But he has no patience with the others who have dared to use the title "Confessions": "As if it ever were to be believed, that penitence and humiliation would ever excite men to call thousands to witness a needless disclosure of what oppresses them with grief and shame."

As the century progressed, higher literacy rates and technological improvements in printing and publishing led to more books of every kind. In the vanguard were memoirs, which poured forth. An 1822 article in *Edinburgh Magazine* commented on "the insatiable appetite of the public for every species of Private Memoirs and Correspondence." William Matthews's definitive bibliography of British autobiography bears this observation out. Matthews lists 48 such books published between 1790 and 1799; 53 from 1800 to 1809; 72 from 1810 to 1819; and (in a more than 100 percent increase from the previous decade) 171 from 1820 to 1829.

All this activity and intense reflection transpired for some years despite the lack of a suitable name for the genre. As Foster pointed out, there were some problems with "Confessions."* "Memoir" (or "Memoirs") was and would continue to be the choice of some, but aside from being of blatantly French origin, it implied a certain subjectivity or narrowness of vision not suitable to authors who wished to tell the whole truth about their whole lives. In his 1796 *Miscellanies*, D'Israeli put forward a Teutonic coinage: "self-biography." (He was all in favor of it, especially if such a work was published posthumously: "When a great man leaves some memorial of his days, his deathbed sanctions the truth, and the grave consecrates the motive.") Reviewing the book in the *Monthly Review*, William Taylor expressed distaste for this term but couldn't come up with an alternative: "It is not very usual in English to employ hybrid words partly Saxon and partly Greek: yet *autobiography* would have seemed pedantic." This is the *Oxford English Dictionary*'s first citation for the word, arm's-length italics and all. By the time of the *OED*'s next cited use, in 1809—Robert Southey's reference to a "very amusing and unique specimen of autobiography"— the hybrid word appears to have been accepted as not pedantic at all. In 1825, an anonymous poem called "Literary Advertisement" appeared in *The Times*. One stanza read:

---

*That did not prevent *Confessions of an English Opium Eater* from begetting a crop of similarly titled works: James Hogg's *Confessions of a Justified Sinner* (1824), John Greenleaf Whittier's *The Confessions of a Bachelor* (1828), Lady Blessington's *Confessions of an Elderly Lady and Gentleman* (1838), and *Confessions of an Inquiring Spirit* (1840), a posthumous work by Coleridge on his religious philosophy. The allure of the word persists, although in recent years the amount of irony invested in it has increased. Since 2004, one has been able to purchase, among other titles, *Confessions of: an Economic Hitman, a Wall Street Analyst, a French Baker*, and *a Video Vixen*.

> There's nothing, at present, so popular growing
> As your Autobiographers—fortunate elves,
> Who manage to know all the best people going,
> Without having ever been heard of themselves!

In 1826, the publishers John Hunt and Cowden Clarke issued a popular series titled *Autobiography: A Collection of the Most Instructive and Amusing Lives Ever Published, Written by the Parties Themselves*. The thirty-four volumes would include scores of texts, both new works and classic ones by the likes of Benvenuto Cellini, John Wesley, and Colley Cibber. Interestingly, the first autobiography to *call* itself an autobiography did not arrive until 1829, with William Brown's *The Autobiography, or Narrative of a Soldier*.*

One of the notable by-products of today's memoir boom, from its beginnings in the early 1990s, has been the anti-memoir screed: periodic complaints about the exhibitionism, unseemliness, and just plain *wrongness* of the genre. Almost precisely the same complaints were made in the wake of the first memoir boom, two centuries earlier. The German philosopher Friedrich Schlegel inflicted some of the first rips in 1798:

---

*In these early years of the word's existence, it was, for some reason, more commonly applied to novelistic ersatz autobiographies than to real ones: Scottish novelist John Galt's 1832 *The Member: An Autobiography* (1832), the pseudonymous, satirical American book *A Yankee Among the Nullifiers: An Auto-biography*, W. P. Scargill's *The Autobiography of a Dissenting Minister* (1834). The most famous nineteenth-century example came in 1847, when Charlotte Brontë titled her pseudonymous novel *Jane Eyre: An Autobiography*. "Hitherto I have recorded in detail the events of my insignificant existence: to the first ten years of my life I have given almost as many chapters. But this is not to be a regular autobiography. I am only bound to invoke Memory where I know her responses will possess some degree of interest; therefore I now pass a space of eight years almost in silence: a few lines only are necessary to keep up the links of connection." Two years later, in 1849, Charles Dickens chose a more antique-sounding title for the serial publication of his most autobiographical work: *David Copperfield, or The Personal History, Adventures, Experience and Observation of David Copperfield the Younger of Blunderstone Rookery (which he never meant to publish on any account)*.

Pure autobiographies are written either by neurotics who are fascinated by their own ego, as in Rousseau's case; or by authors of a robust artistic or adventurous self-love, such as Benvenuto Cellini; or by born historians who regard themselves only as material for historic art; or by women who also coquette with posterity; or by pedantic minds who want to bring even the most minute things in order before they die and cannot let themselves leave the world without commentaries.

The memoir backlash, like the genre itself, arrived a little bit later in Britain but quickly gathered steam. One remarkably common objection related to the egotism and vanity inherent in writing an entire book about oneself. Many reviewers seemed to put autobiographers in the same category as dinner guests who violate decorum by talking incessantly about themselves; a common objection was to the very word "I," sometimes referred to as "the hateful pronoun." Virtually all eighteenth- and nineteenth-century autobiographers began with prefatory remarks that addressed the vanity issue and presented a rationale for their book—usually some variation on the Horatian principles of instruction and amusement.

Another objection was expressed by Isaac D'Israeli himself, in an 1809 review of the memoirs of a poet he felt did not deserve to write his memoirs: "If the populace of writers become thus querulous after fame (to which they have no pretensions) we shall expect to see an epidemical rage for auto-biography break out." That issue—what, precisely, qualified someone to put before the public the story of his or her life?—would be a pointed and heated one in the decades ahead. For a century, more or less, a common if unspoken understanding was that three sorts of people were entitled and expected to produce memoirs: eminences (whether political, military, literary, religious, or social), the pious, and people with exciting, unusual, or somehow stirring stories to tell. Now it seemed as if the genre was being opened up to all sorts and classes of people, who used it for all sorts of purposes. The 1820s saw a flurry of books by tradesmen and artisans, and an article in the *London Magazine* fretted that if current trends continued, "every keeper of an apple-stall might unstore his 'fruits of experience'"—a reference to silver trader Joseph Brasbridge's memoir—"each sweeper at a crossing might give a trifle to the world." An anonymous author in *Blackwood's Magazine* opined that the form should be the province of people of "lofty reputation" or who had something of "historical importance to say," not of the "vulgar" who try to "excite prurient interest that may command a sale." And in 1826, a critic in *Quarterly Review* complained, "England expects every driveller to do his Memorabilia."

In a review the following year of ten autobiographies, John Lockhart erupted: "Cabin boys and drummers are busy with their commentaries . . . thanks to the 'march of intellect,' we are already rich in the autobiography of pickpockets." He complained that the genre itself

> emboldens beings who, at any period, would have been mean and base in all their objects and desires, to demand with hardihood the attention and the sympathy of mankind, for thoughts and deeds that, in any period but the present, must have been as obscure as dirty. . . . The mania for this garbage of Confessions, and Recollections, and Reminiscences . . . "is indeed a vile symptom." It seems as if the ear of that grand impersonation, "the Reading Public," had become as filthily prurient as that of an eavesdropping lackey.

Lockhart's phrase "filthily prurient" was not carelessly chosen: the highborn as well as the low had followed Rousseau in airing various sorts of soiled linen. In 1821, Wordsworth's onetime protégé Thomas De Quincey created a scandal with his anonymous *Confessions of an English Opium Eater*, which is exactly what it says it is. Two years later, the prominent man of letters William Hazlitt wrote an embarrassing narrative of his disastrous infatuation with a nineteen-year-old waitress; he published it anonymously, under the title *Liber Amoris*, but didn't fool anybody. (Nor was it greeted with enthusiasm: one review called it a "wretched compound of folly and nauseous sensibility"; another stated that it "mixed filth and utter despicableness.")

Courtesans' memoirs constituted a subgenre all their own that, in addition to any literary aspirations, were designed as marketing tools. The prototypical work in this category was Harriette Wilson's 1825 *Memoirs*, which begins, "I shall not say why and how I became, at the age of fifteen, the mistress of the Earl of Craven." It's an apt first sentence, because Wilson was all about telling and not telling. Thus she charged her patrons two hundred pounds to *not* include their names in the book. Most accepted her terms. One who did not was the Duke of Wellington, who famously said, "Publish and be damned."

By that time, to complain about the culture of autobiography was a fool's mission. It had arrived, and there was no turning back. Proof of this proposition can be found in Thomas Carlyle's unclassifiable work *Sartor Resartus*, published periodically in 1833–1834 and as a book in 1836. It consists of an autobiographical-philosophical manuscript by the fictional German professor Teufelsdröckh, sandwiched by an anonymous and equally fictional translator-editor's commentary. This includes a letter from yet another character that, in explaining *why* the professor has given his life story, mercilessly mocks the conventions, metaphors, and assumptions of contemporary autobiography. The philosophical portions "could not but awaken" in readers a strange curiosity touching the mind they issued from; the perhaps unparalleled physical mechanism, which manufactured such matter, and emitted it to the light of day. Had Teufelsdröckh also a father and mother; did he, at one time, wear drivel-bibs, and live on spoon-meat? Did he ever, in rapture and tears, clasp a friend's bosom to his; looks he also wistfully into the long burial-aisle of the Past, where only winds, and their low harsh moan, give inarticulate answer? Has he fought duels;—good Heaven! how did he comport himself when in Love?

Teufelsdröckh himself begins with a typically Romantic purple paean to "Happy season of Childhood!"—wherein, he notes, "Kind Nature, that art to all a bountiful mother; that visitest the poor man's hut with auroral radiance; and for thy Nurseling hast provided a soft swathing of Love and infinite Hope, wherein he waxes and slumbers, danced-round [umgaukelt] by sweetest Dreams!"

To the editor's exasperation, Teufelsdröckh seems unable to resist a single detail, including his "friendship for cattle and poultry," the precise rules of all the games he played, and the fact that his first outfit was made of yellow serge cloth. Finally, when he is about to go into the particulars of his education, the editor can take no more and cuts him off: "Thou rogue! Is it by short-clothes of yellow serge, and swineherd horns, that an infant of genius is educated? And yet, as usual, it ever remains doubtful whether he is laughing in his sleeve at these Autobiographical times of ours, or writing from the abundance of his own fond ineptitude."

Chapter 4

THE UNITED STATES
OF AUTOBIOGRAPHY

PROBABLY THE SECOND MOST INFLUENTIAL autobiography of
all time was Benjamin Franklin's. He embarked on it in 1771, the same year
Rousseau finished his. Franklin, sixty-six years old at the time and one of
the most eminent men in all the colonies, begins in the form of a long
letter to his son William, starting with the customary presentation of a
rationale. First of all, he imagines William might find it "agreeable" to
learn some of the circumstances of his father's life. (In the course of
composition, Franklin became bitterly estranged from William, and he
dropped the epistolary motif.) He quickly moves on to other reasons, and
these assume that other people besides family members will eventually
read the book: "Having emerg'd from the Poverty and Obscurity in which
I was born and bred, to a State of Affluence and some Degree of Reputation in the World, and having gone so far thro life with a considerable
share of Felicity . . . my Posterity may like to know, as they may find some
of them suitable to their own Situations, and therefore fit to be imitated."

Franklin also says that he is endeavoring to write about his life because he expects to *enjoy* it. (Here, if nowhere else, he resembles Rousseau, who notes, "In writing about my travels I am as I was when traveling; I cannot bear to arrive.") Finally, Franklin is the rare if not solitary memoirist who concedes that he writes because "perhaps I shall a good deal gratify my own *Vanity.* Indeed I scarce ever heard the introductory Words, *Without Vanity I may say, &c.* but some vain thing immediately follow'd. Most People dislike Vanity in others whatever Share they have of it themselves, but I give it fair Quarter wherever I meet with it."

Immediately it's clear that we are in a different universe from Rousseau's. Franklin is not quite the petit bourgeois shopkeeper that D. H. Lawrence pilloried in *Studies in Classic American Literature,* but he is a confident raconteur of polished anecdotes, most accompanied by a lesson or moral. The book is utterly lacking in scandal; one of the only female presences is his wife, whom he refers to as "Miss Read," and his references to her are discreet and demure. And while Franklin has his low moments, they unanimously involve momentary discomfort or inconvenience, not soul torment or even self-doubt. Thus in an early passage he describes finding himself on the Market Street wharf in Philadelphia in October 1723, at the age of seventeen, having just taken the boat from New Jersey: "I was in my working dress, my best clothes being to come round by sea. I was dirty from my journey; my pockets were stuff'd out with shirts and stockings; I knew no soul, nor where to look for lodging. I was fatigued with traveling, rowing, and want of rest, I was very hungry; and my whole stock of cash consisted of a Dutch dollar, and about a shilling in copper."

No problem! Franklin is directed to a baker, where he asks for "three penny-worth of any sort. He gave me, accordingly, three great puffy rolls. I was surpriz'd at the quantity, but took it, and having no room in my pockets, walk'd off with a roll under each arm, and eating the other." Then he finds comfortable lodging. Then he finds a job as a printer's helper.

The first part of the book is about a young man striving to improve his circumstances and himself; as a visual aid, Franklin reproduces the chart he drew up showing his weekly performance in the thirteen virtues. In other hands this might not be very sufferable, but Franklin is saved by his self-deprecation, his wit, and his sharp eye for the people and the world around him.

After completing about fifty pages and taking the story up to 1730, Franklin put down his pen. As he succinctly explained, "The affairs of the Revolution occasion'd the interruption." He was ready to begin again in 1783, and he reproduces, in their entirety, two letters from friends written in that year urging him to continue with the work. Both stress its great potential as a pedagogical tool. The first, by Abel James, points out that the influence autobiographical writings "have upon the minds of youth is very great, and has nowhere appeared to me so plain, as in our public friend's [Franklin's] journals. It almost insensibly leads the youth into the resolution of endeavoring to become as good and eminent as the journalist." The second correspondent, Benjamin Vaughan, also is in favor of autobiographies, provided that the autobiographer is, like Franklin, of high moral fiber: "If it encourages more writings of the same kind as your own, and induces more men to spend lives fit to be written, it will be worth all Plutarch's Lives put together."

So Franklin started in again. He worked intermittently, and by the time of his death, in 1790, had gotten only to the age of fifty-one. Soon afterward, passages from the manuscript appeared in two American periodicals; the following year a French translation of a pirated manuscript appeared in book form, under the title *Memoirs of the Private Life of Benjamin*

Franklin, Written by Himself (*Mémoires de la vie privée de Benjamin Franklin, écrits par lui-même*). Two years later, two English translations from the French appeared; the editors of the twentieth-century Yale edition calculate that one of them was reprinted 150 times over the next seventy years. Meanwhile, in 1817, Franklin's grandson William Temple Franklin began bringing out the authorized edition of Franklin's writings. Greatly concerned with his grandfather's reputation, he made some 1,200 changes, most of them for the worse, including replacing "stared like a pig poisoned" with "stared with astonishment."

Since then there have been hundreds, perhaps thousands, of editions of the book; an 1868 one provided the title by which we know it, *The Autobiography of Benjamin Franklin*. The future banker Thomas Mellon read the book in 1827, when he was fourteen, and later said he regarded "the reading of Franklin's *Autobiography* as the turning point of my life." Upon reaching an eminent position, Mellon had one thousand copies printed up and distributed to young men who came to him seeking advice. Alternatively, Lawrence is far from the only commentator who has criticized the book. In 1870, Mark Twain descried the way it showed Franklin as "living wholly on bread and water, and studying astronomy at meal time—a thing which has brought affliction to millions of boys since, whose fathers had read Franklin's pernicious biography."

Benjamin Vaughan's 1783 letter encouraging Franklin to continue with his *Autobiography* contains this sentence: "This style of writing seems a little gone out of vogue, and yet it is a very useful one, as it will make a subject of comparison with the lives of various public cut-throats and intriguers, and with absurd monastic self-tormentors or vain literary triflers." "Absurd monastic self-tormentors" was an obvious gibe at Rousseau, whose *Confessions* was published the previous year. The "vain literary triflers" were his growing flock of epigones. All of these would be outnumbered, however, by the "public cut-throats and intriguers." Vaughan was prescient, but even he could not have envisioned how autobiography in early America would become a fertile ground for thieves, murderers, beggars, and marginal individuals of every variety.

To be sure, a substantial number of quite eminent citizens of the period, besides Franklin, were inspired to write their life stories. In a book published in 1779 (and republished at least eighteen times before the Civil War), Colonel Ethan Allen applied some of the conventions of the Indian captivity narrative to his description of cruel treatment by the hands of his British captors. Subsequent autobiographies by notables included *Narrative of the Adventures of an American Navy Officer*, by Nathaniel Fanning, in 1806; Anne Grant's *Memoirs of an American Lady*, in 1808; and the memoirs of Alexander Graydon, a Revolutionary War veteran and Pennsylvania Federalist, in 1811. One of the biggest successes of antebellum American publishing was *A Narrative of the Life of David Crockett, of the State of Tennessee*, the 1834 memoirs of the backwoodsman-turned-Indian-fighter-turned-politician, which self-consciously followed Franklin in telling the story of a self-made American man and which continued to be reprinted well into the twentieth century.

Possibly the best-selling book—in any category—of the first half of the nineteenth century was a personal narrative written by a Connecticut merchant captain, James Riley. In 1815, his ship, the *Commerce*, was wrecked off the coast of Africa. Along with the eleven other survivors, Riley was captured and enslaved by a band of nomadic Arabs. After suffering miserable treatment, Riley eventually came in contact with a British consul who purchased his freedom. Riley's 1817 account of his experiences, *An Authentic Narrative of the Loss of the American Brig* Commerce (often referred to as *Captain Riley's Narrative*), was an immediate bestseller on both sides of the Atlantic. Not only was it a rip-roaring tale, but in its depictions of the pain and indignity Riley suffered in bondage, it provided the young U.S. abolitionist movement with a talking point on the horrors of slavery. At least seven editions came out within two years, and at least sixteen more American editions appeared between 1820 and 1859. According to *American National Biography*, "In 1851 a million Americans then alive were said to have read the book, including Abraham Lincoln, who listed it as one of his favorite works." Equally popular, if less harrowing, was *Two Years Before the Mast* (1840), by Richard Henry Dana, Jr., the young son of a prominent Massachusetts poet and journalist. Dana's book was the true story of his time as a common seaman on a five-month voyage around Cape Horn and on to California.

But what was remarkable was how many life stories were being turned out by those hanging on to the lower rungs of the social ladder. Narratives by criminals, in particular, picked up on a longtime trend on the other side of the Atlantic. As early as the late seventeenth century, miscreants of various kinds were telling their stories in the pages of several different English periodicals. One such publication featured the confessions of prisoners executed at Tyburn prison and, according to a contemporary account, "experienced a ten times greater sale than either the *Spectator*, the *Guardian* or the *Rambler*."

In the colonies, two notable murderers' tales—*A Narrative of the Life Together with the Last Speech, Confession and Solemn Declaration of John Lewis* and *An Authentic and Particular Account of the Life of Francis Burdett Personel, written by Himself*—were published as books in 1762 and 1773, respectively. The narrators were repentant, in the manner of a conversion narrative, but in the books that followed Lewis's and Personel's, readers increasingly began to expect violence and gore. *A Brief Narrative of the Life and Confession of Barnett Davenport Under Sentence of Death, for a series of the most horrid Murders, ever perpetrated in this Country, or perhaps*

any other, published in 1780, tried to justify its title by describing in excru-
ciating detail how Davenport, a nineteen-year-old Continental Army de-
serter, beat to death his landlord, the man's wife, and one of their three
grandchildren, then set fire to the house, causing the death of the remain-
ing two children. Davenport seemed to revel in his crime, referring to the
"shrieks, cries, and doleful lamentations" of his victims and noting how
the face of one of them was "covered with gore and streaming blood."

The first-person criminal genre picked up steam after the turn of the
century. For her book *Interpreting the Self*, Diane Bjorklund collated two
major bibliographies of American autobiography and found that between
1800 (the year the bibliographers began counting) and 1849, the second-
highest occupational category was Criminal/Deviant, accounting for 56
of the 225 published autobiographies, or 24.9 percent. (Clergy/Religious
ranked first and Military third.)* Especially among prisoners sentenced to
death, a printed confessional narrative became expected. Typically, these
texts had an unbeatable combination of chilling details and sanctimonious
remorse. Charles Boyington, a journeyman printer convicted of murder,
wrote in 1835, "It is natural that the public should anticipate some statement from me: yet it is not for the gratification of curiosity, however
laudable, that I have been induced to commence this exposition, but a deep
sense of duty to my distant relatives and friends and to my memory."

Public executions were mass spectacles in the antebellum period. The
great popularity of condemned prisoners' narratives was another reflection of this ghoulish interest, and hack writers competed to get the plum
commission as amanuenses. In her fascinating book *The Unvarnished*

---

*These proportions changed over time. The most recent decade Bjorklund tabulated was the 1970s, in
which she found the most commonly represented profession in autobiographies was Entertainer, with
152 of the 1,175 books, or 12.9 percent, followed by Clergy, Writer, Sports Figure, and Politician.

Truth: Personal Narratives in Nineteenth-Century America, historian Ann Fabian tells the story of John Lechler, a Pennsylvanian who in 1822 "caught his wife Mary in bed with his friend and neighbor, Bernhart Haag. Haag tried to get away, but while he cowered bare-bottomed in the cellar, Lechler strangled his wife." Then he picked up his gun, followed Haag home, attempted to shoot him through the door of his house, but missed, killing Mrs. Haag instead. Before he was hanged, he ended up writing *two* narratives. He explained why in the opening pages of one of them:

> My good old friend, Samuel Carpenter, agrees to receive my confession, and have it published to raise a little money, after paying the printers, to educate my poor children. And I declare with my dying breath that it contains the whole truth. The jailor has frequently, as I have told several people, told me that I must give him my confession, because he gave me such good victuals—and at last I was *compelled*, for I am his poor prisoner, in chains to write a *history* for him, which he intends to have published also.

As the genre solidified, the texts became marbled with bows to convention: a statement of the criminal's remorse, an avowal of the confession's truth, an explanation of how an illiterate prisoner's testimony was (or was not) rendered into proper English and, frequently, a description of how the document was transferred from the condemned man to the publisher. The confession of Jesse Strang, a notorious murderer executed in 1827, contained a third-person framing narrative of his statement on the gallows: "Holding a pamphlet in his hand, he said, 'This contains a full confession of the great transaction for which I am about to die, and every word that it contains, to the best of my knowledge and belief, is true: if there is a single word in it that is not true, it has been inserted by mistake and not by design.'" Then he handed it to a minister, who arranged to have it published.

One of the blockbusters of early-nineteenth-century American letters was the *Memoirs of Stephen Burroughs*. Burroughs, the son of a New Hampshire minister, was a self-admitted rogue, acknowledging, for example, that when he posed as a minister, he "violated that principle of veracity which we implicitly pledge ourselves to maintain toward each other." He also confesses to adultery and details his association with counterfeiters and subsequent three-year imprisonment, his work as an itinerant schoolteacher, his trial on a charge of rape, and his involvement in land fraud. The first volume of the book was published to excellent sales in 1798, the second in 1804, and both together in many editions beginning in 1811.

Autobiography seemed to be sufficiently democratic to embrace all Americans, natives as well as their immigrant captors. In 1832, the Sauk leader and warrior Black Hawk led a party that attempted to reclaim land in Illinois that he believed had been signed away to the United States through illegitimate treaties. Federal and Illinois forces fired on them, even as they waved a surrender flag, eventually killing three hundred of their people (including women and children) and taking Black Hawk and many others prisoner. While in captivity, Black Hawk told his life story to an interpreter. And the result was a bestseller: *Life of Ma-Ka-Tai-Me-She-Kia-Kiak, or Black Hawk, Embracing the Traditions of His Nation, Various Wars in Which He Has Been Engaged, and His Account of the Cause and General History of the Black Hawk War of 1832, His Surrender, and Travels Through the United States*. The diction is clearly a product of Black Hawk's white editors, but recent scholarship has shown that the sense of most of the text came from Black Hawk, and, indeed, a sense of dignified outrage emanates from the page. Here is his description of the initial treaty that ceded Indian lands to whites:

Here, for the first time, I touched the goose quill to the treaty—not know-ing, however, that by that act I consented to give away my village. Had that been explained to me, I should have opposed it, and never would have signed their treaty, as my recent conduct will clearly prove.

What do we know of the manner of the laws and customs of the white people? They might buy our bodies for dissection, and we would touch the goose quill to confirm it, without knowing what we are doing. This was the case with myself and people in touching the goose quill for the first time. . . .

My reason teaches me that *land cannot be sold*. The Great Spirit gave it to his children to live upon, and cultivate, as far as is necessary for their subsistence; and so long as they occupy and cultivate it, they have a right to the soil—but if they voluntarily leave it, then any other people have a right to settle upon it. Nothing can be sold, but such things as can be car-ried away.

Women on the margins told their life stories in striking number as well. In 1809, someone who signed her name "K. White" published a narrative of her *Life, Occurrences, Vicissitudes and Present Situation*. The book begins with the familiar motif of being taken captive by Indians, but within a few pages she has escaped and moved on to other adventures, including the suicide of her fiancé and marriage to another man, "S. White," who se-duces the maid, impregnates his wife, then abandons her, saddled with debt. As a result of the latter condition, White flees the authorities— occasionally disguising herself as a man—but spends some time in jail. Another woman, Elizabeth Munro Fisher, became embroiled in a legal battle over inherited land with her half brother. Not only did she lose, but she was convicted of forgery and sent to prison for six years. She wrote her memoirs when she was released and self-published them in 1810. Four years later, Lucy Brewer published a book, *The Life of Louisa Baker* (later reprinted as *The Female Marine*), telling of her experiences as a prostitute and as a disguised sailor in the War of 1812. The *Memoirs of Mrs. Abigail Bailey*, published in 1815, is the harrowing tale of the author's escape from marriage to a violent husband who sexually abused their daughter.

In the 1830s, two sensational memoirs combined a dizzying mix of genres: captivity narratives, gothic novels, and anti-Catholic screeds. The first was credited to a young woman named Rebecca Reed, who had fled from a Charlestown, Massachusetts, convent in 1832 and immediately began telling stories of the abuse she had suffered there. In large part because of these allegations, rioting townspeople burned the convent to the ground. In 1835, a book titled *Six Months in a Convent* was published under Reed's name; it detailed the bizarre and cruel practices she had sup-posedly witnessed and endured. It concluded: "If, in consequence of my having for a time strayed from the *true religion*, I am enabled to become an humble instrument in the hands of God in warning others of the errors of Romanism, and preventing even *one* from falling into its *snares, and from being* shrouded in its delusions, I shall feel richly rewarded." The book was a smash, selling, according to historian Ray Allen Billington, 200,000 copies in the first month of publication.

The following year saw the publication of *Awful Disclosures of the Hotel Dieu Convent of Montreal, or the Secrets of Black Nunnery Revealed*, by Maria Monk. Monk had also supposedly escaped from a convent and in the book she exposes its lurid secrets, most of which had to do with nuns being forced to have sex with priests. She also describes a lime pit in the convent's basement where the murdered progeny of these unions were thrown. The book became an immediate bestseller and Monk was taken up by New York society. However, even more so than Reed's memoir, Monk's was spurious. Several investigations revealed that she had never in fact *been* in the convent. She disappeared from public life and died in 1849 in a New York prison.

Just as the fictional *Robinson Crusoe* gave a kick-start to actual autobiographical writing in the early eighteenth century, so these varied first-person life stories had a profound influence on the American novel. James Fenimore Cooper traded heavily on the Indian captivity story, and Herman Melville's first six works of fiction—from *Typee* (1846) to *Moby-Dick* (1851)—were all first-person tales that adapted and played on the conventions of the sea-adventure narrative. The novel Melville published in 1856, *Israel Potter: His Fifty Years of Exile*, had a more direct connection to the autobiographical tradition. It was based on the story of a real man who in 1824 published a real book, *The Life and Remarkable Adventures of Israel Potter*. Potter was a destitute veteran of the Battle of Bunker Hill who took pen to paper out of anger that when he petitioned Congress for a pension, as he writes, "on no other principle, than that *I was absent from the country when the pension law passed*—my Petition was REJECTED!!!" In the book, which he sold for twenty-eight cents, Potter describes his meetings with King George III and Benjamin Franklin; Melville invents encounters with Ethan Allen and John Paul Jones as well. More broadly, thanks to these texts, the first person singular insinuated itself into the American literary consciousness until it became the predominant mode. Emerson was writing a veiled autobiography in his essays of the 1840s and 1850s, and Thoreau a more direct one in *Walden* and his other documentary narratives. Whitman's *Leaves of Grass* was autobiography in verse; so was Lowell's *Life Studies* a century later. As for fiction, from *Adventures of Huckleberry Finn*, through *The Great Gatsby*, *The Sun Also Rises*, and

The Catcher in the Rye, to *The Adventures of Augie March* and three-quarters of the works of Philip Roth, it's hard to find an important American novel that's *not* some variation on a memoir.

THE MOST ORIGINAL AND REMARKABLE American autobiographical subgenre that emerged in the first half of the nineteenth century drew on narratives of conversion, repentance, captivity, and adventure. It had a chance to emerge because of the singular American tradition of the lower orders telling their stories. Indeed, the authors of these books inhabited the lowest position society had to offer. The first published work by an African-American was *NARRATIVE Of the UNCOMMON SUFFERINGS, AND Surpriᵹing DELIVERANCE OF Briton Hammon, A Negro Man* . . . , issued in Boston in 1760. The fourteen-page pamphlet actually told a fairly typical captivity narrative: while at sea, Hammon, a slave, was captured by Caribbean Indians and held by them for thirteen years. The ironic (in contemporary minds) happy ending comes when Hammon is reunited with his American master.

Approximately one hundred American slave narratives were published in book or pamphlet form before 1865; until the Depression era, slave narratives outnumbered every other kind of book by African-Americans, including novels. The first widely read narrative was the work of Olaudah Equiano, who, like many earlier and later autobiographers, begins with a self-conscious reflection on his literary project: "It is not a little hazardous in a private and obscure individual, and a stranger, too, thus to solicit the indulgent attention of the public, especially when I own I offer here the history of neither a saint, a hero, nor a tyrant." Equiano was kidnapped by slave traders at age eleven and was eventually purchased by a sea captain, Michael Henry Pascal. He bought his own freedom in 1766, and settled in England, where he became an active abolitionist. And, like most subsequent slave narratives, his book, published in 1789 and reprinted in fifty different editions in Europe and the United States before 1850, was in large part designed to further that cause. It contained many memorable passages, such as Equiano's first view of the slave ship that would take him to the New World. This held "a multitude of black people of every description chained together, every one of their countenances expressing dejection and sorrow, I no longer doubted of my fate; and, quite overpowered with horror and anguish, I fell motionless on the deck and fainted. When I recovered a little I found some black people about me. . . . I asked them if we were not to be eaten by those white men with horrible looks, red faces, and loose hair."

Unlike Equiano's *Narrative*, early works published in this country by former slaves tended to be spiritual autobiographies in familiar forms. Others were confessions by criminals. Sometimes they resembled such narratives by whites, sometimes they were very different. The ostensible author of the most notorious such text was Nat Turner, a Virginia slave who experienced a vision that led him to believe that God had chosen him to lead a great uprising: he "heard a loud noise in the heavens, and the Spirit instantly appeared to me and said the Serpent was loosened, and Christ had laid down the yoke he had borne for the sins of men." He understood that he should watch the heavens for signs, and then "I should arise and . . . slay my enemies with their own weapons." The sign came in the summer of 1831; by the time they were through, Turner and his supporters had killed more than fifty whites. The rebels were arrested and eventually executed (along with dozens of other blacks unfortunate enough to be in the area). But before his hanging, Turner gave an interview to Thomas R. Gray, a white lawyer, and from this testimony Gray produced *The Confessions of Nat Turner*, published in Baltimore and widely distributed. Given that the text was produced by this unsympathetic editor, it's striking if not surprising that Turner's voice is straightforward and not undignified, even as he recounts the acts of terrible violence taken by his confederates and himself. They commenced at the home of his master, Mr. Travis:

> I entered my master's chamber, it being dark, I could not give a death blow, the hatchet glanced from his head, he sprang from the bed and called his wife, it was his last word, Will laid him dead, with a blow of his axe, and Mrs. Travis shared the same fate, as she lay in bed. The murder of this family, five in number, was the work of a moment, not one of them awoke; there was a little infant sleeping in a cradle, that was forgotten, until we had left the house and gone some distance, when Henry and Will returned and killed it.

But a very different sort of slave narrative had started appearing and would continue to do so until the Civil War. The dozens of such texts from this period were so resonant and numerous not only because they were timely, dramatic, and moving; more than that, they took the figurative journey of many past autobiographies, from spiritual bondage to spiritual liberation, and made it absolutely literal. As the genre became closely aligned with the views and aims of abolitionism, it developed certain conventions that were so often present that they reached almost the level of ritual. In the words of the scholar Henry Louis Gates, Jr., the books constituted "a communal utterance, a collective tale." A prefatory apparatus would include an engraved portrait, signed by the author, and several signed statements by white abolitionists and/or editors testifying that not only is every word straight from the ex-slave's mouth and totally true, but that the account, if anything, underestimates the horrors of slav-

ery. The narrative itself starts with the formulaic clause "I was born . . ."
The scholar William Andrews describes some characteristics of the text
itself:

> Usually the antebellum slave narrator portrays slavery as a condition of
> extreme physical, intellectual, emotional, and spiritual deprivation, a kind
> of hell on earth. Precipitating the narrator's decision to escape is some sort
> of personal crisis, such as the sale of a loved one or a dark night of the soul
> in which hope contends with despair for the spirit of the slave. Impelled by
> faith in God and a commitment to liberty and human dignity comparable
> (the slave narrative often stresses) to that of America's Founding Fathers,
> the slave undertakes an arduous quest for freedom that climaxes in his or
> her arrival in the North. In many antebellum narratives, the attainment of
> freedom is signaled not simply by reaching the free states, but by renaming
> oneself and dedicating one's future to antislavery activism.

Almost all slave narratives contain a scene or scenes of a master beat-
ing or cruelly treating a female slave, often the narrator's mother, and
painful scenes of family separation. Harriet Beecher Stowe acknowledged drawing on five separate slave narratives in *Uncle Tom's Cabin*
(1852), and this emotional material was clearly the most powerful thing
she borrowed. Also in the 1850s, a writer who called herself Hannah
Crofts composed a novel in the form of a slave narrative and titled it *The
Bondwoman's Narrative*. The work was not published and lay in obscurity
for some 140 years, until Henry Louis Gates purchased the manuscript at
auction, declared it the first novel written by an African-American woman,
and edited it for publication in 2002. (In recent decades, the "neo-slave
narrative" has become a fertile genre, beginning with Margaret Walker's

Jubilee in 1966, and continuing with such novels as Ishmael Reed's *Flight to Canada*, William Styron's *The Confessions of Nat Turner*, Ernest J. Gaines's *The Autobiography of Miss Jane Pittman*, Sherley Anne Williams's *Dessa Rose*, Toni Morrison's *Beloved*, Charles Johnson's *Middle Passage*, and Edward P. Jones's *The Known World*.)

Working within established conventions, the authors of slave narratives often fashioned passages of great power. At the close of his 1825 book, William Grimes declares, "I am now entirely destitute of property; where and how I shall live I don't know; where and how I shall die I don't know, but I hope I may be prepared. If it were not for the stripes on my back which were made while I was a slave, I would in my will, leave my skin as a legacy to the government, desiring that it might be taken off and made into parchment, and then bind the constitution of glorious, happy *and free* America. Let the skin of an American slave, bind the charter of American liberty." It is impossible to measure the exact mixture in the passage of irony and sincerity, and it is the more striking for it.

There was, in addition, considerable variation in terms of plot; the varied means by which slaves made their escape, often pursued by barking dogs, was rich in picaresque adventure. Henry Brown's narrative of 1849 described how he paid eighty-six dollars to have himself surreptitiously shipped, in a two-foot-by-three-foot box, to Philadelphia abolitionists. (The following year the Fugitive Slave Law forced Brown—by that time he had acquired the nickname "Box"—to flee to England, where he set up a traveling show featuring a replication of his escape, including the famous box.) William and Ellen Craft, a married couple, tell the extraordinary tale of their escape in *Running a Thousand Miles for Freedom* (1860): Ellen presented herself as William's master, that is, a white male.

One of the classic slave narratives is Harriet Jacobs's *Incidents in the*

Life of a Slave Girl: Written by Herself, published pseudonymously in 1861. Born in North Carolina in 1813, Jacobs describes, with a candor rare in any book of the time, how, at the age of sixteen, she felt that the only way to escape the sexual advances of her master was to enter into a liaison with a young white neighbor. Some years later the master renewed his demands, and she ran away. She hid for almost seven years in a tiny space under the roof of her grandmother's home; occasionally she could hear the voices of her two children. In June 1842, she escaped to Philadelphia, and she was eventually reunited with her children in the North. In 1850, she was offered the chance to buy her freedom but declined: "The more my mind had become enlightened, the more difficult it was for me to consider myself an article of property; and to pay money to those who had so grievously oppressed me seemed like taking from my sufferings the glory of triumph."

Freedom and dignity, suffering and triumph, were not the only profound issues confronted by slave narratives. William Wells Brown's *Narrative* of 1847 constitutes to a large extent a meditation on truthfulness and deceit. Slavery, says Brown, "makes its victims lying and mean." He recounts all sorts of lies associated with the institution, including one of his jobs when he worked for a slave trader: "blacking" slaves being sold for auction, that is, coloring their hair to make them seem younger. He describes an episode where he escaped flogging by convincing the overseers that the intended victim was actually somebody else, an innocent free black man who had the misfortune to be wandering by. Like Rousseau, Brown says he "deeply regretted the deception I practiced on this poor fellow." Frederick Douglass, whose three autobiographies, published between 1845 and 1881, constituted the acknowledged masterpiece of the genre, directly addressed the issue of truth, in all its complicated subtlety. Because of their circumstances, he observed, slaves habitually suppress the truth rather than take the consequences of telling it, and in so doing prove themselves a master of the human family. If they have anything to say of their masters, it is generally in the masters' favor, especially when speaking to an untried man. I have been frequently asked, when a slave, if I had a kind master, and do not remember ever to have given a negative answer; nor did I, in pursuing this course, consider myself as uttering what was absolutely false; for I always measured the kindness of my master by the standard of kindness set up among slaveholders around us.

The opening of Douglass's first book, *Narrative of the Life of Frederick Douglass*, shows his commanding, distinctive, and allusive style:

I was born in Tuckahoe, near Hillsborough, and about twelve miles from Easton, in Talbot County, Maryland. I have no accurate knowledge of my age, never having seen any authentic record containing it. By far the larger part of the slaves know as little of their ages as horses know of theirs, and it is the wish of most masters within my knowledge to keep their slaves thus ignorant. I do not remember to have ever met a slave who could tell of his birthday. They seldom come nearer to it than planting-time, harvest-time, cherry-time, spring-time, or fall-time. A want of information concerning my own was a source of unhappiness to me even during childhood. The white children could tell their ages. I could not tell why I ought to be deprived of the same privilege. I was not allowed to make any inquiries of my master concerning it. He deemed all such inquiries on the part of a slave improper and impertinent, and evidence of a restless spirit.

Douglass escaped in 1838, when he was about twenty, and made his way to New Bedford, Massachusetts. He was invited to speak at an anti-slavery convention three years later, and was such a success that, like many former slaves, he was sent on a lecture circuit by the Massachusetts Anti-Slavery Society. He was a riveting and eloquent speaker, which ironically created problems. Audiences, he recounted in his second autobiography, *My Bondage and My Freedom,* "said I did not talk like a slave, look like a slave, nor act like a slave, and that they believed I had never been south of the Mason and Dixon line." And so his abolitionist sponsors "said to me, 'Better have a *little* of the plantation manner of speech than not; 'tis not best that you seem too learned.'" Clearly, as a means of delivering one's story, live recitation has the advantage of sensory and emotional immediacy. The self-editing Douglass was forced into was one drawback. Another, he discovered, was staleness: "It was impossible for me to repeat the same story month after month and keep up my interest in it. It was new to the people, it is true, but it was an old story to me; and to go through with it night after night, was a task altogether too mechanical for my nature."

Writing and publishing his story, obviously, could expose many more people to it. And, as Douglass recognized, the very act of writing had deep implications. The idea of freedom—immediately important to black Americans of the nineteenth century, essential, in some way, to all people in all eras—was tied up with notions of literacy. Douglass quotes his master, Mr. Auld: "'Learning will *spoil* the best nigger in the world. Now,' he said, 'if you teach that nigger (speaking of myself) how to read, there would be no keeping him. It would forever unfit him to be a slave.'" The introductory apparatus to his 1845 *Narrative* stresses that he employed no collaborator, ghostwriter, or editor (revealing, incidentally, that the audience was aware of and perhaps expected such assistance).

The publication of the book was itself a courageous act. Unlike other former slaves who took pen to paper, Douglass did not disguise his own or his former master's names, or any part of his story. As a result, he ran the risk of being captured and re-enslaved. But this did not happen, and the book was greeted in the North, and in England, with near-universal acclaim. The *New York Tribune*'s notice was typical: "Considered merely as a narrative, we have never read one more simple, true, coherent, and warm with genuine feeling." By 1859, thirty thousand copies had been sold and Douglass was a literary and moral luminary. His friend James McCune Smith referred to him as a "Representative American man" who "passed through every gradation of rank comprised in our national make-up, and bears upon his person and upon his soul everything that is American."

Chapter 5

INTERLUDE: TRUTH, MEMORY, AND AUTOBIOGRAPHY

"I have done that," says my memory. "I cannot have done that,"
says my pride, and remains inexorable. Eventually—memory yields.

—FRIEDRICH NIETZSCHE

Of the vast accession of vocabulary, ideas, and emotions; of our
introduction to the world outside; of the successive pictures of society
which are formed in the mental vision of the child—of all this we
retain practically nothing; and so an autobiography of childhood is
nearly always commonplace and untrue, even when the author
himself is sincere.

—ANDRÉ MAUROIS

IN JOHN GREENLEAF WHITTIER'S 1840s short story "Yankee
Gypsies," a beggar wanders the country carrying a written narrative of a
shipwreck in which he lost all his possessions. The story's narrator eventu-

ally finds out that the man is a fraud and bought the manuscript "from one of those ready-writers in New York who manufacture beggar-credentials at the low price of one dollar per copy, with earthquakes, fires, or shipwrecks, to suit customers."

That detail surely struck a chord with Whittier's readers, who had experienced in their lifetimes a string of supposedly factual memoirs that were met with suspicions, or turned out to consist of gross exaggerations or outright fabrications. Each of these texts generated its own brouhaha. But they also reflected lingering enmity between the United States and England, the growing controversy over slavery, and a larger debate about the nature of truth.

In 1816, a volume titled *The narrative of Robert Adams, an American sailor who was wrecked on the Western coast of Africa, in the year 1810; was detained three years in slavery by the Arabs of the great desert, and resided several months in the City of Tombuctoo* was published in four European cities and in Boston. The English editor of the book, Simon Cock, wrote that he found Adams, a mixed-race American sailor, telling his story among the street beggars in London in 1815, and subsequently transcribed the tale. Cock devotes a great deal of his editorial apparatus to countering any suspicion that the story is a fabrication, affirming at one point that "fifty gentlemen" had interrogated Adams, "among whom there was not one who was not struck by the artlessness and good sense of Adams's replies, or who did not feel persuaded that he was relating simply the facts which he had seen, to the best of his recollections and belief." Nevertheless the book was met with widespread skepticism, especially on the western shores of the Atlantic. A writer in *The North American Review* undertook an investigation and reported that, among other falsehoods, there was no Adams family in the New York State town the writer had claimed to be from. He concluded that the book was a "gross attempt to impose on the credulity of the publick. To us, indeed, this appeared so obvious, that we should not think it worthy of any serious examination, had it not excited so much interest, and gained universal belief in England." To this day, scholars have not reached consensus on the truth of Adams's narrative.

About a half-dozen years later, a man who called himself John Dunn Hunter published *Memoirs of a Captivity Among the Indians of North America*, which told of his abduction at the age of two or three and the twenty years he spent with the Osage and Kansas tribes. The book, unusual among captivity narratives for its detailed and respectful description of the Indians and their culture, was, like Adams's narrative, hailed in England, where Hunter spent about a year and was deemed "the *Lion* of the fashionable world." Things were different in the United States, where General Lewis Cass, governor of the Michigan Territory (later Andrew Jackson's secretary of war and, in 1848, the Democratic nominee for president), took it upon himself to prove (in an article written for the same *North American Review*) that Hunter was an imposter and his book "a worthless fabrication."

Hunter had his defenders as well—and continues to attract them among contemporary scholars. Although there are undoubtedly factual errors in his narrative, at this late date it's impossible to determine whether he was who he claimed to be. But the very contentiousness is significant. The book was intended, or at least read, as a didactic entry in an ongoing political argument: as putting forth the humanness if not nobility of Native Americans at a time when the American military was vanquishing them and justifying this course of action by assumptions or contentions about racial inferiority. (Also part of the fight, as in the case of Robert Adams, was lingering American animosity toward the British, who showered both authors with praise.) "True" testimony is always powerful ammunition in a political debate. As a result, one side will be at least tempted to exaggerate or fabricate; the other side will respond with an effort to debunk or expose.

Such a pas de deux was inescapable in the most overarching American debate of the period. In 1836, when the slave narrative had not yet established itself as a genre, a book appeared titled *Archy Moore, The White Slave; Or, Memoirs of a Fugitive*. The text was preceded by an "Advertisement" signed by "The Editor" that began: "It is unnecessary to detain the reader, with a narrative of the somewhat singular manner in which the MS. of the following Memoirs came into my possession. It is sufficient for me to say, that I received it, with an injunction to make it public—an injunction which I have not felt at liberty to disobey." But was it an actual memoir—or was "The Editor" a fiction and the slave Archy Moore an invention? Although the flowery language of the text suggested the latter, it was impossible to say for sure; and in the 1830s, no clues were provided by library call numbers, bookstore sections, bestseller list categories, or author interviews. Abolitionists tried to finesse the question. A sympathetic anonymous reviewer in *The Christian Examiner* opined that "if Archy Moore is a fiction, inasmuch as its particular series of events never actually occurred, it still is fact in a much more important sense, inasmuch as events of a similar character, only we doubt not of even greater horror, are occurring every day wherever slavery exists." But with stakes and passions as high as they were in the debate over abolition, that kind of rationale simply wouldn't do. Pro-slavery forces continued to disparage the book, and finally Richard Hildreth, an abolitionist and historian who had lived for some years in the South, came forward and acknowledged that Archy Moore was an invention and that he, Hildreth, had written every word himself.

There was another awkward step the following year. John Greenleaf Whittier—the same New England poet and abolitionist who would soon sit down to write "Yankee Gypsies"—was engaged by the American Anti-Slavery Society to prepare for publication the life story of an actual fugitive slave, a man who went by the name of James Williams. The resulting book, narrated in Williams's first-person voice, told of his harsh treatment on an Alabama plantation and the torture he had seen inflicted on his fellow slaves. The veracity of the text was almost immediately challenged by an Alabama newspaper editor, who called it "a notorious libel upon our country" and printed a letter claiming that Williams was in fact named Shadrach Wilkins and was a fugitive not only from slavery but from charges of attempted murder. The Anti-Slavery Society initially denied the charges outright; an article in the abolitionist periodical *The Liberator* said the book was "incontrovertibly true; and is additionally valuable, because it so powerfully corroborates other evidence and facts which have been published." But the charges and complaints didn't go away, and the society directed two members to investigate. These men ultimately and reluctantly concluded that "many of the Statements made in the said Narrative were false." Weeks later, the society discontinued sale of the book. James Williams, meanwhile, was nowhere to be found.

The Archy Moore and James Williams episodes were a loud wake-up call for abolitionists. They had worked on the ends-justify-the-means assumption that in a narrative that showed the true horrors of slavery, literal truth wasn't important. Yet the alacrity with which their opponents seized on the falsehoods in the texts proved that in this literary battle, factual accuracy was very important indeed. Knowing that their subsequent books would be subject to intense scrutiny, as in a courtroom, they henceforth accompanied each one with an array of features all designed to establish its truth: prefaces or affidavits by eminent figures (always white), a lithograph of the author, and a reproduction of his or her signature. Equally significant, almost all of the ex-slaves who wrote these books went on the lecture circuit: in person, they could answer questions about their lives, show audiences the physical scars with which slavery had left them, and in general bear witness to the truth of their tales.

Yet another discredited autobiography of the period was written by an African-American who claimed to be white, and who described in the book his many years masquerading as a Native American. This was *The Life and Adventures of James P. Beckwourth, Mountaineer, Scout and Pioneer, and Chief of the Crow Nation of Indians*, a picaresque tale that was an immediate bestseller when it was published in 1856. As Laura Browder notes in her book *Slippery Characters: Ethnic Impersonators and American Identities*, Beckwourth describes in the book how, when he was a boy, "my father" moved to St. Louis, "taking with him all his family and twenty-two negroes," but neglects to say that his father was also his master and that he himself was one of the twenty-two black slaves. The book was a lively yarn—critic Bernard De Voto subsequently said that it "gave our literature its goriest lies"—but few were taken in by Beckwourth's attempted ethnic impersonation. De Voto reports that the historian Francis Parkman, in the margins of his copy of the book, described Beckwourth as "a fellow of bad character—a compound of black and white blood, though he represents otherwise."*

At this point in American history, it was clear that a label of "autobiography" or "memoir" or "personal narrative" on the cover of a book had little bearing on the truth of the statements inside it. Sometimes, as with slave narratives, a demonstration of falsity created an uproar. But in

*Ironically—given his effort to hide his heritage, and the racist attitudes toward both blacks and Native Americans that Beckwourth displays in the book—he has in recent decades been enshrined as a key figure in African-American history, including a juvenile biography in the Black Americans of Achievement series.

less highly charged subjects, the public didn't seem to greatly care. Not uncommonly, people found their own names appropriated on the covers of spurious autobiographies. There were at least three such books purporting to be written by Davy Crockett, in addition to his own 1834 memoir—which itself was not free of tall tales.

The spate of unreliable memoirs reflected an uncertainty and sometimes malleability about "truth" that showed up in the wider culture as well. As the historian Karen Halttunen argues in her book *Confidence Men and Painted Women*, nineteenth-century America was oddly fascinated with the question of what was real and what was fake, who was an imposter and who was the genuine article. One of Melville's most haunting novels is called *The Confidence-Man* and is about a shadowy figure who is constantly changing not only his story but his very appearance. In the novel that bears his name, Huck Finn several times pretends to be someone he's not; his most notable quality, it sometimes seems, is his compulsion to tell lies and "stretchers." P. T. Barnum constructed a fabulous career on the fault line between authenticity and humbug. He first came to prominence in 1835, when he presented to the public Joice Heth, the supposedly 161-year-old ex-nurse of "dear little George Washington," whose birth in 1732 she had attended. Heath died a year later, and an autopsy revealed her age to be about eighty. In 1841, Barnum published an exceedingly odd series of first-person newspaper articles under the minimally disguised name "Barnaby Diddleum." In one section he described how he acquired the services of an elderly black woman—"aunt Joice"—and had her teeth extracted to make her appear even older than she was. That account shows up in Barnum's actual autobiography—first published in 1854, and reprinted annually until his death in 1890. Yet other Barnaby tales are clearly fanciful. Typical of the time, it was impossible for a contemporary reader to discern which was which.

A similar chipping away at autobiography's integrity was taking place in France. The critic Philippe Lejeune notes, "After the fall of the Empire, the public was ravenous for memoirs on the *ancien régime*, which publishers tried to exploit by fabricating false memoirs by people who lived in that other century or by anonymous writers." Lejeune quotes an 1829 newspaper article defending the "apocryphal memoirs," a "third genre" between fiction and memoir: "We acknowledge that the greatest part of the originality of confessions disappears when we know that they are not the work of the penitent. But that these books cannot instruct and entertain at the same time, that is what we think is unacceptable. They can even have a distinguished literary merit."

That may be true. Yet autobiography, more than any other genre, trades on its authenticity and credibility. If those qualities are understood to be lacking in a memoir, why would anyone possibly take it seriously or even bother to read it? At the same time, the temptation to exaggerate for effect or a good story or to prove a point is always present. Given that, and given the high number of discredited books, it isn't surprising that so many American autobiographers should have felt the need to assure readers, at or near the start of their books, that they had been steadfast in resisting the urge to play false with the facts. Thus:

- Stephen Burroughs, 1804: "Are these matters painted to you, sir, in colors too high for the simple statement of facts. No, sir, indeed they are true, the force of which I must feel while poring over the scenes."
- Robert Bailey, 1822: "I do pledge myself upon the honor of a soldier, an officer, and a gentleman to give a true and literal account of every act or transaction relating thereto." He went on to assure readers, "My recollection of past events makes me

confident that no circumstance, with reference to myself, will be forgotten. I can now repeat a sermon almost word for word, or any narrative of not more than one hour's duration."

■ Joseph Martin, 1830: "I wish to have a better opinion of my readers . . . than ever to think that any of them would ever wish me to stretch the truth to furnish them with wonders that I never saw, or acts or deeds I never performed."

■ John Binns, 1854, pointing out the advantage of writing his autobiography late in life: "It ensures a more full and frank disclosure of facts than would, probably, have been given at an earlier period. Nearly all the persons I shall name . . . have been called hence, and their remains consigned to silent graves."

■ Ralph Keeler, 1870: "I am forced to be veracious by the fact that there are scores of people yet in the prime of life who are cognizant of the main events of the ensuing narrative."

■ George Train, 1902: "Thanks to my early Methodist training, I have never knowingly told a lie; and I shall not begin at this time of life."*

Twain himself, like a significant number of autobiographers before (Gibbon, Rousseau) and since (John Addington Symonds, Henry Adams), chose to have his memoirs published posthumously because, he explained in a preface, that was the only way it was possible to be truthful:

I speak from the grave rather than with my living tongue for a good reason: I can speak thence freely. When a man is writing a book dealing with the

---

*All of the quotations in this list, except for the last one, are taken from Diane Bjorklund's *Interpreting the Self*.

privacies of his life—a book which is to be read while he is still alive—he shrinks from speaking his whole frank mind. All his attempts to do it fail; he recognizes that he is trying to do a thing which is wholly impossible to a human being.

But deliberate lies and mendacious omissions are only one way that falsehoods may creep into a memoir. In *The Confessions*, Rousseau writes:

Almost nothing happened of sufficient interest to my heart for me to retrace its memory with any clarity; and it is difficult to see how, amid so many comings and goings, so many removals following one upon the other, I could have avoided making a few transpositions of time and place. I write entirely from memory, unassisted by mementoes or materials of any sort. There are events in my life that remain as present to me as if they had just happened; but there are voids and lacunae, too, which I can fill only with the aid of anecdotes as confused as the memory that remains of them. I may sometimes, then, have made mistakes and may do so again over trifling details, until such time as I have acquired more certain information about myself; but in what truly concerns my subject, I am confident of being precise and faithful, as I will always try to be in everything; that at last is something that may be relied upon.

Later, he repeats the admission that some of his facts may be incorrect. But that doesn't matter, he says: "I cannot be mistaken about what I felt, nor about what my feelings led me to do; and this is what principally concerns me here. . . . It is the history of my soul that I promised, and to relate it faithfully I require no other memorandum; all I need do, as I have done up until now, is to look inside myself."

As in many other matters, Rousseau was prescient. As he recognized, and as a century of psychological research has confirmed, the human memory is very far from a completely trustworthy mechanism. Conventional wisdom casts memory as a retrieval system, like a videotape that plays back information that has been recorded onto it, or a computer that accesses the files of what really happened. In this model, its efficiency would be limited only by its capacity: some piece of data is forgotten when it's pushed out by another piece that's more recent or more pressing. And only special circumstances, like mental illness, might lead to a distorted or fabricated "memory."

This model, almost all psychologists would agree, is utter nonsense. Among the most lasting of Freud's many revolutionary insights concerned the capriciousness of memory: how emotional turmoil can lead it to play tricks on us, how (in what he called "repression") our psychic defenses can purge it of the most painful experiences. In experiment after experiment, study after study, subsequent psychologists have gone a good deal farther, establishing that memory is by nature untrustworthy: contaminated not merely by gaps, but by distortions and fabrications that inevitably and blamelessly creep into it. It is itself a creative writer, cobbling together "actual" memories, beliefs about the world, cues from a variety of sources, and memories of *previous* memories to plausibly imagine what might have been, and then, in a master stroke, packaging this scenario to the mind as the real one. As the psychologist F. C. Bartlett put it in his groundbreaking 1932 book, *Remembering*: "Remembering appears to be far more decisively an affair of reconstruction rather than one of mere reproduction."

And the reconstruction is subject to all kinds of influences, taking a heavier toll with the passage of time. Psychiatrist Daniel Offer asked a group of high schoolers a set of questions about their lives, and thirty-four years later, asked the same men to think back and answer the same questions about their earlier selves. The differences were dramatic. Only a quarter of the grown men recalled that religion had been important to them as teenagers; at the time, nearly 70 percent reported that it was. About a third of the adults remembered receiving physical punishment; as teenagers, nearly 90 percent had answered yes to the same question.

But it's not only time that prompts distortion and errors. They creep in immediately after an event, especially when a person trying to remember it is given prompts or suggestions, even seemingly very subtle ones. The psychologist Elizabeth Loftus, author of a number of pioneering studies in this field, conducted multiple interviews with a couple of dozen young people, in which they were asked to remember "the time they were lost in a shopping mall." None of them had ever been lost in a mall, but after the interviews, about a quarter of them remembered having gone through such an experience. In another experiment, subjects were shown a security video of a man entering a department store, and were told that shortly thereafter the man had murdered a security guard. They were then given a set of photographs and asked to identify the gunman—who was not depicted in any of the photos. Some of the subjects, after (wrongly) choosing one of the photos, were told they picked the right one. Surveyed afterward, psychologist Daniel Schachter writes, these subjects "claimed higher confidence and trust in their memories, a better view, and clearer recollection of the gunman, and heightened recall of facial details." If these people were testifying in court, Schachter notes, their confidence "would have been extremely convincing to a jury."

Or, for that matter, to readers of their autobiography. Suggestibility can arrive in many forms besides a police office or a prosecuting attorney (or a research psychologist) asking leading questions. The act of memoir writing represents something very different from a neutral attempt to remember. Beneath the account of every incident, episode, or character is an interpretation of one's life. Beneath that is the implied need to justify the whole enterprise of putting that life on paper, to show that in some way it makes a good story. The result is all kinds of *internal* suggestion. Even assuming such a thing as accurate memory existed, how could it fail to give in to such temptations?

Summarizing some of this research, the psychologist C. R. Barclay has observed that most of our autobiographical memories are "reconstructions aimed at preserving the essential integrity" of our sense of ourselves and our histories. They are, he wrote, largely "true but inaccurate . . . one conveys the meaning of lived events through plausible reconstructions of those events." Another psychologist who has experimented and written widely on memory, Ulric Neisser, puts it this way:

> We may remember an overall event, perhaps well enough to infer some of its more specific characteristics, but we do not remember those characteristics themselves. That is why memory is so vulnerable to unintended distortion and why it often seems "true" even when it is false. We can never do full justice to . . . "historical truth," because what really happened was too rich for anyone's memory to preserve. But it is relatively easy to remember events in a way that is accurate with respect to some overall characteristic of the situation; such a recollection always has some degree of validity even if it suggests nested details that are by no means accurate themselves.

In 1973, former White House counsel John Dean testified before the Senate Watergate Committee. He offered the committee a 245-page opening statement, then described his meetings with President Nixon and other aides at such great length and with such specificity that Senator Daniel Inouye asked him, "Have you always had a facility for recalling the details of conversations which took place many months ago?" In his reply, Dean suggested that the nature of the events he was describing spurred his memory: "When you meet with the President of the United States it is a very momentous occasion, and you tend to remember what the President of the United States says when you have a conversation with him. . . . So I would say that I have an ability to recall not specific words necessarily but certainly the tenor of a conversation and the gist of a conversation."

It turned out, remarkably, that Dean's memory could be objectively tested. Not long after his appearance before the committee, it was discovered that Nixon secretly tape-recorded all conversations in the Oval Office; the following year, transcripts of many of the tapes were published. Ulric Neisser compared the transcripts of two particular meetings with Dean's accounts—which, of course, were given under oath—and concluded that in many if not most cases, he got the tenor of the conversations and the gist of the conversations almost completely wrong.

Here is part of Dean's testimony about a September 15, 1972, meeting:

When I arrived at the Oval Office I found [aide Robert] Haldeman and the President. The President asked me to sit down. . . . The President then told me that Bob—referring to Haldeman—had kept him posted on my handling of the Watergate case. The President told me I had done a good job and he appreciated how difficult a task it had been, and the President was pleased that the case had stopped with [Gordon] Liddy. I responded that I could not take credit because others had done much more difficult things than I had done. As the President discussed the present status of the situation I told him that all I had been able to do was to contain the case and assist in keeping it out of the White House.

Neisser observes:

Comparison with the transcript shows that hardly a word of Dean's account is true. Nixon did not say *any* of the things attributed to him here: he didn't ask Dean to sit down, he didn't say Haldeman had kept him posted, he didn't say Dean had done a good job (at least not in that part of the conversation), he didn't say anything about Liddy or the indictments. Nor had Dean himself said the things he later described himself as saying: that he couldn't take credit, that the matter might unravel some day, etc. (Indeed, he said just the opposite later on: "Nothing is going to come crashing down.")

Neisser points out similar discrepancies between the tape-recorded transcript of the other meeting and Dean's account of it. It is worth noting, however, that even though his representations of the particular conversations were not accurate, much of what he reported Nixon as saying had been said by Nixon on *other* occasions, though not necessarily to Dean. His testimony offered sort of the gist of the gist. As Neisser concludes, Dean "remembered how he had felt himself and what he wanted, together with the general state of affairs; he didn't remember what anyone had actually said. His testimony had much truth to it, but not at the level of 'gist.' It was true at a deeper level. Nixon was the kind of man Dean described, he had the knowledge Dean attributed to him, there was a cover-up. Dean remembered all of that; he just didn't recall the actual conversation he was testifying about."

Psychologist Daniel Schachter is the most prolific chronicler of memory's flaws. Especially pertinent to autobiography, as well as to informal recollections of the past, is a fallacy he calls "bias": innocent ways in which our memory consistently distorts the past. In his book *The Seven Sins of Memory*, he identifies five persistent memory biases, all borne out by multiple studies (emphasis added):

> *Consistency and change* biases show how our theories about ourselves can lead us to reconstruct the past as overly similar to, or different from, the present. *Hindsight* biases reveal that recollections of past events are filtered by current knowledge. *Egocentric* biases illustrate the powerful role of the self in orchestrating perceptions and memories of reality. And *stereotypical* biases demonstrate how generic memories shape interpretations of the world, even when we are unaware of their existence or influence.

What some of the biases have in common is that, as opposed to the frequent randomness of real life, they make for more compelling or dramatic stories. One study asked graduate students to record how nervous they were before taking an important examination. A month later, asked to describe their state of mind before taking the test, they consistently exaggerated their anxiety levels. The effect was most pronounced among those who had passed. That little tale—"I was really worried, but I passed"—would be memoir-worthy. The "truth"—"I wasn't that worried, and I passed"—would not.

These effects hold true for even the most dramatic occurrences. Decades ago, psychiatrists coined the term "flashbulb memories" to indicate people's recollections of momentous events, whether personal (the death of a parent, the birth of a baby) or public (the assassination of a president). The initial research more or less assumed that because these memories are enduring and vivid, they are accurate. But that has turned out not to be true. To cite just one of many studies demonstrating this, Neisser and a colleague interviewed a group of college students less than twenty-four hours after the crash of the space shuttle *Challenger*, asking questions not only about the event but also about the circumstances under which they heard about it. The same students were re-interviewed two and a half years later. Although the subjects reported very vivid memories of the crash, and claimed great confidence in their accuracy, on the whole their recall was dismal. The majority answered fewer than 50 percent of the seven questions correctly, and eleven out of the forty-four subjects got all of them wrong. Maybe even more striking was that when presented with their original responses, the subjects could not remember them. "The original memories," write the authors, "seem to have disappeared entirely."

That combination—memory like Swiss cheese, arrogant confidence in its integrity—seems to be a human trait, and is certainly reflected in most autobiographies (Rousseau's humility is exceptional), which do not grant even the possibility that the chronicle they offer—including the word-for-word transcription of conversations held half a century before—is less than 100 percent accurate. In fact, there is an inherent and irresolvable conflict between the capabilities of memory and the demands of narrative. The latter demands specifics; the former is really bad at them. To cite one final psychological study, Neisser described an experiment where college students asked "What did you do last summer?" were much less able to describe concrete events than to summarize recurrent patterns or make general comments. Not only that, but the request for specificity "appeared to disturb" the subjects. He observed, "Individual episodes have no privileged status in memory; it is at least as natural to remember extended situations or typical patterns. Why not? The latter are often far more important in the long run."

However, the vast majority of memoirs and autobiographies are composed mainly of "individual episodes" rather than "extended situations or typical patterns." And not just episodes. In recent years, they have tended to include page after page of he-said, she-said dialogue. This is understandable: quotation is much more readable and forceful than paraphrase. But exact words are even harder to remember than your typical concrete event. I couldn't accurately quote you a single sentence my wife said to me at breakfast this morning, much less my first-grade teacher's wording half a century ago. One of the few memoirists to recognize this limitation is Robert de Roquebrune, who in his *Testament de mon enfance* (1958) said that he could accurately reproduce only two words spoken in his entire childhood—when his mother once forcefully said, "It's *tomorrow!*" (He could not, however, remember what the "it" was.) So, immediately, all those autobiographies lose the ironclad accuracy demanded by scientific proofs, courtroom testimony, and *New Yorker* articles.

A sort of self-imposed suggestibility is a problem as well, and no less powerful than the kind imposed by a police officer or a prosecuting attorney asking leading questions. The act of writing an autobiography represents something very different from a neutral attempt to remember. Beneath the account of every incident, episode, or character is one's interpretation of one's life. Beneath *that* is the implied need to justify the whole enterprise of putting that life on paper, to show that in some way it makes a good and valuable story. One more factor is what the critic Georges Gusdorf termed the "original sin" of autobiographers: the way knowing the outcome of an experience inevitably imposes itself on, and distorts, the memory of that experience. Even assuming such a thing as accurate memory existed, how could it not buckle under such pressure?

So the reality is: Once you begin to write the true story of your life in a form that anyone would possibly want to read, you start to make compromises with the truth. This paradox was recognized by some of the more sophisticated of Rousseau's nineteenth-century heirs, including Stendhal, who observed, "I do not claim to write a history, but quite simply to note down memories in order to guess what sort of man I may have been." The English critic Leslie Stephen, the father of Virginia Woolf and an enthusiastic late-nineteenth-century advocate of life writing, went farther—and anticipated later observers who actually celebrated the gap between memory and certainty: "An autobiography, alone of all books, may be more valuable in proportion to the amount of misrepresentation it contains."

By the turn of the twentieth century, autobiography was at the breaking point. There were a number of points on which it was experiencing great tension, some of which—social class, public versus private, the limits of candor—will be examined in the next chapter. But one of the key issues of contention concerned the fallibility of memory and the troubled nature of "truth." Being aware of this, how could a serious writer proceed with the project of writing about himself or herself? One option, magnificently chosen by Marcel Proust in the early twentieth century, was to let autobiography simmer and develop under the heat of the imagination, and present the result as fiction. Another was to acknowledge the predicament and move on. Referring to himself in his characteristic third person, Henry Adams was candid, unapologetic, and ahead of his time, a straight-talking American Rousseau:

> This was the journey he remembered. The actual journey may have been quite different, but the actual journey has no interest for education. The memory was all that mattered.

Adams composed those words in 1905. Writing his own autobiography at almost exactly the same time, Mark Twain also wryly acknowledged, and accepted, the limitations of recall:

I used to remember my brother Henry walking into a fire outdoors when he was a week old. It was remarkable in me to remember a thing like that and it was still more remarkable that I should cling to the delusion for thirty years that I did remember it—for of course it never happened; he would not have been able to walk at that age. . . . For many years I remembered helping my grandfather drinking his whisky when I was six weeks old but I do not tell about that any more now; I am grown old and my memory is not as active as it used to be. When I was younger I could remember anything, whether it had happened or not; but my faculties are decaying now and soon I shall be so I cannot remember any but the things that never happened.

EMINENT VICTORIAN
AUTOBIOGRAPHY

THE MEMOIR BOOM OF THE BRITISH 1820s was duplicated in the United States some three decades later. Louis Kaplan's definitive *Bibliography of American Autobiographies* lists 198 works published between 1850 and 1859—a fourfold increase in just thirty years—and the number kept going up for the rest of the century, reaching 448 in the 1890s.* Most of the writers of these books were male, but not all. Three works by women particularly stand out, for both their literary qualities and the way they prefigured later subgenres. I start with the one published last. Poet Lucy Larcom's *A New England Girlhood* (1889) was a memoir of an on-balance happy childhood, in the same vein as works written a hundred

---

*British autobiographies, meanwhile, held fairly steady: 194 in the 1840s compared with 171 in the 1820s, according to William Matthews's *British Autobiographies: An Annotated Bibliography of British Autobiographies Published or Written Before 1951*. The first decade in which American autobiographies outnumbered British ones was the 1860s, but just barely, by a count of 236 to 234. By the end of the century, the British were ahead again, with 489 in the 1890s.

years later by Russell Baker, Annie Dillard, or Bill Bryson. At the time, the reading public did not expect a memoir by a more or less normal person that had no fire, brimstone, melodrama, or overarching moral, which led Larcom to an impressive compound justification in her preface. Among her points were that the book was written at the urging of friends; that it would forever excuse her from the many annoying requests she got for "personal facts, data for biographical paragraphs, and the like"; that it shed light on a vanished time and place; that since the "most enjoyable thing" about writing is the "mutual friendship" between author and readers, an autobiography is like the sharing of confidences among friends; that "there may be more egotism in withdrawing mysteriously into one's self, than in frankly unfolding one's life-story, for better or worse"; and, reflecting the pantheism she developed in her later life, that a true autobiography is actually "a picture of the outer and inner universes photographed upon one little life's consciousness." She explained, "If an apple blossom or a ripe apple could tell its one story, it would be still more than its own, the story of the sunshine that smiled upon it, of the winds that whispered to it, of the birds that sang around it, of the storms that visited it, and of the motherly tree that held it and fed it until its petals were unfolded and its form developed."

Larcom, who was born in Beverly, Massachusetts, in 1824, would become a protégée of none other than John Greenleaf Whittier and eventually achieve success enough that *The Boston Globe* faintly praised her as the "best of America's minor poets." Her comfortable and secure early childhood ended at the age of seven, with the death of her father, a sea captain. Her mother moved the family to Lowell, where she took in boarders, and Lucy, for ten years starting at the age of eleven, went to work, becoming one of the textile factories' famous "mill girls." While her description of the experience has been of great value to subsequent historians, it is in no way a brief against the system; the memoir uncovering the exploitation and suffering of young factory workers, so common in nineteenth-century Britain, never took hold in the United States. Rather, the book focuses on the way her time in the mills shaped her as a person and, eventually, a poet. Although she "loved quietness," she grew not to mind the incessant din, finding "that I could so accustom myself to the noise that it became like a silence to me. And I defied the machinery to make me its slave. Its incessant discords could not drown the music of my thoughts if I would let them fly high enough. Even the long hours, the early rising, and the regularity enforced by the clangor of the bell were good discipline for one who was naturally inclined to dally and to dream, and who loved her own personal liberty with a willful rebellion against control."

Another common type of modern-day memoir is the true-life saga of living through traumatic or at least dramatic historical events. The nineteenth-century precursor here is *My Cave Life in Vicksburg* (even the title has a modern tabloidy feel), whose author, listed on the title page as "A Lady," in fact was Mary Ann Webster Loughborough, the wife of a major in the Confederate army. The book recounts several months, in the spring and summer of 1863, in which she and her two-year-old daughter and many other Vicksburg civilians lived in makeshift caves meant to protect them from Union mortar and artillery shells that poured down on the city day and night. The vividness and humaneness of the writing explain why the New York publishing firm Appleton would put out the book the following year, while the Civil War was still raging. Loughborough describes universal emotions in the face of war, as every sense is assaulted:

I shall never forget my extreme fear during the night, and my utter hopelessness of ever seeing the morning light. Terror stricken, we remained crouched in the cave, while shell after shell followed each other in quick succession. I endeavored by constant prayer to prepare myself for the sudden death I was almost certain awaited me. My heart stood still as we would hear the reports from the guns, and the rushing and fearful sound of the shell as it came toward us. As it neared, the noise became more deafening; the air was full of the rushing sound; pains darted through my temples; my ears were full of the confusing noise; and, as it exploded, the report flashed through my head like an electric shock, leaving me in a quiet state of terror the most painful that I can imagine—cowering in a corner, holding my child to my heart—the only feeling of my life being the choking throbs of my heart, that rendered me almost breathless.

A fascinating hybrid text is Elizabeth Hobbs Keckley's *Behind the Scenes; or, Thirty Years a Slave, and Four Years in the White House*, published in 1868.* The beginning is classic slave narrative (Frederick Douglass was a friend of Keckley's, and no doubt an inspiration), with a key difference: writing after the end of slavery, Keckley recalls a vanished world, not the horrors of still-uncorrected wrongs, and so her main task is not abetting abolition but telling a good story (while at the same time making sure that the evils of the institution are not forgotten). That may be why she starts the book with the statement "My life has been an eventful one," delaying until the second sentence the formulaic "I was born . . ." There are sadly familiar elements of lashings (the first one suffered at the age of five), family separation, and Keckley's own impregnation by a white man (she says she was "persecuted" by him), but by the third chapter she is in St. Louis and, while still a slave, has started a business making

---

*The scholar Jennifer Fleischner has determined that the author's actual last name was "Keckly," but since it was given with an *e* on the title page of the memoir and in all subsequent references until the 2003 appearance of Fleischner's book *Mrs. Lincoln and Mrs. Keckly*, I use the traditional spelling here.

dresses for the city's elite women. Her clients lent her $1,200—enough to buy her freedom, which she did in 1855. Keckley moved to Washington in 1860 and set up a dressmaking business. She was an immediate success, making gowns for Mrs. Stephen Douglas, Mrs. Jefferson Davis, and, soon after her husband was inaugurated, Mary Todd Lincoln. Keckley became not only the First Lady's regular dressmaker but also her confidante and, eventually, her "best living friend," as Mrs. Lincoln put it in a letter quoted by Keckley. The book has been the principle source for all biographies of Mary Lincoln, as well as a prime one for any account of life in the Lincoln White House.

Today we're used to celebrities' underlings (or relatives) writing books that air all sorts of dirty laundry; *Behind the Scenes* may have originated the genre. It certainly had the behind-the-scenes intimacy we have come to expect. Keckley's description of the family on the day after Lincoln's assassination (she was, she characteristically informs the reader, Mrs. Lincoln's "only companion, except her children, in the days of her great sorrow") is, if anything, too raw in its baring of the family's pain:

Returning to Mrs. Lincoln's room, I found her in a new paroxysm of grief. Robert was bending over his mother with tender affection, and little Tad was crouched at the foot of the bed with a world of agony in his young face. I shall never forget the scene—the wails of a broken heart, the unearthly shrieks, the terrible convulsions, the wild, tempestuous outbursts of grief from the soul. I bathed Mrs. Lincoln's head with cold water, and soothed the terrible tornado as best I could. Tad's grief at his father's death was as great as the grief of his mother, but her terrible outbursts awed the boy into silence. Sometimes he would throw his arms around her neck, and exclaim, between his broken sobs, "Don't cry so, Mamma! don't cry, or you will make me cry, too! You will break my heart."

Mrs. Lincoln could not bear to hear Tad cry, and when he would plead to her not to break his heart, she would calm herself with a great effort and clasp her child in her arms.

The passive-aggressive attitude that often creeps into the book can be explained by its reason for being. By 1867, Mrs. Lincoln, who had moved to Chicago after the president's death, was about $70,000 in debt from expenses incurred during the White House years. She devised a plan—savaged by the newspapers as beneath the dignity of a former First Lady—to get funds by selling her clothes and jewelry in New York. Undignified or not, it did not succeed in raising a cent. Keckley, summoned to New York by Mrs. Lincoln to help, had to stay there for several months "to look after her interests," and was not too happy about it: "Mrs. Lincoln's venture proved so disastrous that she was unable to reward me for my services, and I was compelled to take in sewing to pay for my daily bread."

Clearly, and understandably, Keckley resented what she had been put through, but in 1868 there was no established discourse for an ex-slave to express resentment regarding a president's widow. And so she wrote a book, and included in it excerpts from dozens of letters from Mrs. Lincoln to her. (Copyright law today would not let a kiss-and-tell tome publish correspondence from the subject in full without permission.) All of them were private—that was what letters were, when people still wrote letters—but some cut very close to the bone, for example, this one, mailed to Keckley just months before the book's publication:

I am writing this morning with a broken heart after a sleepless night of great mental suffering. R. [her son Robert] came up last evening like a maniac, and almost threatening his life, looking like death because [Mrs. Lincoln's letters regarding the proposed sale of clothing] were published in yesterday's paper. I could not refrain from weeping when I saw him so miserable. . . . I pray for death this morning. Only my darling Taddie prevents my taking my life.

Keckley's justification for printing this material is tortured. Claiming that she has been "prompted by the purest motive," she notes, in a typically qualified sentence, "Mrs. Lincoln may have been imprudent, but since her intentions were good, she should be judged more kindly." And therefore, she writes,

if I have betrayed confidence in anything I have published, it has been to place Mrs. Lincoln in a better light before the world. . . . I have written nothing that can place Mrs. Lincoln in a worse light before the world than the light in which she now stands, therefore the secret history that I publish can do her no harm. . . . These letters were not written for publication, for which reason they are all the more valuable; they are the frank overflowings of the heart, the outcropping of impulse, the key to genuine motives.

Keckley's publisher took a different tack, advertising the book as "The Great Sensational Disclosure by Mrs. Keckley." And the newspapers, so quick to vilify Mrs. Lincoln just months earlier, now turned on Keckley. "Has the American public no word of protest against the assumption that its literary taste is of so low grade as to tolerate the back-stairs gossip of negro servant girls?" asked one reviewer. *The New York Times* resisted bringing up the subject of race but was equally disdainful: "We cannot but look upon many of the disclosures made in this book as gross violations of confidence. Mrs. Lincoln evidently reposed implicit trust in [the author], and this trust, under unwise advice no doubt, she has betrayed." Mary Lincoln was indeed offended by the revealing of confidences and never spoke to Keckley again. Robert Lincoln was irate as well, and Keckley speculated that he made an effort to suppress the book. In any case, it sold poorly. The author returned to Washington and her seamstress business. In 1892, at the age of seventy-four, she took a position as head of the Department of Sewing and Domestic Science Arts at Wilberforce University in Ohio. Health problems compelled her to return to Washington again, and she died there in 1907, forgotten and destitute. A photograph of Mary Todd Lincoln hung on the wall of her room.

As prescient and interesting as these books are, they had little impact at the time. If American autobiography in the period could be said to have a face, it combined the features of three very famous white males who were connected in multiple ways. These men—Ulysses S. Grant, P. T. Barnum, and Mark Twain—also were emblematic of a sea change in the kinds of Americans who were inspired to write their autobiographies. In the first half of the nineteenth century, people whom the bibliographer Louis Kaplan classified as either Clergy/Religious or Criminal/Deviant accounted for 57 percent of such books. Then the moral middle opened up. By the first decade of the twentieth century, Clergy/Religious was still the most common category, at 22.7 percent, but Criminal/Deviant was down to 4.4 percent, and other categories made strong showings, neatly exemplified by these three authors. Grant stood for Military Life (13.2 percent) and Politician (7.2 percent), Barnum for Business (6.3 percent), and Twain for Writer (5.6 percent) and Frontier Life (7.9 percent).*

*In the 1970s, the last decade calculated by the scholar who took up Kaplan's work, Mary Louise Briscoe, 1,175 autobiographies were published and the leading categories were: Entertainer (12.9 percent), Clergy/Religious (9.2 percent), Writer (8.5 percent), Sports Figure (9.8 percent), and Politician (6.3 percent).

The Life of P. T. Barnum, Written by Himself appeared in 1854, when the author was forty-four years old. Barnum gave detailed accounts of the deceptions and humbug he was well known for perpetrating—notably the Joice Heth hoax, and the "Feejee Mermaid," one of the most popular exhibits ever at his American Museum, which he described in the book as "an ugly, dried-up, black-looking, and diminutive specimen" that was likely the result of someone surgically connecting a fish tail with a monkey's torso and head. Reaction to the book tended to focus on Barnum's candor, which was unapologetic and sometimes bordered on defiant. Some critics praised it, but it put off others, including a reviewer from *The New York Times*, who was shocked that Barnum so willingly admitted to "the systematic, adroit, and persevering plan of *obtaining money under false pretenses from the public at large.*" *Harvard Magazine*'s critic, meanwhile, was bothered by his honesty: "Excess of frankness is a fault of which it is seldom necessary to complain. But Mr. Barnum has carried his frankness too far. It is his very sincerity which makes his book so bad." It was a peculiar criticism, suggesting that at this point, some members of the public preferred some boundaries even in true stories.

As in other cases before and since, bad reviews did not dissuade the public from buying the book, and it sold an impressive 160,000 copies. Considering Barnum's unmatched commercial instincts, lack of shyness, and relatively young age at the time of publication, it's not surprising that he should have eventually produced a second autobiography. This was *Struggles and Triumphs, or, Forty Years' Recollections of P. T. Barnum*, published in 1869. I should say *first* published in 1869. By this point, Barnum was mainly involved in presenting circus and menagerie shows, and until his death (in 1891), at each year's show he distributed a new edition of the autobiography carrying the story up to the present. Barnum biographer A. H. Saxon observes, wearily, "The subject of the continuing evolution of Barnum's book becomes from this point on a bibliographer's nightmare, further complicated by the showman's grandiloquently announcing in the 1880s that anyone who wished to was free to publish his own edition."

In one of the final editions of the book, Barnum wrote that during a dinner with Ulysses S. Grant in 1880, the former president talked of discovering on a recent round-the-world trip that Barnum's name was "familiar to multitudes who had not heard of me." A few years later, Grant, in poor health and reeling from the collapse of a banking firm of which he was a partner, needed money. He understood that he could, through an accumulation of words, mortgage his fame—which, while perhaps not on the level of Barnum's, was considerable. He began writing articles for a *Century Magazine* series on the Civil War, at $500 a piece. Their success prompted him to embark on a book of memoirs. It's hard to imagine today, when presidents—and their wives—characteristically finance their post–White House years with door-stopping narratives containing accounts of every meeting with a foreign potentate (Jimmy Carter alone has a double-digit backlist), but at the time only two such works had been written. The first had come from the pen of Martin Van Buren, the eighth president, who worked on his memoirs from 1854 until his death in 1862—largely, it would appear, because he didn't have much else to occupy his time. His son's widow gave the 1,247-page manuscript to the Library of Congress, and it was finally published in 1920. It is a long-winded and in some ways peculiar work: Van Buren does not mention his wife a single time, and devotes more space to a brief mission to England than to his two years as secretary of state or four years as vice president. (The manuscript breaks off before his election as president in 1840.) But it has its charms, including Van Buren's sincere modesty, for example, in his regret over what he saw as a deeply ingrained resistance to scholarship and study, even when he was faced with important court cases or political debates: "I am now amazed that with such disadvantages I should have been able to pass through such contests as it has been my lot to encounter with such few discomfitures."

The second presidential memoir to be written, and the first to be published, was James Buchanan's 1866 work, *Mr. Buchanan's Administration on the Eve of the Rebellion*. It was (as the title suggests) a third-person work clearly intended to secure a favorable legacy for Buchanan's presidency. It did not succeed.

When Grant floated his idea for a memoir, the Century Company presented him with a contract offering a 10 percent sales royalty—which, on the basis of projected sales of the book, would bring him $20,000 to $30,000. Grant was apparently prepared to accept those terms. But then Samuel Clemens—the same Sam Clemens who wrote and published his own books as "Mark Twain"—intervened. Hearing of the proposed contract during a visit to Grant, he advised that its terms were unacceptable and proposed that the firm he had set up to bring out his own *Adventures of Huckleberry Finn*, Charles L. Webster & Company, publish the memoirs by subscription, paying the general 70 percent of net profits. Grant ultimately accepted the offer and set to work.

At one point during the writing process, Grant let it be known that he would be interested in Twain's opinion of the manuscript. Twain recalled in his own posthumously published autobiography:

> By chance I had been comparing the memoirs with Caesar's "Commentaries" and was qualified to deliver judgment. I was able to say in all sincerity that the same high merits distinguished both books—clarity of statement,

directness, simplicity, unpretentiousness, manifest truthfulness, fairness and justice towards friend and foe alike, soldierly candor and frankness and soldierly avoidance of flowery speech. I placed the two books side by side upon the same high level and I still think that they belonged there.

Twain's praise does not, I should make clear, stem from the fact that he ghostwrote the memoirs, as rumors have persistently claimed. Grant's best biographer, William McFeeley, and other historians agree that this wasn't the case: Grant wrote the whole thing himself. The praise, in any case, is just. Rare if not unique among autobiographies, the book is almost completely lacking in ego, and thus a reader implicitly credits its characterizations and accounts; as for the writing, the clarity and simple diction and syntax make it, to this day, a paragon of the plain style. (Among its many admirers was Gertrude Stein.) All those qualities are on display in Grant's description of his meeting with Lee at Appomattox:

> When I had left camp that morning I had not expected so soon the result that was then taking place, and consequently was in rough garb. I was without a sword, as I usually was when on horseback in the field, and wore a soldier's blouse for a coat, with the shoulder straps of my rank to indicate to the army who I was. When I went into the house I found General Lee. We greeted each other, and after shaking hands took our seats. I had my staff with me, a good portion of whom were in the room during the whole of the interview.
>
> What General Lee's feelings were I do not know. As he was a man of much dignity, with an impassible face, it was impossible to say whether he felt inwardly glad that the end had finally come, or felt sad over the results, and was too manly to show it. Whatever his feelings, they were entirely concealed from my observation; but my own feelings, which had been quite

jubilant on the receipt of his letter, were sad and depressed. I felt like anything rather than rejoicing at the downfall of a foe who had fought so long and valiantly, and had suffered so much for a cause, though that cause was, I believe, one of the worst for which a people ever fought, and one for which there was the least excuse.

While writing the book, Grant was diagnosed with throat cancer, and valiantly continued with the work of composition in the face of steadily declining health. The manuscript of the second volume was delivered to the publisher on June 18, 1885, and he died five days later. The book was one of the biggest bestsellers of the century. More than 300,000 two-volume sets were sold by subscription agents, netting Grant's widow, Julia, some $450,000 in royalties.*

The third member of the late-nineteenth-century autobiographical trio was Mark Twain himself, a Connecticut neighbor and friend of Barnum's in the 1870s.† Where Barnum and Grant were both early exemplars

---

*Two years after Grant's death, Julia Grant embarked on her own memoirs. She started, she told an interviewer, "more to gratify my children's wishes than my own. Soon I became an inveterate scribbler. I preferred writing to eating or driving or seeing friends. The children said I had found a fad at last. But it wasn't a fad; it was joy. I was living again, with the aid of my fancy and my pen, the life that had been so sweet to me." She completed the manuscript in 1892 but never published it, for reasons that are not clear, though in one letter she blamed unnamed "critics" who pronounced it "*too* near, *too* close to the private life of the Genl for the public, and I thought this was just what they wanted." The manuscript stayed in the Grant family until it was finally published in 1975. The first First Lady whose memoirs saw the light of print was Helen Herron Taft, wife of William Howard Taft, whose *Recollections of Full Years* came out in 1914.

†For years, Barnum took the strangest and most audacious of the unsolicited letters he continually received from people who wanted him to display them or their possessions, and forwarded them to Twain, who planned to turn them into a piece of comic writing. After one shipment, Twain wrote Barnum to thank him for "the admirable lot of letters. Headless mice, four-legged hens, human-handed sacred bulls, 'professional' Gypsies, ditto 'Sacasians,' deformed human beings anxious to trade on their horrors, school-teachers who can't spell—it is a perfect feast of queer literature." To Barnum's dismay, Twain never did anything with the letters.

of the celebrity autobiography, a book justified in large or (in many future cases) complete part by the author's fame, as opposed to his or her having anything to say, Twain was a writer who achieved fame *through* memoir. Twain's posthumous official *Autobiography*, commenced late in life, is actually one of his weaker books, with too many long digressions, cranky asides, score settlings, and detailed accounts of royalties and book sales. But his early work, fresh and groundbreaking, was a kind of memoir in installments: four of his first seven books, and the ones that thrust him into the public consciousness, were nonfiction explorations of his past and his experiences.

The first of this series, *The Innocents Abroad*, was published in 1869, when Twain was thirty-four and at the end of an eight-year stint as a tramp newspaperman. His only published book to this point was a collection of sketches called *The Celebrated Jumping Frog of Calaveras County*, but for several years he had been lecturing widely around the country, and was beginning to develop a reputation as the best of the Western humorists. Handsomely published, sold by subscription, and amply illustrated (many of the pictures included likenesses of the already recognizable author), *The Innocents Abroad* chronicled the first American organized tour of Europe and the Holy Land. It was an immense success, selling an estimated 500,000 copies in Twain's lifetime. The book—like its eventual sequel, *A Tramp Abroad* (1880)—was more a comic travelogue than a memoir, but it absolutely depended on Twain as a character and personality.

Twain was a profoundly autobiographical artist, of a sort familiar today but unprecedented at the time. His appearances on the lecture circuit and, eventually, on the front pages of newspapers and in the public consciousness depended on the palpable sense of a real man telling his own real story (with a few stretchers thrown in). In his writing, he was drawn again and again to autobiographical forms. (*Adventures of Huckleberry Finn*, no less than *David Copperfield* or *Jane Eyre*, is a memoir in fiction.) While deliberating on a follow-up to *Innocents Abroad*, he put together a peculiar sketch called "Mark Twain's (Burlesque) Autobiography." Presumably in parody of a feature commonly overdone in the memoirs, he devoted about 95 percent of it to a faux genealogy of the "Twain" clan, with such knee-slappers as "Augustus Twain seems to have made something of a stir about the year 1160. He was as full of fun as he could be, and used to take his old sabre and sharpen it up, and get in a convenient place on a dark night, and stick it through people as they went by, to see them jump. He was a born humorist." Twain paired this with another piece, equally unfunny, and published them as a pamphlet in 1870; later he had the sense to buy up all the plates and have them destroyed.*

His next proper book was less successful than *The Innocents Abroad* but more autobiographical. In *Roughing It* (1872), he decided to tell the story of his time in the West, commencing in 1861. The then twenty-six-year-old Twain, a riverboat pilot for more than a year, was at liberty because traffic on the Mississippi had been disrupted by the Civil War; he had just finished an extremely brief stint in the Confederate Army (he would tell *that* story a decade hence in "The Private History of a Campaign That Failed"). "My brother," he writes in the opening sentence, referring to Orion Clemens, ten years his senior, "had just been appointed Secretary of Nevada Territory—an office of such majesty that it concentrated in itself the duties and dignities of Treasurer, Comptroller, Secretary of State, and Acting Governor in the Governor's absence. A salary of eigh-

---

*Twain would also embark on a mock memoir based on the life of his feckless brother Orion, and complete some one hundred pages before abandoning the project.

teen hundred dollars a year and the title of 'Mr. Secretary,' gave to the
great position an air of wild and imposing grandeur. I was young and
ignorant, and I envied my brother. I coveted his distinction and his finan-
cial splendor, but particularly and especially the long, strange journey he
was going to make, and the curious new world he was going to explore."
So Twain lit out for the territory with Orion. The book tells the story of
that journey, of his years as a freelance writer and newspaperman in Nevada and California, of the many colorful characters and locales he encountered, and finally his 1866 journey to Hawaii (then known as the
Sandwich Islands). The autobiographical details, of course, are far less
important than Twain's wonderful and enormously influential voice,
which introduced to subsequent comic memoirists from James Thurber to
David Sedaris the near-nuclear power of a self-deprecating narrator de-
ploying hyperbole based on shrewd and perceptive observation.

Twain's autobiographical books kept going farther back in time and
getting less facetious. In *Life on the Mississippi* (1883), composed during
the period when he was writing *The Adventures of Tom Sawyer* and *Adventures of Huckleberry Finn*, he went all the way back to his boyhood in
Hannibal, Missouri, and his time as a riverboat apprentice and pilot on the
Mississippi. It's much too long—it was sold by subscription, too, and to
achieve the required six-hundred-page length, Twain larded the manuscript with digressions, lengthy descriptions, assorted musings, and as
much trivia about the river as Melville had on whales in *Moby-Dick*. But
the stuff on his boyhood and youth is prime. In this characteristic passage he tells of his first day as a cub pilot, under the tutelage of the captain,
Mr. Bixby:

> Now and then Mr. Bixby called my attention to certain things. Said he,
> "This is Six-Mile Point." I assented. It was pleasant enough information,

but I could not see the bearing of it. I was not conscious that it was a matter of any interest to me. Another time he said, "This is Nine-Mile Point." Later he said, "This is Twelve-Mile Point." They were all about level with the water's edge; they all looked about alike to me; they were monotonously unpicturesque. I hoped Mr. Bixby would change the subject. But no; he would crowd up around a point, hugging the shore with affection, and then say: "The slack water ends here, abreast this bunch of China-trees; now we cross over." So he crossed over. He gave me the wheel once or twice, but I had no luck. I either came near clipping off the edge of a sugar plantation, or I yawed too far from shore, and so dropped back into disgrace again and got abused.

The watch finally ends, but after what seems only a few minutes of sleep Twain is summoned back to the pilothouse: "Here was something fresh— this thing of getting up in the middle of the night to go to work. It was a detail in piloting that had never occurred to me at all. I knew that boats ran all night, but somehow I had never happened to reflect that somebody had to get up out of a warm bed to run them." After a few minutes, Mr. Bixby asks him:

"What's the name of the first point above New Orleans?"

I was gratified to be able to answer promptly, and I did. I said I didn't know.

"Don't know?"

This manner jolted me. I was down at the foot again, in a moment. But I had to say just what I had said before.

"Well, you're a smart one," said Mr. Bixby. "What's the name of the next point?"

Once more I didn't know.

"Well, this beats anything. Tell me the name of any point or place I told you."

I studied a while and decided that I couldn't. . . .

"Look here! What do you suppose I told you the names of those points for?"

I tremblingly considered a moment, and then the devil of temptation provoked me to say:—

"Well—to—to—be entertaining, I thought."

This was a red rag to the bull. He raged and stormed so (he was crossing the river at the time) that I judge it made him blind, because he ran over the steering-oar of a trading-scow. Of course the traders sent up a volley of red-hot profanity. Never was a man so grateful as Mr. Bixby was: because he was brim full, and here were subjects who could talk back. He threw open a window, thrust his head out, and such an irruption followed as I never had heard before. The fainter and farther away the scowmen's curses drifted, the higher Mr. Bixby lifted his voice and the weightier his adjectives grew. When he closed the window he was empty. You could have drawn a seine through his system and not caught curses enough to disturb your mother with. Presently he said to me in the gentlest way:—

"My boy, you must get a little memorandum-book, and every time I tell you a thing, put it down right away. There's only one way to be a pilot, and that is to get this entire river by heart. You have to know it just like A B C."

MOST OF THE DIFFERENCE between American and British autobiography in the nineteenth century can be understood by a consideration of the year 1854. That was when the United States saw the autobiography of

P. T. Barnum, who was perhaps the greatest self-promoter of all time. Embarking on his memoirs on the other side of the Atlantic that year was John Stuart Mill, who . . . wasn't. Like many eminent Victorian autobiographers—including Harriet Martineau, Charles Darwin, Anthony Trollope, John Addington Symonds, and Herbert Spencer—Mill stipulated that his memoirs not be published until after his death (which ended up occurring in 1873). Even from the grave, he was sheepish about the seeming egotism involved in presenting the story of his life to the public: "I do not for a moment imagine that any part of what I have to relate, can be interesting to the public as a narrative, or as being connected with myself," he wrote in the first chapter. "But . . . it may be useful that there should be some record of an education which was unusual and remarkable."

Those last two adjectives are good examples of Mill's propensity for very British understatement. His father, the historian, philosopher, and economist James Mill, used young John as a laboratory for his theories of education, commenting to his friend and colleague Jeremy Bentham that the boy was being brought up "to be a successor worthy of both of us." (James Mill was the dominant parent in the household; John does not mention his mother a single time in his autobiography.) John embarked on the study of Greek at age three, Latin at seven, logic at twelve, and political economy at thirteen. That was all well and good, perhaps, except that all the cramming kept him away from other things, like friends, fun, and feelings. "For passionate emotions of all sorts, and for everything which has been said or written in exaltation of them, he professed the greatest contempt," Mill writes of his father. "He regarded them as a form of madness." At the age of twenty, Mill had a mental and emotional breakdown—the chapter describing it is called "A Crisis in My Mental History"—stemming from a fear that he would never be able to feel happiness or pleasure. He emerged from it when he found he was moved to tears by an emotional passage in Jean-François Marmontel's *Mémoires*: "I was no longer hopeless: I was not a stock or a stone."

In the hands of a current-day memoirist, this material would be gold, with a high concept of intellectual abuse at the hands of a salably eccentric dad. But Mill, even from the safe fortress of the grave, is determined to play down any intrafamily conflict, and to blunt the edges of his hurt feelings. In an early draft, he noted, "It must be mentioned . . . that my father's children neither loved him, nor, with any warmth of affection, anyone else." The line was gone in the final version. Repeatedly, when Mill bared his soul in the draft, or mentioned Mrs. Mill, the passage would be excised. In the published text, he writes that his father "carefully kept me from having any great amount of intercourse with other boys. He was earnestly bent upon my escaping not only the ordinary corrupting influence which boys exercise over boys, but the contagion of vulgar modes of thought and feeling; and for this he was willing that I should pay the price of inferiority in the accomplishments which schoolboys in all countries chiefly cultivate." Only in the original manuscript does he give a detailed description of that price, which was steep:

I grew up with great inaptness in the common affairs of every day life. I was far longer than children generally are before I could put on my clothes. I know not how many years passed before I could tie a knot. My articulation was long imperfect; one letter, *r*, I could not pronounce until I was nearly sixteen. I never could, nor can I now, do anything requiring the smallest manual dexterity. . . . I was continually acquiring odd or disagreeable tricks which I very slowly and imperfectly got rid of. I was, besides, utterly unobservant: I was, as my father continually told me, like a person who had not the organs of sense: my eyes and ears seemed of no use to me, so little did I see or hear what was before me, and so little, even of what I did see or hear, did I observe and remember. . . . He could not endure stupidity, nor feeble and lax habits, in whatever manner displayed, and I was perpetually exciting his anger by manifestations of them. From the earliest time I can remember he used to reproach me, and most truly, with a general habit of inattention; owing to which, he said, I was . . . judging and acting like a person devoid of common sense; and which would make me, he said, grow up a mere oddity, looked down upon by everybody, and unfit for all the common purposes of life.

Posthumously published or (as in the cases of John Ruskin and Cardinal Newman) not, almost all Victorian autobiographies were circumspect, sometimes defiantly so. Consider:

- Novelist Anthony Trollope, on why he devoted very little space to his relationship with his wife: "My marriage was like the marriage of other people and of no special interest to any one except my wife and me."
- Herbert Spencer, the theory-of-everything philosopher: It would "be out of taste to address the public as though it consisted of personal friends."
- The politician Samuel Smith: "Things essentially private are rarely touched upon, and only when necessary to the general narrative."
- The judge Sir Edmund Parry: "I do not propose to write of my mother in these pages, since I could do no justice to the grace of her memory, and the dim vision of it is my own affair."

The poet and painter William Bell Scott, in his *Autobiographical Notes* (posthumously published in 1892), was a little more thoughtful and less defensive, noting that "to write one's mental history is too difficult as well as too dreadful." He said such an attempt would be "like walking into the street naked, and it only likely to frighten our neighbors." The critic Wayne Shumaker comments that in nineteenth-century memoirs, one only rarely comes upon "the flavor of real living, the feeling of immediacy, of the confrontation of pressing problems in the here and now."

The marvel is that, in the face of this reticence by consensus, autobiography was so extraordinarily popular among the Victorians. Harriet Martineau was not alone in the sentiment she expressed at the outset of her work: "From my youth upwards I have felt that it was one of the duties of my life to write my autobiography." The extremely minor writer Augustus Hare produced a staggering six volumes of memoir between 1896 and 1900, consisting of, in the words of critic A. O. J. Cockshut, "immense prolixity and innumerable boring anecdotes." The Irish novelist George Moore put forth six separate memoirs as well, published between 1888 and 1933. (The first, *Confessions of a Young Man*, was published when he was a mere thirty-six; in the words of critic Ann Thwaite, "No one earlier had thought of writing an autobiography before reaching the age of fifty.")

The pervasive desire to relate one's life, inhibited by the severe restrictions on what could be included *in* that narrative, pressured autobiography close to the breaking point. In response, it stretched and changed shape. William Hale White and Samuel Butler felt empowered to give a candid account of their difficult lives only by presenting them in novels, in *The Autobiography of Mark Rutherford* (1881) and *The Way of All Flesh* (published posthumously in 1903), respectively.

A special case, for multiple reasons, is *My Secret Life,* which was first printed in a small private edition of eleven volumes, containing some 4,200 pages and well over a million words, beginning around 1888. (Its first public edition did not appear until 1966.) The book is a first-person history, staggering in its capaciousness and detail, of the sexual experiences of the author, who calls himself "Walter." His professed rationale for the venture is a sort of public-spirited sharing of information: he wonders, "Have all men had the strange letches which late in life have enraptured me, though in early days the idea of them revolted me? I can never know this; my experience if printed may enable others to compare as I cannot." Walter insists, at the outset, on the truthfulness of the contents: he was determined, he says, "to write my private acts freely as to fact, and in the spirit of the lustful acts done by me, or witnessed; it is written therefore with absolute truth, and for without any regard for what the world calls decency." Nevertheless, it has never been conclusively determined whether *My Secret Life* is autobiography or fiction or something in between; Walter's identity is an unresolved question as well. In his 2001 book *The Erotomaniac: The Secret Life of Henry Spencer Ashbee,* Ian Gibson makes a convincing though admittedly circumstantial case that the book was fiction and the author was Henry Ashbee (1834–1900), an obsessive collector and bibliographer of erotica.

But even less acceptable to Victorian society was the secret life of John Addington Symonds (1840–1893), a poet, critic, biographer, translator, and scholar of the Renaissance, who concluded, roughly at the age of twenty, that he was a homosexual. Some thirty years later, inspired by the candid memoirs of Count Carlo Gozzi and of Benvenuto Cellini, both of which he had recently translated from the Italian, he embarked on his autobiography. A principal subject—perhaps *the* principal subject—of it was his sexual feelings and life. "This is a foolish thing to do," he wrote to a friend, Henry Graham Dakyns, "because I do not think they will ever be fit to publish." (Even if there were no other reasons for this assessment, Symonds was well aware of the customary sentence for someone convicted of sodomy: two years' hard labor.) He went ahead, he wrote in the same letter, with reasoning similar to Walter's, because a study of his evolution and development, "written with the candour & precision I feel capable of using, would I am sure be interesting to psychologists and not without its utility. There does not exist anything like it in print; & I am certain that 999 men out of 1000 do not believe in the existence of a personality like mine."

Parts of Symonds's memoir make for riveting reading today, not so much for the incidents it describes as for the continuing but never resolved internal debate it contains. The culture in which Symonds has been formed tells him that his sexuality is unnatural and depraved. Part of him accepts this, yet another part knows that, though the way he is has caused him considerable unhappiness, it has also given him great joy and fulfillment, and so there must be something wrong with society's standards. Near the end of the book, a short passage contains both views. Symonds writes, "I carry within me the seeds of what I know to be an incurable malady . . . that . . . deeply rooted perversion of the sexual instincts (uncontrollable, ineradicable, amounting to monomania) . . . expose which in its relation to my whole nature has been the principal object of this memoir. It is a singular life history; and yet, for aught I know, it may be commoner than I imagine." When he prepared a final version of the manuscript, he inserted a footnote after the word "imagine" that read: "When I wrote the above, I had not yet read . . ." and here he listed several contemporary works by German scholars that protested laws against homosexuality and suggested it was more common than had been thought. He concluded: "I have recently done so, and am now aware that my history is only one out of a thousand." So the same percentage of the population Symonds had previously given (in his letter to Dakyns) as being *aware* of "a personality like mine," he now estimates *possesses* such a personality. It was a remarkable change in perception, and after completing the memoirs, Symonds was moved to write and actually publish (albeit in a private edition of just fifty copies) a pamphlet called *A Problem in Modern Ethics*, described by the *Dictionary of National Biography* as the first "psychological-sociological analysis of homosexuality in English, exposing vulgar errors by a well-judged mixture of sarcasm, science, and common sense."*

One of the people to whom Symonds sent the pamphlet was his friend Edmund Gosse, a prominent and prolific poet, critic, and biographer. (Gosse was so much the prototypical Victorian man of letters that shortly after his death in 1928, T. S. Eliot remarked that "the place that Sir Edmund Gosse filled in the literary and social life of London is one that no one can ever fill again, because it is, so to speak, an office that has been abolished.") Gosse responded with a letter that some, though not all, critics have taken to be an acknowledgment of his own "inversion": "I know all you speak of,—the solitude, the rebellion, the despair. Yet I have been

---

*In 1892, Symonds proposed to Havelock Ellis a book on homosexuality, a subject that he felt was "fearfully mishandled by pathologists and psychiatrical [*sic*] professors, who know nothing whatsoever about its real nature." They decided to collaborate, but Symonds died before the project took final shape. In Ellis's 1897 book *Sexual Inversion*, the anonymous "Case XVII," described as "one of the leaders of English literature," is Symonds. After Symonds's death in 1893, the manuscript of his autobiography became the possession of his literary executor, Horatio Brown. Brown died in 1926, bequeathing the autobiography to the London Library, with instructions that nothing be published for fifty years. The manuscript, in a green cloth box, was opened for the first time in 1949, when Symonds's daughter requested permission to read it. Five years later the library decided to make the manuscript available to "*bona fide* scholars." But by then so much time had passed that no scholar was even aware of the existence of the manuscript, and it remained unexamined. Not until the 1980s did the critic Phyllis Grosskurth stumble upon it, and she edited an edition published in 1984.

happy, too; I hope you have also been happy,—that all with you has not been disappointment & the revulsion of hope? Either way, I entirely & deeply sympathise with you. Years ago I wanted to write to you about all this, and withdrew through cowardice." Whatever Gosse was acknowledging in private, in public he was and would continue to be a pillar of heterosexual rectitude. In an unsigned obituary for *The Saturday Review* after Symonds's death in 1893, Gosse damned him with faint praise as "one who aimed at the highest things and came a little short." Decades later, Gosse helped to burn a mass of the older man's more compromising papers; Symonds's granddaughter later reported being disgusted by the "smug gloating delight" with which Gosse recounted the incident.

Given this snippy behavior, it's ironic that Gosse should have received a precious literary gift from Symonds. In 1890, Gosse had written a biography of his father, Philip. After it appeared, Symonds wrote him a letter of praise, but added: "I wish there were more of *you* in your Father's *Life*. You could write a fascinating autobiography if you chose; and I hope you will do this." It took Gosse about fifteen years to follow that counsel, but he ultimately did so. The result, *Father and Son: A Study of Conflicting Temperaments* (1907), is the only one of his approximately eighty-five books that is still in print. And deservedly so. Not only did it break the impasse of the Victorian autobiography, but it stands as the progenitor of the modern memoir

Unlike Symonds, Gosse was willing to let his autobiography appear in his lifetime; unlike Butler or White, he was willing to present it as nonfiction without any novelistic veneer. But he did take the absurd measure of initially publishing the book anonymously. Absurd, because any educated person of the time would recognize "my Father" as Philip Gosse. Gosse the elder is a great character, who would not be out of place in a Dickens novel. He had developed a reputation as a naturalist but ran into a major roadblock when Darwin's early publications and the emerging geologic and fossil evidence demonstrated that the world was much, much older than any literal reading of the Bible would allow. The central challenge of Philip Gosse's life was to reconcile his fundamentalist religious beliefs with his scientist's values.

As challenges go, this was a beauty, and some of the best passages of *Father and Son* describe Philip Gosse's effort to meet it in a misguided earlier-day version of intelligent design. His 1857 book *Omphalos: An Attempt to Untie the Geological Knot* (the title is the ancient Greek word for "navel") argued that just as Adam showed up with a superfluous belly button, so, too, when God created the Earth, he furnished it ancient fossils and rocks that were brand-new but had the appearance of being millions of years old. Gosse felt his hypothesis would reconcile science and religion. "He offered it," his son writes, "with a glowing gesture, to atheists and Christians alike. This was to be the universal panacea; this the system of intellectual therapeutics which could not but heal all the maladies of the age. But, alas! Atheists and Christians alike looked at it, and laughed, and threw it away."

Among the many prophetic aspects of *Father and Son*, maybe the most striking is the way it prefigures the narrative of a beleaguered, constricted, abusive, or otherwise troubled childhood, in the manner of *Angela's Ashes*, *Running with Scissors*, *The Glass Castle*, and dozens of new additions every year. Young Edmund, an only child, suffers his mother's death, of cancer, when he is seven. After that his father becomes warped by his religious fanaticism, and single-handedly tries to mold the boy into a sort of pint-sized holy man, not letting him read anything secular, and keeping him away from all other kids, and pretty much all human contact outside the church, till the age of ten or eleven. The book also anticipates later memoirs in its form. The earlier model, in secular as well as religious autobiographies, had been a movement toward resolution and acceptance of society or God or both. At the end of *Father and Son*, Edmund breaks with Philip Gosse and his church.

Subtler, but equally prescient, are the book's literary qualities. Throughout, one is aware of the presence of two Edmund Gosses: the fifty-eight-year-old littérateur—he comes through clearly in the sentences quoted above—and the boy who went through it all and is presented via the grown man's memory, induction, and imagination. Throughout the book, Gosse looks at himself looking at the strange stuff that transpired, and the dual perspective deepens the sadness and our understanding. The household gloom over the *Omphalos* debacle, he writes, "thickened day by day, as hope and self-confidence evaporated in thin clouds of disappointment." Philip, no barrel of laughs to begin with, turned more morose; he assumed that his book had failed because he had offended God:

> In brooding tramps, round and round the garden, his soul was on his knees searching the corners of his conscience for some sin of omission or commission, and one by one every pleasure, every recreation, every trifle scraped out of the dust of past experience, was magnified into a huge offence. He thought that the smallest evidence of levity, the least unbending to human instinct, might lead the weaker brethren into offence.

A groundbreaking feature of the book is its use, seen in few previous autobiographies and only sparingly in those, of the kinds of scenes normally found in novels. In one of them, Gosse records, heartbreakingly, the last bit of his father's levity to go. Philip sometimes sang songs from his Dorsetshire youth. One day a workman heard him and made an approving comment; then, Gosse reports, "my Father, who was holding my hand loosely, clutched it, and looking up, I saw his eyes darken. He never sang a secular song again during the whole of his life."

In two sentences, Gosse moves from a freeze-frame moment to a span of decades: a heady move. Stepping back that way is risky. It can break the narrative mood and let the door open for banality and bathos. But if you can do it with a clear eye, as Gosse does, it suddenly raises the stakes of your narrative and opens up vast fertile territories for generations of memoirists.

Chapter 7

ONE HUNDRED
PERCENT AMERICANS

IN 1999, THE EDITORIAL BOARD of the Modern Library compiled a list of the one hundred best English-language nonfiction books of
the twentieth century. Seven of the top twenty were memoirs or autobiographies: Booker T. Washington's *Up from Slavery*, James Watson's *The
Double Helix*, Vladimir Nabokov's *Speak, Memory*, Richard Wright's
Black Boy, James Baldwin's *Notes of a Native Son*, Gertrude Stein's *The
Autobiography of Alice B. Toklas*, and the first-place winner, *The Education
of Henry Adams*. (The other memoirs to make the top 100 were the collected autobiographical writings of W. B. Yeats; *The Autobiography of
Mark Twain*, Robert Graves's *Goodbye to All That*, Isak Dinesen's *Out
of Africa*, Dean Acheson's *Present at the Creation*, Beryl Markham's
West with the Night, Tobias Wolff's *This Boy's Life*, George Orwell's
Homage to Catalonia, William Styron's *Darkness Visible*, *The Autobiography of Malcolm X*, and Anne Lamott's *Operating Instructions*.) Adams—
great-grandson of President John Adams, grandson of President John

Quincy Adams, son of Senator Charles Francis Adams, journalist, historian, novelist—embarked on the book in 1905, when he was sixty-seven. His plan was always posthumous publication—he commented to Henry James that the book would be "a shield of protection in the grave"—and it was published in 1918, shortly after Adams's death. The following year it was awarded the Pulitzer Prize for Biography or Autobiography, and it quickly achieved the status of American classic.

The most striking and famous thing about the book is that Adams, like Caesar and Pope Pius II before him and Gertrude Stein and Norman Mailer after, referred to himself in the third person. It was a brilliant choice, suiting both his allusive style and the bemused diffidence with which he regarded himself: someone born into an eighteenth-century world and destined to live to the twentieth; a product of almost-too-distinguished forebears whose achievements, no matter how substantial, would always be considered disappointing; a man whose lifelong search for "education" seemed always to fall short. Here he partakes in that favorite trope of autobiographers, the recollection of earliest memory:

> He first found himself sitting on a yellow kitchen-floor in strong sunlight. He was three years old when he took his earliest step in education; a lesson of color. The second followed soon; a lesson of taste. On December 3, 1841, he developed scarlet fever. For several days he was as good as dead, reviving only under the careful nursing of his family. When he began to discover strength, about January 1, 1842, his hunger must have been stronger than any other pleasure or pain, for while in after life he retained not the faintest recollection of his illness, he remembered quite clearly his aunt entering the sick room bearing in her hand a saucer with a baked apple.

Two years after Adams was awarded the Pulitzer, the same prize went to another third-person autobiography with a similar title, *The American-ization of Edward Bok*. Bok, the Dutch-born longtime editor of the *Ladies' Home Journal*, explains at the outset his stylistic rationale: "I had always felt the most effective method of writing an autobiography, for the sake of a better perspective, was mentally to separate the writer from his subject by this device." However, after reading the book, one has a hard time escaping the conclusion that Bok's real reason was that if he had referred to himself as "I," he would have been revealed as the insufferably smug egotist that he was. Consider the section in which he boasts about the *Journal*'s circulation of a million and three-quarter copies, and imagine how it would sound with every "Bok" and "Bok's" replaced by an "I" and "my":

On every hand, the question was being asked: "How is it done? How is such a high circulation obtained?" Bok's invariable answer was that he gave his readers the very best of the class of reading that he believed would interest them, and that he spared neither effort nor expense to obtain it for them. When Mr. [William Dean] Howells once asked him how he classified his audience, Bok replied, "We appeal to the intelligent American woman rather than to the intellectual type." And he gave her the best he could obtain. As he knew her to be fond of the personal type of literature, he gave her in succession Jane Addams's story of "My Fifteen Years at Hull House," and the remarkable narration of Helen Keller's "Story of My Life"; he invited Henry Van Dyke, who had never been in the Holy Land, to go there, camp out in a tent, and then write a series of sketches, "Out of Doors in the Holy Land"; he induced Lyman Abbott to tell the story of "My Fifty Years as a Minister." He asked Gene Stratton Porter to tell of her bird-experiences in the series: "What I Have Done with Birds." . . . He got Kate

Douglas Wiggin to tell a country church experience of hers in "The Old Peabody Pew."

I quote this passage not only to illustrate Bok's self-regard, but because of the light it sheds on turn-of-the-twentieth-century autobiography. Bok's high opinion of himself was to some extent justified. He shrewdly recognized that readers were interested in the life stories of prominent people (the word "celebrity" was not yet in wide circulation), told by themselves, and he went out and solicited such stories for the *Ladies' Home Journal*. In many cases, they had a life beyond the magazine: all of the articles or series mentioned above eventually were turned into books. To say that the memoirs of Van Dyke (a minister and author), Abbott (another minister), Porter (a popular novelist), and Wiggin (also a novelist, notably of *Rebecca of Sunnybrook Farm*) are little read today would be perhaps to overstate their popularity. But Addams's and Keller's books are classics of American memoir.

Keller's book, *The Story of My Life* (1902), has a strikingly modern feel for three distinct reasons. The first is her (extremely young) age at publication: just twenty-two. The second is her status as a media figure. Born in Alabama in 1880, Keller suffered an illness at the age of nineteen months that left her deaf and blind, and as a result she was also unable to speak. When she was seven, through the offices of Alexander Graham Bell, she was referred to Michael Anagnos, director of the Perkins Institution for the Blind in Boston, who in turn assigned a young teacher named Anne Sullivan to live and work with her. Decades before Edward Bernays and Ivy Lee institutionalized the field of "public relations," Anagnos proved to be a master at getting Keller's name and remarkable story before the public. In 1889, she arrived at Perkins for a four-year residence. That year, an article about her appeared in *The New York Times* under the headline "The Deaf, Dumb, and Blind Girl." Between then and the appearance of her autobiography thirteen years later, Keller was featured in the *Times* on more than three dozen occasions, recounting the progress of her education, her visits with Bell and President Grover Cleveland, and her graduation from Perkins, where she recited thirty-six lines from Longfellow's "Flowers," and, the newspaper somewhat creepily reported, appeared a "a tall, noble-looking girl, finely proportioned and appearing much older than her 13 years." Her photograph often appeared in national magazines; favorite poses showed her stroking her dog or reading Shakespeare in Braille. By May of 1900, a *Times* writer wondered whether "altogether too much has been written concerning Miss Helen Keller." The next year the *Times* excerpted an article from *Christian Endeavor World* that gave a resoundingly negative answer: "Who tires of reading about Helen Keller? This wonderful girl . . . is perhaps the best-known and best-beloved young woman in all the land."

The third modern aspect of Keller's book is the way it prefigures— albeit with a much more uplifting finale than the ambivalent conclusion we have become used to—the multitudinous contemporary disability memoir, represented in such works as *My Left Foot, The Diving Bell and the Butterfly, Autobiography of a Face, My Lobotomy, Poster Child,* and many more. Today, the public is ready for and indeed expects such narratives; in Keller's time, if it had not been for her fame, her story would surely have gone unpublished. Also relevant was the socially acceptable nature of her particular disability. In Louis Kaplan's bibliography of American autobiography through 1945, the overwhelming majority of memoirists indexed under "Physically handicapped" or "Illnesses, accounts of " suffered from one of just two conditions: blindness and tuberculosis. For an explanation, the world awaits a doctoral dissertation.

In this environment, it was all the more remarkable that *A Mind That*

Found Itself should have appeared in the nation's bookshops in 1908. Its author was Clifford W. Beers, who graduated from Yale in 1897 and three years later suffered a mental breakdown (subsequent writers have described it as a manic-depressive disorder, with elements of delusion) and tried to kill himself by jumping out a high window of the family home. He was committed to a series of institutions, in one of which he "found his mind" and recovered his reason, in his account, when he suddenly realized that the man claiming to be his brother, whom Beers had viewed as an imposter, was actually telling the truth. He was still subject to severe mood swings but was lucid enough to begin to be outraged at the treatment he received. In 1887, the journalist Nellie Bly had published *Ten Days in a Mad-House*, an undercover account of a stunt in which she feigned madness and was committed to a New York lunatic asylum. Beers doesn't mention Bly, but he took on something of the character of an investigative reporter. At one point, he deliberately broke rules so as to be transferred to a more severe ward and experience the worst conditions the hospital had to offer. He was not disappointed: at various points he was strangled, force-fed against his wishes, secluded in a cold cell without coverings, and placed in a straitjacket for about three hundred hours.

Beers's manic episodes were characterized by bursts of creative activity, especially writing; after his release, he took to the composition of the book with gusto. With the editorial help of a college friend, he emerged with a riveting account of his experience; as the great psychologist William James wrote in a letter to him that serves as the book's epigraph, "It reads like fiction, but it is not fiction; and this I state emphatically, knowing how prone the uninitiated are to doubt the truthfulness of descriptions of abnormal mental processes." The title notwithstanding, it seems that the single most important factor in Beers's recovery was his very determination to write an account of his ordeal, and thus seek to improve conditions in such institutions and the care and treatment of the mentally ill generally. He predicted that as *Uncle Tom's Cabin* was to slavery, his book would be to mental illness, and he rejected James's advice to publish under a pseudonym: "I must fight in the open." Beers writes in the first chapter, "I am not telling the story of my life just to write a book. I tell it because it seems my plain duty to do so. A narrow escape from death and a seemingly miraculous return to health after an apparently fatal illness are enough to make a man ask himself: For what purpose was my life spared? That question I have asked myself, and this book is, in part, an answer."

Remarkably enough, what might have seemed delusions of grandeur proved not to be delusions at all. The year after the book's initial publication (it was reprinted dozens of times over the next three decades), Beers founded an organization he called National Committee for Mental Hygiene (a term he coined) that eventually established branches in fifty-three countries. He was the first to propose the establishment of halfway houses, in which recovering patients could be monitored outside of a hospital setting. In an editorial published after his death in 1943, *The New York Times* called him "the most successful champion that the insane ever had."*

The notion of autobiography as more a means to a social end, less an instrument of personal expression, was characteristic of the era, which is referred to as "Progressive" for a reason. Women's rights activists Elizabeth Cady Stanton (1898) and Anna Howard Shaw (1915) and urban reformers Jacob Riis (1901) and Jane Addams (1910) all used their memoirs to advance the cause. The founder of the Tuskeegee Institute, Booker T. Washington (1856–1915), published an autobiography in 1900 (*The Story of My Life and Work*) and another (*Up from Slavery*) in 1901. In both

---

*Four years earlier, Beers had suffered a relapse, of depression and paranoia, and committed himself to a Rhode Island hospital, where he died.

books, which appear to have been influenced equally by the slave narrative tradition, Benjamin Franklin's autobiography, and the novels of Horatio Alger, Washington explicitly argues for the creed of hard work, self-reliance, and industrial education, while more subtly nominating himself as Frederick Douglass's successor as the leader of American blacks.

Maybe the most striking work in this vein is *Prison Memoirs of an Anarchist* (1912), by Alexander Berkman, who, in protest against treatment of the Homestead Strikers in 1892, had tried to murder industrialist Henry Frick. Although the book begins with an account of his radicalization, his attack on Frick, and his trial, more than three-quarters of it is a present-tense account of his years in prison. And a remarkable account it is, gripping and unflinching and unsparing in any details, notably the sexual relations among prisoners. As Hutchins Hapgood wrote in an introduction to the original edition, "This is the only book that I know which goes deeply into the corrupting, demoralizing psychology of prison life. It shows, in picture after picture, sketch after sketch, not only the obvious brutality, stupidity, ugliness permeating the institution, but, very touching, it shows the good qualities and instincts of the human heart perverted, demoralized, helplessly struggling for life."

Also reflective of the times' progressive cast was a purposeful widening of the autobiographical playing field. Writing in his editor's column in *Harper's* magazine in 1909, William Dean Howells hailed works of autobiography as "the most delightful of all reading," in large part because they constituted the "most democratic province of the republic of letters." He asserted, "We would not restrict autobiography to any age or sex, creed, class or color," and he called for the memoirs of "some entirely unknown person." Actually, things were already moving in this direction. The aforementioned Hutchins Hapgood, a reform-minded American journalist, had been responsible in 1903 for a book accurately called *The*

Autobiography of a Thief, the product of four months of interviews with a reformed miscreant identified only as Jim. The editor of the New York newspaper *The Independent*, the similarly named Hamilton Holt, began publishing at around the same time what he called "lifelets": short autobiographical sketches by people from all walks of life. A selection of sixteen of them was published in 1906, under the title *The Life Stories of Undistinguished Americans as Told by Themselves*. Included, as Holt explained in a preface, were "the story of the butcher, the sweatshop worker, the bootblack, the push-cart peddler, the lumber man, the dressmaker, the nurse girl, the cook, the cotton-picker, the head-hunter, the trained nurse, the minister, the butler and the laundryman."

It's not just that these people's jobs were diverse; so were their countries of origin, which included Lithuania, Poland, Sweden, Ireland, France, Germany, Italy, Greece, Syria, China, and Japan. The United States was in the midst of the greatest immigration wave in its history. At the same time, it was poised at the beginning of what would later be termed the "American Century." Is it any wonder that a major, maybe *the* major, theme of the autobiographies of the time was the meaning of being an American?

This was true even of books by Americans whose roots were very deep indeed. Perhaps the most ambivalent tale of Americanization was told by a Sioux Indian, born in Minnesota in 1858. His original name was Ohiyesa, but his father converted to Christianity, took the name Jacob Eastman, and called the boy Charles. Charles Eastman received a bachelor's degree from Dartmouth College and a medical degree from Boston University, and went on to a varied career that included government service and advocacy of the Native American cause. He also wrote two autobiographies, *Indian Boyhood* (1902) and *From the Deep Woods to Civilization* (1916), that, in their narrative of Eastman's progression from his tribal childhood to full participation in American life, neatly reversed the progression of the traditional captivity narrative. But in both books he is always mindful of both the good things he experienced as a boy and the flaws of "civilization." He concludes the second in sterling fashion by musing on the "evil and wickedness practised by the nations composed of professedly 'Christian' individuals":

> Behind the material and intellectual splendor of our civilization, primitive savagery and lust hold sway, undiminished, and as it seems, unheeded. When I let go of my simple instinctive nature religion, I hoped to gain something far loftier as well as more satisfying to the reason. Alas! It is also more confusing and contradictory. . . .
>
> Yet even in deep jungles God's own sunlight penetrates, and I stand before my own people still as an advocate of civilization. Why? First, because there is no chance for our former simple life any more; and second, because I realize that the white man's religion is not responsible for his mistakes. . . .
>
> I am an Indian; and while I have learned much from civilization, for which I am grateful, I have never lost my Indian sense of right and justice. I am for development and progress along social and spiritual lines, rather than those of commerce, nationalism, or material efficiency. Nevertheless, so long as I live, I am an American.

As for newcomers to the country, they could, for a time, afford to be more upbeat, and they were. Jacob Riis's description of his arrival in New York after emigrating from Denmark communicates the general sense of almost unlimited possibility: "It was a beautiful spring morning, and as I looked over the rail at the miles of straight streets, the green heights of Brooklyn, and the stir of ferryboats and pleasure craft on the river, my hopes rose high there would be a place for me. . . . I had a pair of strong hands, and stubbornness enough to do for two; also a strong belief that in a free country, free from the dominion of custom, of caste, as well as of men, things would somehow come right in the end." Riis arrived in New York in 1870, when the great wave of immigration was still to come. Edward Bok came from the Netherlands the same year. More than eighteen million souls journeyed to the United States between 1890 and 1920, a large proportion of them with points of origin well south of Denmark and east of Holland. The first great autobiographer who was part of that wave was Moshke Antin, born in 1881 in Polotsk, Russia. Her father immigrated to Boston in 1891; her mother and the four children followed three years later. Moshke—she would soon change her name to Mary—was placed in the first grade but within half a year was promoted to fifth. In her high school years, she got to know Edward Everett Hale and other literary and cultural figures in the city, and was encouraged to translate (from Yiddish) into English letters she'd written to her uncle describing the passage to America. She edited them into a short book that was published in 1899 with the title *From Plot͡zk [sic] to Boston*, with a foreword by the noted English Jewish writer Israel Zangwill (whose 1908 play *The Melting-Pot* would introduce that phrase to the popular lexicon and provide the young century's most forceful brief in favor of immigration). The short review of Antin's book in the *Boston Transcript* shows how much of a novelty her experiences still seemed: "She wrote the narrative in her native dialect called Yiddish . . . with what purpose is not known, but it evidently was written with all the fervor and enthusiasm of an exceptional girl of her age after what were to her most thrilling experiences." By 1912, when Antin published her next book, it was no longer necessary to explain what Yiddish was. The main story of that book, *The Promised Land*—and there was not a molecule of irony in the title—was

Antin's life from childhood up through her teen years, but the subtext was America itself: what it meant and continued to mean to immigrants like herself, and how their presence had changed the nature of the country. Those issues are present on every page of the book, but in the introduction, Antin highlights them as part of her rationale for publishing an autobiography at the tender age of thirty. She admits that she has

> not accomplished anything, I have not discovered anything, not even by accident, as Columbus discovered America. My life has been unusual, but by no means unique. And this is the very core of the matter. It is because I understand my history, in its larger outlines, to be typical of many, that I consider it worth recording. . . . I am only one of many whose fate it has been to live a page of modern history. We are the strands of the cable that binds the Old World to the New. As the ships that brought us link the shores of Europe and America, so our lives span the bitter sea of racial difference and misunderstandings. Before we came, the New World knew not the Old; but since we have begun to come, the Young World has taken the Old by the hand, and the two are learning to march side by side, seeking a common destiny.

Indeed, Antin asserts that in the process of becoming an American, her former self was obliterated: "I am just as much out of the way as if I were dead, for I am absolutely other than the person whose story I have to tell. . . . My life I have still to live; her life ended when mine began."

The Promised Land was a smashing success, as much for its assimilationist optimism as for its undeniable literary qualities. *The New York Times*'s rave review concluded, "In the moving, vividly interesting pages of her autobiography, Mary Antin has presented the case of the Russian Jew's American citizenship as it has not been presented before. And she has made a unique contribution to our modern literature and our modern history." *Publishers Weekly* ranked it the best-selling nonfiction book of the year. In Antin's lifetime (she died in 1949), *The Promised Land* went through thirty-four printings and sold an estimated 85,000 copies.

The Promised Land represented a high-water mark of immigrant optimism. The mid-teens saw a growth in nativist resentment against the unwashed millions. This could be seen in *The Passing of the Great Race*, a massive 1916 bestseller that put forth a theory of "Nordic superiority"; in the resurgence of the Ku Klux Klan; and even in the success of D. W. Griffith's 1915 film *The Birth of a Nation*. Not surprisingly, there was a change in mood among new Americans and those otherwise on the margins. The optimism of a Jacob Riis, a Booker T. Washington, or a Mary Antin was no longer operative. The very act of sitting down and composing an autobiography, in one's own voice and under one's own name, required a level of confidence that was harder to come by. Identity was becoming tenuous; the cultural ground was shifting under everyone's feet. It was two centuries after Defoe, but the system where all books were unequivocally classified as complete truth or complete fiction was not yet in place. A series of autobiographical works by members of marginal groups explores that misty middle ground.

A book called *The Autobiography of an Ex-Colored Man* was published in 1912. It told the story of a light-skinned black man, never named in the text, who, after witnessing a lynching, decides that for the rest of his life he will pass as white. No author was listed on the title page. Nor was there any indication that the book was not a factual autobiography. In reality it was a novel by an African-American lawyer, songwriter, and diplomat named James Weldon Johnson, who had decided on this course of publication, he wrote to a friend, because if "the author is known, and known to be the one who could not be the main character, the book will fall flat."

Reviewers and the public fell for the ruse as well. In his actual autobiog-raphy, *Along This Way*—published in 1933, after he had gained promi-nence as an activist and NAACP officer—Johnson described "being introduced to and talking with one man who tacitly admitted to those present that he was the author of the book."

First-person texts by Jewish immigrants came from a wide range of stances, few of them unambiguous. As in Defoe's time, it was often dif-ficult or impossible to tell whether a printed testimony was the work of the "I" of the text or a masked fabricator. Abraham Cahan's *The Rise of David Levinsky*, an admittedly fictional autobiography, was published in 1917. The very first paragraph showed a marked contrast with Antin: to the narrator, Levinsky, the kind of transformation she talked about, the magical casting of an old self in the new world, wasn't really possible: "I was born and reared in the lowest depths of poverty and I arrived in America—in 1885—with four cents in my pocket. I am now worth more than two million dollars and recognized as one of the two or three leading men in the cloak-and-suit trade in the United States. And yet when I take a look at my inner identity it impresses me as being precisely the same as it was thirty or forty years ago."

Published in 1923 with a cloudier provenance was *Haunch, Paunch, and Jowl: The Making of a Professional Jew*. There was no name on the title page, and the publisher stated it was the "anonymous autobiography" of a judge who had died five years previously and who gives himself the name "Meyer Hirsch." This time, reviewers were divided on the actuality question. *The New York Times* hedged its bets, allowing that it is "probably about one-half fiction." The real percentage was one hundred: the author, Samuel Ornitz, made up the story of Hirsch, a thoroughly corrupt figure, who boasts about being a "professional Jew," someone who exploits and sometimes invents threats of anti-Semitism to advance his own interests or, as a character in the book puts it, stirs up "rumpuses, alarms, furors over every fancied grievance, insult and reflection." Ornitz was in fact a Jew, but the book played into the hands of those who felt that the newcomers were less than 100 percent American. (Ornitz went to Hollywood in the late 1920s and was a successful screenwriter until 1947, when he was called before the House Un-American Activities Committee. Along with other members of the "Hollywood Ten," he refused to testify, and served nine months in prison.)

In October 1916, Edward Bok published in his *Ladies' Home Journal* an anonymous article called "My Mother and I: The Story of How I Became an American Woman." It was accompanied by an appreciation from the pen of none other than former president Theodore Roosevelt, a friend of Bok's, who called the piece "a really noteworthy story—a profoundly touching story—of the Americanizing of a young girl, who between babyhood and young womanhood leaps over a space which in all cultural and humanizing essentials is far more important than the distance painfully traversed by her fore-fathers during the preceding thousand years." The following year the article was expanded into a book called *My Mother and I*, now with an author's name on the title page: E. G. Stern. The narrative touches many of the same notes as *The Promised Land*, but underpinning them were ambivalent chords. The narrator, who never refers to herself by name, came from the old country as a baby but, she tells us in the opening chapter, has shaken off every remnant of the ghetto in which she grew up: "I am a college woman. My husband is engaged in an honorable profession. Our home is unpretentious but pretty, and is situated in a charming old suburb of an American city where attractive modern residences stand by the side of stately old colonial houses, as if typifying young America in the shadow of old America." At the end of the book, her mother comes to visit that home for the first time and is baffled: by the

English her grandson speaks, by the non-kosher food her daughter serves ("Her plate at meals was left almost untouched"), by the "white kitchen, used only for cooking." And then the narrator realizes that the price of her journey and her happiness is an irreparable break with her heritage.

Neither the front matter nor the text offered any clue as to whether E. G. Stern, who was a Philadelphia journalist and former social worker named Elizabeth Gertrude Stern, was telling her own story or a made-up one. The publisher called the book autobiography, but reviewers again were divided. *The New York Times* commented that the story was "told vividly and with so great an effect that one is often impelled to wonder whether this is not, in essentials at least, a genuine autobiography rather than a work of fiction." That anonymous critic was perceptive. The book was in essence Stern's own story of growing up in Pittsburgh, Pennsylvania, as the daughter of Aaron Kleine Levin, a cantor, and his wife, Sarah.

Stern's next book, *I Am a Woman—and a Jew*, was published in 1927 under the name Leah Morton. Again, it was officially an autobiography, and again reviewers were puzzled. The *Times* said it "purports and ap-pears to be . . . the actual experiences of a real woman" but didn't take a stand on whether it was. The *Boston Transcript* assumed the book con-tained "Morton's" own story, but felt that it also constituted "virtually a composite autobiography of the Jew in America." The truth was compli-cated. As late as 1986, in the introduction to a new edition of the book, the scholar Ellen Umansky described the main outlines of the story as factual, with some embellishments and alterations. However, shortly after the edi-tion appeared, Umansky received a letter from Stern's older son, Thomas Noel Stern, a retired history professor, in which he asserted (Umansky later wrote) that "Elizabeth Stern was not born in East Prussia to Sarah and Aaron Levin as she publicly claimed throughout her life, but rather was born in 1889 in Pittsburgh, the illegitimate daughter of Christian Limburg, a German Lutheran, and Elizabeth Morgan, a Welsh Baptist. 'After shifting from home to home in early years,' he wrote, 'Mother was placed with Aaron and Sara Leah Levin, near the Pittsburgh railway depot.'" In a memoir of his own published in 1988, *Secret Family*, Thomas Stern made additional revelations, most scandalously that Aaron Levin had sexually abused his mother from the age of seven to fourteen, when she became pregnant and underwent an illegal abortion. Umansky set about investigating these claims and was unable to find any records of Elizabeth Stern's birth, possibly because, "according to Thomas Stern, his mother deliberately destroyed all records alluding to her true identity." She concluded, "It may well be impossible, then, to establish with certainty the true circumstances surrounding Elizabeth Stern's birth." But there is little doubt that Stern—who gave herself the middle name Gertrude, and who was also known as Bessie Levin (the name under which she was listed in Aaron Levin's will), E. G. Stern, Leah Morton, and Eleanor Morton (the name under which she published most of her other books, and by which her 1954 *New York Times* obituary identified her)—was the classic case of an early-twentieth-century American who used autobiographical forms to address her own deep questions of identity.

It also seems clear that Stern only partially believed the stories she told in her books. You could not say the same for the man who called himself Chief Buffalo Child Long Lance, and whose 1928 autobiography, *Long Lance*, was praised in the *New York Herald Tribune* by the anthropologist Paul Radin as "an unusually faithful account" of the author's youth among the Plains Indians. The book included a preface by the novelist Irvin S. Cobb, stating, "I claim there is authentic history in these pages and verity and most of all a power to describe in English words the thoughts, the instincts, the events which originally were framed in a native language."

As the historian Donald B. Smith revealed in his 1982 book *Chief Buffalo Long Lance: The True Story of an Imposter*, Long Lance's native language was actually English. He had been born in North Carolina as Sylvester Long, the son of former slaves, with some black, white, and Native American blood. In 1903, at age thirteen, he ran away from home to join a Wild West show, where he presented himself as an Indian and performed as such. Six years later he exaggerated his Cherokee blood to successfully apply to the Carlisle Indian School in Pennsylvania, under the name Sylvester Long Lance, and he graduated in the same class as the great athlete Jim Thorpe. He went on to college in New York and fought in World War I for the Canadian forces. After his discharge, he worked as a journalist in Calgary and Winnipeg, where he took the final step in his representational journey by adopting the name Chief Buffalo Child Long Lance and the identity of a full-blooded Blackfoot.

In New York in 1925 on a lecture tour, Long Lance met Ray Long, the editor of *Cosmopolitan* magazine, who commissioned him to write an autobiographical article. Long Lance gave himself a boyhood among the Blackfoot, a stint working on western cattle ranches, and some time with Buffalo Bill's Wild West Show (much more renowned than the show he actually had toured with), then picked up his true story at Carlisle. The article was so well received that Long, also an editor with William Randolph Hearst's book publishing operation, commissioned him to expand it into a full-blown autobiography, which he did. The result was a combination of research, stories Long Lance borrowed from Blackfoot friends' childhoods, and pure fancy. The opening line was "The first thing in my life that I can remember is the exciting aftermath of an Indian fight in northern Montana," and Long Lance went on to tell of buffalo hunts on the plains (never mind that the last buffalo hunt had taken place long before his birth). The combination of retroactive nostalgia for the vanished

Native American past, on the one hand, and Long Lance's undeniable skill as a writer and poseur, on the other, was such that not a single murmur of doubt was heard. The first edition of the book was sold out; it was followed by an English edition and Dutch and German translations. Long Lance became a celebrity and a fixture on the social circuit; the syndicated columnist O. O. McIntyre, who informed the country at large about Gotham doings, called him "an amazing paradox, a vanishing Red Man with an Oxonian accent, spats and a monocle." So successful was his mingling that a 1930 *New York Herald Tribune* article titled "One Hundred Percent American" commented, with unintended irony, "There is romance always in the man who can play the game and live the life of another race." That same year, a Hollywood producer hired Long Lance to appear in a film called *The Silent Enemy*, an anthropological docudrama, in the vein of *Nanook of the North*, about the life of the Indians of northern Canada before the arrival of the Europeans. He got rave reviews, including one from *Variety* that noted: "Chief Long Lance is an ideal picture Indian, because he is a full-blooded one." But the film was the beginning of the end of Long Lance's trail. His costar, Chief Chauncey Yellow Robe, was an actual Native American, a grandnephew of Sitting Bull. He expressed doubts about Long Lance's professed identity to the film's producers, who discovered the truth, and confronted Long Lance with it. They never went public, for a revelation of Long Lance's fakery would destroy *The Silent Enemy*'s claims of authenticity. But Long Lance knew that before long he would be exposed. In 1931, he fatally shot himself in the head. He did not leave a note.

The late 1920s were the golden age of autobiographical hoaxes. Postwar and pre-crash, possibility and ballyhoo were in the air, and imagination ran wild. One day in 1925, an elderly peddler named Alfred Aloysius Smith came to the door of Ethelreda Lewis, an English novelist living in

South Africa. He got to talking and told her, among other things, that, when living in Utah, he had helped quell an uprising of the Ute Indians; that he had been a London newspaper reporter and a Scotland Yard detective; and that in Africa he had been a big-game hunter, an explorer, and a miner and had once saved Cecil Rhodes from an alligator attack. Mrs. Lewis persuaded him to collaborate with her on his autobiography. A year later it was published in England and was chosen in America as the first selection of the Literary Guild. A trade edition was put out by the three-year-old publishing firm Simon & Schuster, which had made its reputation and a great deal of money with a series of crossword-puzzle books but had yet to have any success with a book of the conventional sort, under the title *Trader Horn; being the life and works of Alfred Aloysius Horn: an "old visiter"* . . . *the works written by himself at the age of seventy-three and the life, with such of his philosophy as is the gift of age and experience, taken down and here edited by Ethelreda Lewis.* Perhaps the book's self-consciously eighteenth-centuryish title was a hint that the accuracy of its contents was not absolute. Some critics were skeptical; the *Times Literary Supplement* commented that the author's "unaffected simplicity is at times indistinguishable from the diabolical guile of those who are experts in the fashions of the American book market. Nevertheless, a miracle may have happened, it is true; it is not that we cynically doubt the possibility of miracles. Mr. Horn seems to us to be rather too good, at times." A recent writer, Tim Couzens, spent years checking out Smith's tales and concluded, in his 1992 book *Tramp Royal,* that many of them happened roughly as Smith recounted them. The public, which bought 170,000 copies of the book, didn't seem to much care. *Publishers Weekly* assigned it to the nonfiction bestseller list, where for the years 1927 and 1928 it was in fourth place and third, respectively. Aiding in the sales effort was Simon & Schuster's decision to bring Smith, now universally known as "Trader

Horn," to New York City for a publicity lap. Like Long Lance the following year, he traveled the social circuit and was interviewed by many reporters, including E. B. White of *The New Yorker*, who wrote:

> The old man's childish simplicity in the midst of exploitation was lovely. Nobody quite like him ever visited these shores—a fabulous man, only half real, a sort of ancient mariner. We met him at the Literary Guild's birthday party. He was wedged in between Zona Gale and Elinor Wylie,[*] cameras clicking, caterers catering, book circulation mounting; but withal he was rather enjoying it, his long life among cannibals and animals having fitted him to withstand booksy folk and cameramen. He enjoys being picturesque, and does it without offense.

Smith issued two further volumes of autobiography before his death in 1931. That year MGM released *Trader Horn*, recounting selected adventures, starring Harry Carey in the title role. The film included some classic dialogue, as when Horn's sidekick, Peru, asks, "There are cannibals?" and he replies: "Aye. A God-fearing race they are. Except, as you say, in the matter of diet." The movie was nominated for an Academy Award for Best Picture, but lost to *Cimarron*.

Trader Horn came right in the middle of a wave of first-person travel/adventure memoirs. One or more books by T. E. Lawrence (Lawrence of Arabia), Peter Fleming, Richard Halliburton, Negley Farson, and Richard E. Byrd all appeared on *Publishers Weekly*'s list of top ten bestselling books of the year. One of the first in the genre, and perhaps the most successful, was Frederick O'Brien's 1920 *White Shadows in the South Seas*.

---

*Gale and Wylie were popular novelists at the time.

Seeing its success—forty-four weeks on the *Publishers Weekly* bestseller list in 1920 and 1921—George Putnam, the young heir to the venerable publisher G. P. Putnam's Sons, who had recently taken the reins of the firm, asked a friend of his named George S. Chappell to write a South Seas burlesque. This came out under the title *The Cruise of the Kawa*, credited to Walter E. Traprock, F.R.S.S.E.U. (Fellow, Royal South Seas Explorers Union), and included staged photos of such Manhattan notables as Heywood Broun, Frank Crowninshield, Rockwell Kent, and Ralph Barton. It sold close to 100,000 copies and was followed by two sequels, *My Northern Exposure* and *Sarah of the Sahara.*

Like George Putnam, but maybe even more so, Richard L. Simon and M. Lincoln Schuster, the founders and proprietors of Simon & Schuster, were known for aggressively marketing their books and authors—a marked contrast to the traditionally genteel business ethos of American publishers at the time. So it wasn't surprising that they would have seen the potential in Joan Lowell, a minor movie actress who had given lectures on her nautical experiences and who came to their offices one day early in 1929. Geoffrey Hellman, in a 1939 *New Yorker* profile of the firm, recounted that "Schuster was impressed by Miss Lowell, a well-built girl with dark, flashing eyes and powerful biceps." He brought her in to see his partner,

who was even more impressed. They got her to work up her reminiscences into a book-length account of her first seventeen years, in which she stated, among other things, that her father was the Australian-born son of a Montenegrin landowner and had for seventeen years been owner and captain of the four-masted schooner Minnie A. Caine; that her mother, whose surname she had taken, was a member of the Lowell family of Boston; that from the age of eleven months to seventeen years she had been the only female on board the Minnie A. Caine; that she had seen her father break up a waterspout half a mile away by shooting it with a rifle; that she had watched nine virgins and their bridegrooms consummate their marriage in a rather public wedding ceremony on one of the South Sea Islands; that finally the Minnie A. Caine, sailing for Australia with 900 tons of copra, had burned and sunk, and she had to swim over a mile against a high-running sea to a lightship, carrying a kitten on each shoulder; and that she could spit a curve in the wind.

Simon & Schuster worked their marketing magic, and Lowell briefly seized the national publicity spotlight. One article, syndicated by the Newspaper Enterprise Association in papers across the country, started this way:

Gangway for Skipper Joan!

Gangway for the 26-year-old girl who has licked the world!

Her name is Joan Lowell. She is sort of a "Trader Horn in petticoats" and her life story is the most alluring you ever read. Here is a real story of the South Seas, more fascinating even than the fiction tales of Herman Melville and Robert Louis Stevenson.

Cradle of the Deep was selected by the Literary Guild's main competitor, the Book-of-the-Month Club, and got some strong reviews. *The New York Times* said, "It's a jolly yarn, mates; told with dash and ardor and employing a vocabulary as replete with expletives as one will encounter at sea or in a highly modern Broadway show." The book shot up to the number-one spot on nonfiction bestseller lists, and eventually was purchased by some 107,000 souls. However, early doubts were raised as well. A review in the *New York Herald Tribune* by Lincoln Colcord, a writer with excellent credentials in the maritime field (according to a biographi-cal reference work, he "was born at sea off Cape Horn in the bark Char-lotte A. Littlefield, commanded by his father, Captain Lincoln Alden Colcord of Searsport, Maine. His family had been seafarers for five gen-erations"), said the book was "such a good yarn that one wishes it had been presented frankly as a work of fiction, so that the question of its nautical authenticity had never arisen. . . . Space does not permit the cata-loging of all the genuine nautical errors in the book. . . . Their sum total is rather staggering." Soon afterward, residents of Berkeley, California, told the *San Francisco Chronicle* that Lowell, whose real name was Helen Joan Wagner, had spent most of her childhood as a neighbor of theirs. Then the *Minnie A. Caine* was spotted shipshape, anchored in Oakland Harbor, California. It emerged that Lowell and her father had been aboard the boat, but only for a total of fifteen months. The Book-of-the-Month Club offered its 65,000 subscribers refunds on the book, and Simon & Schuster issued a statement acknowledging that the book had "a consider-ably larger element of romanticized fact interwoven with the underlying sequence of truthful narrative than we had at first realized." However, the firm pronounced itself "still satisfied that the essential honesty of Joan's yarn remains unassailable."

The humorist Will Rogers, in his syndicated column, had some sport with the scandal. He said he had been looking forward to reading *Cradle of the Deep*: "Never mind all this Fiction, I want some facts, and all the things I had read about this book said here is the real McCoy." He enjoyed the book, he wrote, though he was "a little leary right from the start as to how a Mother could part with a seven month old Baby Girl, but not know-ing sea people much I thought well maby they part with their young young." It was an "awful blow" when it turned out that "most of Joan's Deep Seaing was on the Ferry from an Apartment in Jersey City over to her Publishers. And that profanity was all gathered from two trips to the 'Front Page.'"*

The Bookman conducted a debate in its pages: "Are Literary Hoaxes Harmful?" To an early-twenty-first-century reader, the arguments ring eerily familiar. Taking the affirmative side was Lincoln Colcord, who was less shocked by Lowell's fabrications than the *lack* of shock (and continued strong sales) with which they had been greeted: "If charlatanism is to be more successful than honest writing, and win its way through advertising and publicity on which there is no check, the foundations of literary effort are seriously threatened." Arguing the negative was the columnist Heywood Broun, who invoked the principle of the Higher Truth:

> Ancients admitted the difficulty of drawing hairlines between the false and true and this feat has hardly grown more simple in the Age of the Unconscious. If I record with factual accuracy some series of events which happened to me I have arrived at a truth of sorts. But it is not the only sort of truth. Suppose I color and heighten and even fabricate episodes more exciting, I am still not beyond all contact with the truth, for in this case I am drawing material out of visions and deepest longings.

Writing in *The New Yorker*, E. B. White was less inclined to be indulgent than he had been in the Trader Horn affair. Noting that Broun had defended Lowell by referring to "a fundamental verity in fairy tales," White commented: "All of this gives us what can briefly be described as a pain. The old balderdash pain."

---

*The quotation is as written by Rogers, who was notoriously loose with his capitalization, punctuation, and spelling. *The Front Page* was a Broadway newspaper drama with salty language.

Chapter 8

MODERNISTS AND
MOVIE STARS

EVEN AS TRADER HORN and Joan Lowell provoked debates in the popular press about the nature of autobiographical truth, writers of a more elevated stature were posing similar questions. Some of these authors, indeed, rejected autobiography altogether because of its inherent unreliability. The young George Bernard Shaw, writing in 1898, emphatically stated: "All autobiographies are lies. I do not mean unconscious, unintentional lies; I mean deliberate lies. No man is bad enough to tell the truth about himself during his lifetime, involving, as it must, the truth about his family and friends and colleagues. And no man is good enough to tell the truth in a document which he suppresses until there is nobody left alive to contradict him." (Shaw, who died in 1950 at the age of ninety-four, stayed true to this conviction. He is, by the measures of longevity and eminence, the most notable modern person of letters *not* to have written an autobiography.) Sigmund Freud struck a similar theme in a letter to the public relations pioneer Edward Bernays, his son-in-law, who had reported that a publisher was interested in publishing Freud's memoirs: "That is of course an impossible suggestion. . . . A psychologically complete and honest confession of my life . . . would require so much indiscretion (on my part as well as on that of others) about family, friends, and enemies, most of them still alive, that it is simply out of the question. What makes all autobiographies worthless is, after all, their mendacity."* But mendacity wasn't the only issue. Through the work of Freud, F. C. Bartlett, and others, a general awareness of the severe limitations of memory, discussed in chapter 5, was coalescing. The French writer André Maurois gave a series of lectures in 1928 published as *Aspects of Biography*, and in them he touched on some of the problems inherent in auto- biography, especially when it deals with the author's early years. He observed: "Of the vast accession of vocabulary, ideas, and emotions; of our introduction to the world outside; of the successive pictures of society which are formed in the mental vision of the child—of all this we retain practically nothing; and so an autobiography of childhood is nearly al- ways commonplace and untrue, even when the author himself is sincere." Another shortcoming of memory, according to Maurois, is the way it "ra- tionalizes; it creates, after the event, the feelings or the ideas which might have been the cause of the event, but which in fact are invented by us after it has occurred."

Memory was not the only constraining factor. The philosopher Friedrich Nietzsche devoted much of his intellectual resources to doubt- ing the possibility, much less the likelihood or even the desirability, of expressing objective truth. "Granted, we want truth: *why not rather un-*

---

*Freud added: "Incidentally, it is American naivete on the part of your publisher to expect a hitherto decent person to commit to so base a deed for $5,000. For me temptation might begin at a hundred times that sum, but even then it would be turned down after half an hour."

truth?" he asked in *Beyond Good and Evil.* "And uncertainty? Even igno-
rance?" Nietzsche wrote late in the nineteenth century; his ideas would
prove to be influential and attractive in the twentieth. The pragmatist philosopher William James defined truth as what is convenient for a person
to believe; the linguist Ferdinand de Saussure stressed the inherent lack of
correspondence between language and the world; the philosopher Ludwig
Wittgenstein endorsed the value of "language games," in which lying has
as much value as truth (whatever that is); and Freud dismissed the therapeutic value of "truth": he argued that, as Jeremy Campbell put it in his
recent book *The Liar's Tale,* "false memories, invented connections between unconnected things, might be more useful than the literal truth in
guiding the analyst to the discovery of psychic reality . . . the emphasis
shifts towards meaning and away from truth." All of this led directly to
the more recent poststructuralism and deconstruction of Jacques Lacan,
Michel Foucault, Jacques Derrida, Roland Barthes, and others, in which
the traditional idea of truth has no value, and indeed is pretty much a
bourgeois plot against the people.

It was surely in part because of such concerns that so many of the
canonical modernist writers transformed the stuff of their lives into fiction: Marcel Proust with *Remembrance of Things Past* (written between
1909 and 1922), D. H. Lawrence with *Sons and Lovers* (1913), James Joyce
with *A Portrait of the Artist as a Young Man* (1916), and even Franz Kafka
with *Metamorphosis* (1915). A highbrow-to-middlebrow trickle-down effect led from these models to such works as F. Scott Fitzgerald's *This Side
of Paradise* (1920), Ernest Hemingway's short story collection *In Our
Time* (1925), Thomas Wolfe's *Look Homeward, Angel* (1929), and Henry
Miller's *Tropic of Cancer* (1937), and from them to the mid-century tradition of the autobiographical first novel, as in James Agee's *A Death in the
Family* and Sylvia Plath's *The Bell Jar,* which was on its last legs even

before the memoir boom and is now for the most part defunct.* (Jay McInerney's *Bright Lights, Big City* was one of the few notable entries in recent years.)

Virginia Woolf never embarked on a memoir for the first fifty-nine years of her life, in part, it would seem, because she was so aware of the limitations of the genre. But then, when she was in the middle of work on a biography of her friend and fellow Bloomsburyite Roger Fry, she sat down at the typewriter, put in a fresh sheet of paper, and began to write: "Two days ago—Sunday 16th April 1939 to be precise—Nessa [her sister, Vanessa] said that if I did not start writing my memoirs I should soon be too old. I should be eighty-five, and should have forgotten. . . . As it happens that I am sick of writing Roger's life, perhaps I will spend two or three mornings making a sketch."

But almost immediately she finds herself focusing on the pitfalls of the enterprise. Writing about her memories is "misleading," she says, "because the things one does not remember are as important; perhaps they are more important." She can bring to the surface her earliest memory— sitting on her mother's lap on a train or bus—but after sketching it out she stops herself, saying that to try to describe the fullness of that moment would inevitably be to fail. And that is because of a fatal flaw of memoir writers: "They leave out the person to whom things happened. The reason is that it is so difficult to describe any human being." It is equally difficult, Woolf goes on, to fully explain any particular moment. She talks about her recollection, at the age of six or seven, of being ashamed to look at

---

*Miller's book, which was banned in the United States for its alleged obscenity until 1961, was audacious not only in its sexual content but in its blending of fact and fiction: although the narrator is "Henry Miller" and many of the episodes are taken from Miller's life, the book was conceived and presented as a novel. Similar strategies were taken up thirty or more years later by such writers as Frederick Exley, Philip Roth, and Paul Theroux.

herself in the looking glass in the hall of her family's house. But where to go from there?

> Though I have done my best to explain why I was ashamed of looking at my own face I have only been able to discover some possible reasons; there may be others; I do not suppose I have got at the truth; yet this is a simple incident; and it happened to me personally; and I have no motive for lying about it. In spite of this, people write what they call "lives" of other people; that is, they collect a number of events, and leave the person to whom it happened unknown.

Despite her doubts, Woolf continues with the "sketch" and explores her feeling of shame when she looked in the mirror.

> I must have been ashamed or afraid of my own body. Another memory, also of the hall, may help to explain this. There was a slab outside the dining room door for standing dishes upon. Once when I was very small Gerald Duckworth [her half brother, who was twelve years older] lifted me onto this, and as I sat there he began to explore my body. I can remember the feel of his hands going under my clothes; going firmly and steadily lower and lower, I remember how I hoped that he would stop; how I stiffened and wriggled as his hand approached my private parts. But it did not stop. His hand explored my private parts too.

That kind of revelation is now standard memoir fare. In 1939, it was amazing for Woolf even to have written it. To have published it—even though Gerald Duckworth had been dead for two years—would have been unthinkable. Woolf kept on with her sketch, however, well beyond the two or three mornings she envisioned—right up until the autumn of

1940, four months before her death, at which point she had amassed some 45,000 words. (It did not appear in print until 1976, under the title "A Sketch of the Past," as part of a collection of Woolf's unpublished auto-biographical work called *Moments of Being*.)

Yet there was another side to this argument about autobiography and "truth." Woolf's father, Leslie Stephen, who was not a modernist at all—he preceded Edmund Gosse as the prototypical British man of letters—may actually have been the first to take it up, when he remarked, in the 1870s, "An autobiography, alone of all books, may be more valuable in proportion to the amount of misrepresentation it contains. We do not wonder when a man gives a false character to a neighbor, but it is always curious to see how a man contrives to give a false testimonial to himself." The idea that autobiography is worth pursuing despite or in fact *because* of its inevitable errors and distortions was frequently invoked in the years following the turn of the century. W. B. Yeats embarked on a series of autobiographical works in 1914, and in a preface to the first of them, *Reveries Over Childhood and Youth*, he wrote, "I have changed nothing of my memories to my knowledge; and yet it must be that I have changed many things without my knowledge." In his 1920 memoir, *If It Die*, which is notable both for its immersion in childhood and youth and for its candor about homosexual feelings and acts, André Gide admitted, "It is the fatal defect of my account, as of all memoirs; one presents what is most appar-ent; the most important things, without contours, elude one's grasp." Ford Madox Ford recognized the phenomenon as well, but for him it was not a "defect" but rather a defiant credo. In his 1911 book of reminiscences of his childhood among the Pre-Raphaelites, *Ancient Lights and Certain New Reflections: Being the Memories of a Young Man*, he writes that the text is full of inaccuracies as to facts, but its accuracy as to impressions is absolute:

For the facts, when you have a little time to waste, I should suggest that you go through the book carefully, noting the errors. To the one of you who succeeds in finding the largest number I will cheerfully present a copy of the ninth edition of the Encyclopaedia Britannica, so that you may still further perfect yourself in the hunting out of errors. But if one of you can discover in it any single impression that can be demonstrably proved not sincere on my part, I will draw you a check for whatever happens to be my balance at the bank for the next ten succeeding years. This is a handsome offer, but I can afford to make it, for you will not gain a single penny in the transaction. My business in life, in short, is to attempt to discover, and to try to let you see, where we stand. I don't really deal in facts, I have for facts a most profound contempt. I try to give you what I see to be the spirit of an age, of a town, of a movement. This can not be done with facts.

Anatole France gave himself a different name and changed a few circumstances in his memoir, *La vie en fleur* (1922), and, he wrote, "this disguise has enabled me to conceal the gaps in my recollection, which is very faulty, and to compound the wrongs of memory with the rights of imagination. I have been able to invent concatenations of circumstance to supply the place of those which eluded me . . . but I am persuaded that no man ever told lies with a deeper concern for the truth." (The translation is by Richard Coe.)

For some writers, memory became an end rather than a means. In 1924, the American novelist Sherwood Anderson published *A Story Teller's Story: The tale of an American writer's journey through his own imaginative world, and through the world of facts, with many of his experiences and impressions among other writers—told in many notes—in four books—and an Epilogue.* As the long-winded subtitle—and the repetition of the word "story" in the title—suggests, the book was rather uncomfortably lodged between the "imaginative world" and "the world of facts." Clearly he preferred the former. In the realm of fancy, he writes, "no man is ugly." He associates fact, by contrast, with "the Puritan, the reformer who scolds at the Puritans, the dry intellectuals, all who desire to uplift." So he doesn't apologize when his imagination runs away with his story; indeed, he continually calls attention to it, with interjections like, "I again find myself plunging forward into a more advanced and sophisticated point of view than could have been held by the boy, beginning to remake his own life more to his own liking by plunging into a fanciful life." But the reader can't even trust the self-described fancies. After describing at length a daydream he had while lying in a hayloft, he asks: "Did I, as I lay deeply buried in the warm hay, really imagine the absurd scene depicted above." He does not answer.

Disappointed with the poor sales of *A Story Teller's Story*, Anderson signed a contract with a new publisher, Horace Liveright, that promised him a salary of one hundred dollars a week in exchange for the delivery of one book a year. His first one under the agreement was *Dark Laughter*, an experimental novel that sold well (but is best known today for being parodied by Ernest Hemingway, a protégé of Anderson's, in *The Torrents of Spring*). The second was a collection of his articles and sketches. Lacking another idea and with his annual deadline looming, he embarked on yet another boyhood autobiography. It gave him a bad case of writer's block. That was because, as he explained in a foreword, he had decided that for once he would go against his nature and tell the truth: "I pursued Truth back through my own memory like a dog chasing a rabbit through dense bushes. What toil, what sweat dropped upon the sheets of paper before me." But it just didn't work. "I am a story teller starting to tell a story and cannot be expected to tell the truth," he concluded. "Truth is impossible to me." He was able to proceed with the book only after he came up with the "writer's trick" of inventing a character, Tar Moorehead, to stand for himself (the book's title is *Tar: A Midwest Childhood*): "'If you are a born liar, a man of the fancy, why not be what you are?' I said to myself, and having said it, I at once began writing with a new feeling of comfort."

That makes sense philosophically, but practically, as Anderson found out, you can run into trouble when some of the people you're not telling the truth about are alive and well. In all his autobiographical writings, he portrayed one of his grandmothers as being Italian. Other members of his family objected and pointed out that she was actually German. Anderson stood his ground, while acknowledging that "it was difficult for my brothers to understand my position. If I choose to have an Italian, rather than a German, grandmother, what is it to you? If you prefer that your own grandmother be an old German, all right. Shall a man who has spent all of his life creating people not have the privilege of creating his grandmother?"

He wrote one final autobiographical work, published in 1942, a year after his death, under the title *Sherwood Anderson's Memoirs*. In the foreword he strikes a familiar note: "Facts elude me. I cannot remember dates. When I deal in facts, at once I begin to lie." And he is as good as his word. In the book he writes that his mother died at age thirty-five (she was actually forty-three) and told her children on her deathbed, "I do not fear to leave you. You are of the stuff of which kings are made." Anderson goes on to comment: "What nonsense! The poor woman couldn't have said that but she did say something that fixed a certain impression in our minds, of that I am quite sure."

In *A Story Teller's Story*, Anderson writes of being inspired to a new way of thinking about literature and writing when he came across a copy of Gertrude Stein's experimental 1914 prose poem *Tender Buttons*, which included many passages along the lines of "Out of kindness comes redness and out of rudeness comes rapid same question, out of an eye comes research, out of selection comes painful cattle." Anderson eventually became friendly with Stein and performed the key act in American literary history of giving the young Ernest Hemingway a letter of introduction to her. Stein had moved to Paris in 1903, at the age of twenty-nine, and over the years had become famous for three things: her amazing collections of art; the many painters and writers who came to her salon and became her friends (not only Hemingway and Anderson, but Picasso, Matisse, Juan Gris, Ezra Pound, and many lesser lights); and the obscurity of her prose, most of which remained unpublished and nearly all of which remained unread.* Adding to the mystique was her unconventional appearance and her unconventional relationship with her companion, Alice B. Toklas. In the early 1930s, fame had come to have a considerable currency, and as a result, Toklas supposedly wrote:

> For some time now many people, and publishers, have been asking Gertrude Stein to write her autobiography and she had always replied, not possibly.
>
> She began to tease me and say that I should write my autobiography. Just think, she would say, what a lot of money you would make. She then began to invent titles for my autobiography. My Life With The Great, Wives of Geniuses I Have Sat With, My Twenty-five Years With Gertrude Stein.
>
> Then she began to get serious and say, but really seriously you ought

---

*Thus a humorous item that appeared in *The New Yorker* in 1927: "We are told of a gentleman who, at a recent bachelor dinner, suspected himself of intemperance and slipped off to a guest room. Reaching the chamber he hit upon a plan to test his condition. He would, he said to himself, pick up a magazine, open it and read the first paragraph he saw. If it made sense all was well. If not, a nap. Friends found him sound asleep a few minutes later, a near-by periodical opened to a poem by Gertrude Stein."

to write your autobiography. Finally I promised that if during the summer I could find time I would write my autobiography. . . .

About six weeks ago Gertrude Stein said, it does not look to me as if you were ever going to write that autobiography. You know what I am going to do. I am going to write it for you. I am going to write it as simply as Defoe did the autobiography of Robinson Crusoe. And she has and this is it.

"This" is *The Autobiography of Alice B. Toklas*, which, though no author's name appeared on the title page when it was published in 1933, was known by everyone to be the work of Stein herself. Choosing to ventriloquially narrate the book in Toklas's voice was brilliant. For one thing, although one still hears echoes of Stein's difficult style, she actually incorporated Toklas's plainspokenness into her prose, and thus was able to produce the most accessible book of her career. Its commercial potential was immediately recognized. Stein's agent sold four installments to *The Atlantic Monthly*, the venerable beacon of the literary establishment, which the author had been unsuccessfully trying to break into for years. The magazine's editor, Ellery Sedgwick, wrote her, "During our long correspondence, I think you felt my constant hope that the time would come when the real Miss Stein would pierce the smokescreen with which she has always so mischievously surrounded herself. . . . Hail Gertrude Stein about to arrive!" The book turned up on the *Publishers Weekly* bestseller list shortly after publication and stayed there for four weeks, which was four weeks more than any of the other memoirists named in this chapter managed to achieve.

In addition, writing as Alice gave Stein freedom of speech. She could indulge, first, her cattiness—and this is one of the cattier memoirs of all time—and, second, à la Edward Bok, her grand sense of herself. The first two pages of the book are actually about Toklas's own early life in San Francisco, but then she goes to Paris and meets Stein:

> I may say that only three times in my life have I met a genius and each time a bell within me rang and I was not mistaken, and I may say in each case it was before there was any general recognition of the quality of genius in them. The three geniuses of whom I wish to speak are Gertrude Stein, Pablo Picasso and Alfred Whitehead.

So Gertrude Stein, who knows that the reader knows that she is pretending to be Alice Toklas, is saying that Gertude Stein is one of the three geniuses of the modern age. What is a reader to make of that? Well, for one thing, that Stein not only had a large ego but also a sense of humor, probably a better one (as she often maintained) than most of the wags who got cheap laughs out of variations on roses being roses. But the game she's playing isn't just a joke. An autobiography is, on the surface, a straight-forward document. In reality, she is suggesting, it is a Chinese box of identity where the "I" of the text and the name on the title page are not, and can never be, completely equivalent.

Stein cemented the success of the book with a lengthy tour of America, in which she gave speeches to community groups and college audiences, and interviews to reporters who enthusiastically took down and printed her gnomic aperçus. In a 1937 book she wrote as herself, *Everybody's Autobiography* (this one was most definitely *not* a bestseller), she acknowledged that the fame she was acquiring was based as much on her personality, and the gossipy Alice Toklas book, as on the works she considered the true evidence of her genius. But that was not so terrible: "Perhaps they were right the Americans in being more interested in you than

in the work you have done although they would not be interested in you
if you had not done the work you had done."

> Marion: There's something about it—I don't know—
> Kurt: What?
> Marion: Vulgar. *Everybody* spouting memoirs. Who cares?
> —*Biography*, by s. n. behrman, 1932

> "What was all that noise in your room last night? Ghosts?" said
> Frank Hogan to Andy Cohen.
> "Not ghosts," answered Andy; "ghost-writers."
> —*The New York Times*, April 29, 1928
> (Hogan and Cohen were baseball players
> for the New York Giants.)

GERTRUDE STEIN WAS NOT your usual celebrity; but then, in the early 1930s America had a strange and powerful need to bestow the mantle of fame, and it often landed on unlikely shoulders. Once it did, a strange process began; the public strongly desired to somehow participate in, almost to *consume*, these people's lives. That could be achieved by watching them perform onstage or in boxing rings or at the movies, by listening to them on the radio or on phonograph records, by taking part in the odd new fad of collecting their signatures, or by reading their true stories. Certainly, memoirs by entertainers boomed in the early twentieth century. Accounting for just 1.1 percent of American autobiographies in the decade 1900–1909, they shot up to 5.4 percent in the 1920s and kept growing from there, reaching 11.8 percent in the 1950s and 14 percent in the 1960s, when they finally and permanently overtook Clergy/Religious as the most populous subcategory. More broadly, from the early years of the twentieth century through the early years of the twenty-first, celebrity autobiographies have been perhaps the most capacious and reliable category in publishing. They were also, roughly through the mid-1960s, cut from the same cloth: meant to burnish what would later be called the "brand," these narratives were sanitized and inspirational, emphasizing the obstacles surmounted on the way to eminence, with amusing anecdotes liberally sprinkled in. The uncomfortable and the unseemly were strenuously avoided.

There was a flaw in the proposition that each new crop of celebrities should universally put forth their memoirs: many of them were uneducated and hardly any were professional writers, and thus they were not really equipped to produce lengthy manuscripts. In 1915, the *San Francisco Chronicle* assigned a young staff member named Rose Wilder Lane to talk to an even younger aviator named Art Smith—known as the originator of skywriting and possibly the first American flyer to loop the loop—and render his musings into prose. (Aviation, which intriguingly paralleled cinema in its technological development and star system, was similarly a boom occupation for the generation of fame.) The result, published as a series in the *Chronicle,* was so popular that the newspaper put it out as a book, *Art Smith's Story: The Autobiography of the Boy Aviator.* A credit on the title page read "Edited by Rose Wilder Lane."

Someone even more famous than Art Smith—within a couple of years, he would probably be the most famous person in the world, setting the tone for a new sort of viral, global mass-media celebrity in which the twentieth century would specialize—was Charlie Chaplin, who began making his wildly popular movie shorts in late 1913. In 1916, he published *Charlie Chaplin's own story: being a faithful recital of a romantic career, beginning with early recollections of boyhood in London and closing with the signing of his latest motion-picture contract.* Not on the title page but, less prominently, on the copyright page could be found the following sentence:

"The subject of this biography takes great pleasure in expressing his obligations and his thanks to Mrs. Rose Wilder Lane for invaluable editorial assistance."*

The term "ghost," used to indicate the writer actually responsible for the creation for which a prominent person takes credit, had been around since the 1880s, according to the *Oxford English Dictionary*, but it was now clear for the first time how necessary ghost writers would be for the production of celebrity autobiographies. In these early days, the protocol was still being established. Rose Wilder Lane was not technically a ghost, because she was credited in the memoirs of Smith and Chaplin. A 1917 book, *Henry Ford's Own Story: How a Farmer Boy Rose to the Power That Goes with Many Millions, yet Never Lost Touch with Humanity,* used a new formulation that would become extremely popular: "as told to Rose Wilder Lane."

Before leaving the remarkable Mrs. Lane, it is worth pointing out that her most lasting collaboration came some fifteen years later, when she helped her mother turn her memories of growing up in the upper Midwest into a series of autobiographical novels. Her mother was Laura Ingalls Wilder, and the books were *Little House on the Prairie* and its much-beloved companions.

Publisher George Putnam, in his autobiography *Wide Margins*, described how one of the first truly ghostwritten memoirs originated in the years just after World War I, when Arthur Guy Empey, who had been a British private in the war, was speaking to catch-as-catch-can audiences at small clubs around New York:

---

*Contemporary critics charged, and Chaplin biographers confirm, that the book was shot through with misstatements and errors, including the patently false claim that he was born "in a small town in France." Chagrined by the reaction, Chaplin ordered the publisher, Bobbs-Merrill, to destroy all available copies. Harry M. Geduld, who edited an edition of the book in 1985, reported that he knew of only four extant copies, one of them in the Library of Congress.

Robert Gordon Anderson was our sales manager, who doubled with writing now and then. Bob saw Empey, heard him captivate an audience, and had a hunch his story was exactly what America would like to read. So Bob Anderson got together with Guy Empey and helped him make a book. I have forgotten how many hundreds of thousands of copies of "Over the Top" were sold, but shortly Empey was filling Carnegie Hall, and we were filling his and Bob's bank accounts with royalties. He had a telling trick of standing with one foot on the seat of a single chair in the middle of a stage, that being the firing step of a frontline trench, while with words he took listeners over the top.

Chaplin had another ghostwriter, Monta Bell, for another autobiographical book he published in 1922, *My Trip Abroad*. Actors Pearl White, William S. Hart, and John Barrymore, dancer Isadora Duncan, baseball manager John McGraw, and boxers James Corbett and Jack Johnson all published ghosted memoirs in the early and middle 1920s. (Ironically, golfer Bobby Jones, probably more literate than anyone in this bunch, credited his collaborator, O. B. Keeler.) In 1927, a new star surpassed Chaplin in the firmament: Charles Lindbergh, who made the first solo flight across the Atlantic and in the process captured the world's fancy. True to custom, after landing, Lindbergh hired an American newspaperman, Carlisle MacDonald, to ghostwrite the story of his flight and his life, which George Putnam's firm would then publish. MacDonald interviewed Lindbergh on the ship back to America, and quickly completed his manuscript. Lindbergh read the galley proofs, and immediately changed his mind about the whole project: the words attributed to him, he felt, did not *sound* like him. He resolved to write the book himself, and did so at the Long Island house of a friend, the financier Harry Guggenheim. "He wrote every page in long-hand, on legal-size paper," Putnam recalled in his own autobiography. "In the upper-right corner of each page, as he completed it, he wrote the number of words on that page." Lindbergh was finished in three weeks, and the book, simply and eloquently titled *We*, was in stores on July 27, barely two months after his flight. *We* made its appearance on the *Publishers Weekly* bestseller list on August 27, reached the number-one spot a month later, stayed on the list for thirty-two weeks, and ultimately sold more than 635,000 copies.

Part of the book's appeal was the sense, put forth by the publisher and picked up by readers and reviewers, that it was *not* ghostwritten. *We* was "Lindbergh's own writing, original material from his pen and not by some 'ghost writer,'" asserted one newspaper. "When the publishers announced Lindbergh's book within a few days after his memorable flight, the critical world showed little interest in it, for it was believed that it would be another one of those things written by some newspaper potboiler. But it is nothing of the kind. It is a straight forward autobiography written without flourish and not for effect." But few celebrities followed Lindbergh's example. In 1928, the heavyweight prizefighter Jack Dempsey's former manager sued him for several hundred thousand dollars. On the witness stand, Dempsey was questioned about a point in some autobiographical articles that had recently been published under his name. The fighter (anticipating a comment for which the basketball player Charles Barkley would be well known more than half a century hence) said that not only had he not written the articles, he hadn't read them.*

In 1929, Frederic Van de Water, the book critic for the New York *Evening Post*, made a full confession in *Scribner's Magazine*, in an essay

---

*Barkley and footballer Terrell Owens, a couple of years later, both protested that they had been "misquoted" in their autobiographies. General Omar Bradley was unable to complain about the autobiography published under his name, because his ghostwriter wrote it after Bradley's death.

that detailed the tradition and practice of ghostwriting. The article opened: "I have been a beauty specialist. I have been a social secretary. I have been a dowager with twelve generations of Manhattan aristocrats behind me, and a secretary of state, and a surgeon-general of the United States and many others. I never have been president yet, but I have been several United States senators and I was, also, early in my career, a tong-leader of Chinatown for a few memorably uncomfortable hours." In the light of Van de Water's confession, Dempsey's testimony, and the sheer unlikelihood that celebrities could have written the hundreds of volumes attributed to them, *The New York Times* commented that although the public was at one time "completely credulous . . . now it seems unlikely that it believes in any of the noted athletes, singers or politicians who break out in print. The few honest ones are discredited along with the many who employ writers."

Because of the widespread skepticism, the locution "as told to" began to appear with great frequency before the name of the collaborator, for example in entertainer Eddie Cantor's 1928 autobiography, *My Life Is in Your Hands*, "as told to" David Freedman. Freedman was also the first of many collaborators to bitterly break with their employers. In 1936, Freedman sued Cantor for $250,000 "on the ground," the *Times* reported, "that the comedian had coasted to radio fame on the witticisms that he [Freedman] had furnished on oral contract." (The suit was never settled because on the night before the second day of the trial, Freedman died in his sleep of a heart attack.) Subsequently, lawsuits were brought by the disgruntled ghosts of Sol Hurok, Mickey Rooney, and Milton Berle. Even when things did not reach the stage of legal action, ghostwriters have often had reason to gripe: they do most of the work, yet get little or none of the glory and in most cases a small fraction of the proceeds. A classic case came in 1984, when a young journalist named William Novak was paid $45,000 to ghostwrite the autobiography of an automobile executive. The executive was Lee Iacocca, and his book, according to a 1990 *Wall Street Journal* article, eventually "sold more copies than any other nonfiction hardcover in history, except for a few reference works, Betty Crocker's cookbook and the Bible," and earned Iacocca royalties well in excess of $6 million. Novak petitioned for more money, pointing out that he wrote all the words; the publisher threw him an estimated $40,000 bonus: peanuts. Ghostwriters' indignities go beyond money: they find themselves pleading for time, truthfulness, even information. The unfunny comedian Jackie Mason refused to tell his ghost how old he was, a decision that Mason later defended to a reporter: "So I didn't want to tell him my age. What am I, married to him?"

But such complaints are rarely aired for an obvious reason: kicking up a fuss sabotages a ghostwriter's future marketability. I am aware of only one instance where a ghost was emboldened to publicly tell, in detail, his side of the story. In 1960, Ty Cobb, a great baseball player and a miserable human being, engaged a journalist named Al Stump to write his autobiography; they split $6,000. Cobb's unpleasantness (Stump soon discovered) went far beyond ordinary meanness: he was a drunken, abusive, racist, violent, disruptive, and truly hateful old man. He was also very ill. Stump quit the project twice and was fired once. But he always came back. He was living out a ghostwriter's weird version of Stockholm syndrome. Stump would later recount:

> During the final ten months of his life I was his one constant companion. Eventually, I put him to bed, prepared his insulin, picked him up when he fell down, warded off irate taxi drivers, bartenders, waiters, clerks, and private citizens whom Cobb was inclined to punch, cooked what food he could digest, drew his bath, got drunk with him, and knelt with him in

prayer on black nights when he knew death was near. I ducked a few bottles he threw, too.

A 1994 film starring Tommy Lee Jones as the ballplayer and Robert Wuhl as the ghost was based on Stump's love-hate-hate relationship with Cobb. In one scene, the writer tells Cobb that he knows the autobiography has to be the whitewashed official version, but when the player dies, he'll tell it like it really was. "I'll write slow," Stump says. "I'll die slow," Cobb retorts. This proved not to be the case. Cobb passed away in July 1961 and the autobiography—titled, with unintentional irony, *My Life in Baseball: The True Record*—came out just a few months later. Stump later said the book was "a cover-up. I felt very bad about it. I felt I wasn't being a good newspaperman." He set the record straight the following year with a *True* magazine article, from which the above quotation is taken.

In recent decades, collaborators have tended to be credited with a "with" or (more prestigiously) with an "and." A fairly recent convention is sole credit for the celeb but fulsome appreciation in the front matter for the individual who actually sets down the words. From the acknowledgments of Tatum O'Neal's *A Paper Life*: "The person who really brought this book to life was my loyal and courageous cowriter, Elisa Petrini. She sat with me though hours and hours of sometimes incoherent ramblings as I fought to resurrect memories that were almost too painful to recount out loud. Her loving patience is evident on every page of this book." But like the action movie stars who insist they do their own stunts, there are always some celebrities who have been quoted as claiming to have written their opus "without a ghostwriter." A partial list includes: Raquel Welch, Shirley Temple Black, Ginger Rogers, Ronald Reagan, Leontyne Price, Ralph Abernathy, Michael Caine, Lee Radziwill, professional wrestler Mick Foley, Ali MacGraw, Bill Clinton, Valerie Bertinelli, Cherie Blair,

Jane Alexander, Donald Trump, Carly Fiorina, Charlton Heston, Ben Gazzara, Steve Martin, Mary Tyler Moore, Hillary Clinton, Jane Fonda, Peter Fonda, rock and roll's Ray Davies, Senator James Webb, football coach Marv Levy, Fred Astaire, Joel Osteen, Michael J. Fox, Clarence Thomas, and Simone Signoret.

Signoret, the French film star, is the only one on the list whose claim has been verified. The writer Maurice Pons spent many hours interviewing her, from which he compiled a six-hundred-page manuscript. Signoret was appalled when she read it: "Of course, the facts were accounted for. I was born there where I was born; of course, we had done the little dinner with Khrushchev and the Praesidium; of course, I spoke of Marilyn [Monroe] . . . [but] I refused it. It was all the more serious that I couldn't accuse anyone. No one had distorted my words, no one had made me say other than what I said. I had said all that, eh! yes, but I had said it with the words, the absences of links, the slang and the lack of true reflection that corresponded perfectly with the image that my popular roles had given to me." She ripped up the typescript, à la Lindbergh, and started in on her own version: as she said in a subsequent work, she found that she "started to become 'the ghost writer of the ghost writer.'" Signoret was so proud of her autobiography, which had the unforgettable title *Nostalgia Isn't What It Used to Be*, that she sued two journalists who asserted she didn't write it herself. She won.

Chapter 9

LOOKING ON THE BRIGHT SIDE, MAINLY: MID-CENTURY MEMOIRS

CLARENCE DAY GREW UP on the Upper East Side of Manhattan, graduated from Yale in 1896, and went to work at the New York Stock Exchange, of which his father was a governor. He was forced to retire in 1903 because of crippling arthritis and subsequently juggled business interests with humorous writing and illustration, including such popular books as *This Simian World* and *The Crow's Nest*. (His arthritis was so severe that he was able to write and draw only with the use of an elaborate pulley arrangement.) In 1929, he published *God and My Father*, a slim volume that humorously recounted his mother's ultimately successful stratagems for bringing his father, more or less an agnostic, into the Episcopalian fold. The book had moderate success and good reviews. Late in 1932, Day wrote a sketch about the time his mother "was persuaded, by a beautifully dressed woman book-agent, to buy on installment a set of *Memoirs of the French Court*"; she hates them and tells Father they are a gift from her, but he is not convinced. Day sent the piece to Harold Ross, the editor of *The*

New Yorker, who accepted it and wrote Day (in a move that proves the aptness of the title of Thomas Kunkel's biography of Ross, *Genius in Disguise*), "We would like to get further pieces from you—anything, including things on your father. We would be very glad to run a little series on him if you saw fit, which is a very bright idea for an editor to have." Showing his own swift recognition that he was onto something good, Day started submitting more short pieces to the magazine, and ended up publishing an impressive thirty-nine of them until his death in 1935, at the age of sixty-one. Many of the pieces were collected in a book titled *Life with Father*, which was a massive bestseller, ending up as the third-best-selling nonfiction book of 1935 and number nine the following year. A posthumous collection, *Life with Mother*, reached the number-one spot on the *New York Times* bestseller list in 1937. The public's fascination with the Day family's genteel 1880s doings continued when a Broadway version of *Life with Father*, by Howard Lindsay and Russel Crouse, opened in 1939. It ran until 1947, by which time it had passed *Tobacco Road* as the longest-running nonmusical Broadway production in history, a record that still stands.

Day kicked off a remarkably popular and durable subgenre that set the pattern for memoirs by ordinary Americans (as opposed to celebrities, politicians, business leaders, and Notable Authors) for the next three decades. In their comic stance and their inclination to nostalgia and exaggeration, these books were descendants of *Life on the Mississippi*, but they had a warmhearted and (the authors hoped) heartwarming glow that would have raised Twain's eyebrows, if not his ire. It sounds simplistic but may be correct to say that the main appeal of these books was the contrast they offered to grim world events—that is, the Depression, World War II and the Holocaust, the Cold War, and McCarthyism. On another level, they were narrative correlatives of what the British writer

Godfrey Hodgson has termed "the liberal consensus"—the shared sense that the United States was the best place on earth, capable of overcoming any setbacks and fixing any flaws. Whatever the deeper explanation, they were united in their determination to look on the bright side of nearly everything. Consider: if Clarence Day were embarking on a memoir today, it would in all likelihood center on his battle with arthritis. In *Life with Father* and *Life with Mother*, he does not even mention the ailment.

In the late 1930s and early 1940s, a number of these books originated as articles in the same *New Yorker* magazine that had first published Day's "Father" sketches, including Ruth McKenney's series about the Manhattan adventures she shared with her eccentric sister, later collected as *My Sister Eileen*; Ludwig Bemelmans's recollections of his youthful days working in a Manhattan hotel, published as *Hotel Splendide*; and Sally Benson's lightly fictionalized tales of her childhood in St. Louis, collected as *Meet Me in St. Louis*. At least two things about these texts are worth noting. First, they did not go out in the world with a clear label of fiction or fact. In the case of Day, McKenney, and Bemelmans, the "I" of the story shared the author's name and, apparently, many elements of his or her life, but beyond that, a reader had no grounds for making a judgment. In *The New Yorker*, the articles were considered "casuals"—the magazine's name for relatively light, relatively short pieces—and were given no gloss in its pages other than a title at the beginning and the author's name at the end. Humor pieces by Robert Benchley or S. J. Perelman were casuals; so were short stories by John Cheever or Irwin Shaw. And, in the magazine's internal reference system, they were all labeled "fiction." The second significant aspect of this form of writing was its capacity to resonate. The *New Yorker* articles became books, and then the books took on new forms: *My Sister Eileen* joined *Life with Father* on Broadway and later was turned into a Broadway musical, *Wonderful Town*; *Meet Me in St. Louis*, of course, became the classic movie musical with Judy Garland. In the decades ahead, the most successful of the light autobiographies would follow the same pattern and be adapted as plays, musicals, movies, and/or television series. In so doing, they lost much or all of their standing as factual documents and became stories, pure and simple. A Broadway audience watching Rosalind Russell as Ruth in *Wonderful Town*, or a movie audience watching William Powell as Father in *Life with Father*, would have no reason to view them as historical figures. They were literary characters, like Hamlet or Nathan Detroit.

Probably the greatest *New Yorker* series in this vein was the work of a thirty-eight-year-old staff writer at the magazine at the time Day was publishing his sketches. In a stretch of thirteen weeks in the summer and early fall of 1933, James Thurber contributed eight casuals about his youthful exploits in Columbus, Ohio; they were collected later that year in the book *My Life and Hard Times*. The opening paragraph gave notice that Thurber was a compelling new voice, perhaps even a literary heir of Twain himself:

> Benvenuto Cellini said that a man should be at least forty years old before he undertakes so fine an enterprise as that of setting down the story of his life. He also said that an autobiographer should have accomplished something of excellence. Nowadays nobody who has a typewriter pays any attention to the old master's rules. I myself have accomplished nothing of excellence except a remarkable and, to some of my friends, unaccountable expertness in hitting empty ginger ale bottles with small rocks at a distance of thirty paces. Moreover, I am not yet forty years old. But the grim date moves toward me apace; my legs are beginning to go, things blur before my eyes, and the faces of the rosy-lipped maids I knew in my twenties are misty as dreams.

My Life and Hard Times was turned into a forgettable film with Jack Oakie, but there was no Broadway show. Alone among the books discussed in this section, it did not crack the bestseller list. It had too much irony and ambivalence, and not enough sentiment, for that sort of mass appeal. There is nothing warm or fuzzy in the book, not even in the chapter about the family Airedale, Muggs: "A big, burly, choleric dog, he always acted as if he thought I wasn't one of the family. There was a slight advantage in being one of the family, for he didn't bite the family as often as he bit strangers."

The worse the news of the world got, the more people seemed to eat up this sort of stuff. The biggest bestseller of 1942—and one of the biggest of all time, with some 2,786,000 copies sold—was *See Here, Private Hargrove*, by Marion Hargrove, a lighthearted romp through basic training in Fort Benning, Georgia. (The journal *Books* praised it as "a contribution to the lighter side of war.") The next year, in the rosy-hued-nostalgia tradition of *Life with Father*, came *Mama's Bank Account*, author Kathryn Anderson McLean's bestselling reminiscences of growing up in a Norwegian immigrant family in San Francisco in the 1910s. (The book was published under the pen name Kathryn Forbes.) Once more the material resonated: it was adapted into a play called *I Remember Mama* the following year—Marlon Brando made his Broadway debut playing the author's brother, Nels—then a 1948 film starring Irene Dunne, then a long-running television series in the 1950s with Dick Van Patten as Nels, then a Broadway musical in 1979 starring Liv Ullmann.

Jostling with *Mama's Bank Account* on the bestseller list was *Roughly Speaking*, by Louise Randall Pierson, who was born in 1890 to an upper-class family in Massachusetts. Her fortunes reversed twelve years later when her father died and left the family penniless. In adulthood, her fortunes just kept reversing, as she dealt with the death of one young son in a swimming-pool accident, bouts of infantile paralysis suffered by her other four children, divorce, and business failure and poverty in the Depression, before remarrying and rebounding at book's end. Un-accountably, the tone is for the most part comic; writing in *The New Yorker*, Clifton Fadiman described the book as "a high-spirited autobiographical failure story written as though it were the most triumphant of success stories." Five years later came *Cheaper by the Dozen*, by Frank B. Gilbreth and Ernestine Gilbreth Carey, about their wacky misadventures grow-ing up in the 1910s and 1920s as two of the twelve children of time-and-motion experts. In keeping with the cheerful demeanor of the genre, the authors did not mention that one of the dozen died of diphtheria at the age of six. The book spent forty-seven weeks on the *New York Times* bestseller list, including twenty-two weeks in the number-one spot, and was made into a film with Clifton Webb and Myrna Loy in 1950 (and an ongoing series of remakes with Steve Martin half a century later).

A characteristic of these light memoirs was their pronounced distance from the quotidian world of the here and now. For all the ones just mentioned—even Hargrove's, which takes place before Pearl Harbor but was published after—the distance was chronological, but in other cases it was a matter of geography. In 1938, Thurber's friend and onetime *New Yorker* officemate E. B. White moved from New York City to a farm on the coast of Maine, where he raised geese, chickens, and sheep. He wrote about this modified Thoreauvian experiment in essays for *Harper's* maga-zine, collected in 1942 in the book *One Man's Meat*. White may have been living remotely, but the pressures of world events were never far from his mind or his pen. In his foreword, he seems almost embarrassed to be publishing such a book at such a time: "It seems a bit of effrontery, or unawareness. The author feels that the blurb on the jacket should say: 'There isn't time to read this book. Put it in your pocket, and when the moment arrives, throw it straight and hard." Yet White did publish it, for he was, as he well knew, a writer to whom the very notion of "escape" was uncongenial; the foreground of the book may have been the country, but the subtext was the global crisis. Rose Feld, who reviewed the book for *The New York Times*, picked this up: "It is clear that beneath the deceptively gentle tenor of his writing lies a deep awareness of the dreadful things that are happening in the world and a stinging irritation with man's reaction to them, his own, perhaps, included." Another author escaped more completely into Maine, which may be why her memoir, also published in 1942, sold a lot more copies. In *We Took to the Woods*, Louise Dickinson Rich (a distant relative of Emily Dickinson) described her and her husband's retreat to the backwoods of Maine, as opposed to the coast. The book was a modest bestseller, but more significant was the way it inspired scores of other Thoreauvian chronicles, paradoxically more alluring than ever now that the country was becoming seemingly one large suburb.

A combination of *Roughly Speaking* and *We Took to the Woods*, and the most successful of all these books, was the very funny *The Egg and I* (1945), by Betty MacDonald. In the late 1920s, MacDonald, a teenage bride, moved with her husband, Bob, to a remote section of Washington's Olympic Mountain region, where they raised chickens and inhabited a dilapidated ranch lacking any and all modern conveniences. Their nearest neighbors were a family—a couple with fifteen children—she called the Kettles. MacDonald's description of Mrs. Kettle in *The Egg and I* gives a good sense of her comedy, which springs from well-observed detail, skillful use of simile, and disinclination to euphemize: "Mrs. Kettle had pretty light brown hair . . . clear blue eyes, a creamy skin . . . a straight delicate nose . . . and a small rounded chin. From this dainty pretty head cascaded a series of busts and stomachs which made her look like a cooky jar shaped like a woman. Her whole front was dirty and spotted and she wiped her hands continually on one or the other of her stomachs. She had also a disconcerting habit of reaching up under her dress and adjusting something in the vicinity of her navel. . . . 'I itch—so I scratch—so what!' was Mrs. Kettle's motto."

The Egg and I was a mammoth success: it sold more than two million copies and was on the *New York Times* bestseller list for nearly two years (including forty-two weeks at number one), and was eventually translated into more than thirty different languages. The book became a film in 1947, with Fred MacMurray and Claudette Colbert playing Bob and Betty, and the first television comedy serial in 1951. Marjorie Main and Percy Kilbride were so striking as Ma and Pa Kettle in the film that the characters were spun off into their own movie, with the setting transposed from rural Washington to Appalachia, and after that came seven more, including two that chronicled their trips to Paris and Hawaii. The success of the films prompted what may have been the first libel suit provoked by a memoir— and what remains, along with the Turcotte family's action against Augusten Burroughs, one of the surprisingly small number of such suits. In 1951, a man named Albert Bishop and his six sons, two daughters, and one daughter-in-law sued MacDonald and her publishers, claiming that, as the models for the Kettle family, they had been subjected to shame, ridicule, and humiliation. (Mrs. Bishop was deceased.) In her defense, MacDonald essentially testified that the book was fiction: that the characters were products of her imagination, loosely based on a variety of different people. The defense also introduced evidence that the Bishop family had tried to profit from the fame *The Egg and I* had brought them, including testimony that Albert Bishop's son Walter had arranged for his father to appear onstage at a local dance hall with chickens under his arm, introducing him as "Pa Kettle." The jury decided in MacDonald's favor.

The Egg and I ends with the good news that Bob has located and made arrangements to purchase another chicken farm, closer to civilization. A contemporary reader would gather that this new place is where Betty Mac-Donald could now be found. A contemporary reader would gather wrong. In fact, MacDonald and Bob had divorced more than a decade earlier, in 1931. In the divorce proceedings, she alleged that Bob "struck and kicked plaintiff on a number of occasions and threatened to shoot plaintiff and children." She was granted a divorce, after which (but before writing *The Egg and I*) she scraped through the Depression as a single mother of two young daughters; in 1938, she was diagnosed with tuberculosis and spent six months in a sanatorium. That she would look back past those happenings, sit down at her desk, and write what *The New York Times* rightly called "an astoundingly light-hearted book" was, well, astounding.*

But people need to put a bright face on things, and they responded to MacDonald because she did it so well. As a reviewer in the *San Francisco Chronicle* remarked, "Betty writes for 'folks,' for the happy, confident majority who respond readily to a gallant facing of trouble."

MacDonald dedicated *The Egg and I* to "my sister Mary who has always believed that I can do anything she puts her mind to." In 1949, that sister, Mary Bard, dedicated her own memoir, *The Doctor Wears Three Faces*, to "my sister Betty, who egged me on." Here is a description of Mary Bard's book:

> In an entertaining account, she describes her courtship and marriage to a
> young doctor; she soon learns the drawbacks of being a doctor's wife which

---

*MacDonald went on to write three additional memoirs, including *The Plague and I* (1948), about her tuberculosis (the dust jacket trumpeted "The New Adventures of This Witty and Irrepressible Author"), and the Mrs. Piggle-Wiggle children's book series, before her death in 1958 at age fifty.

include constant disruptions, automatic membership in a group of doctors' wives known as the "Neglected Ones," and a woeful lack of drama in her first pregnancy; she focuses on the domestic details of being a harried but earnest wife and mother.

That quotation comes from a volume I consider myself fortunate to possess: *Through a Woman's I: An Annotated Bibliography of American Women's Autobiographical Writings, 1946–1976*, by Patricia K. Addis. It is, obviously, a reference work, consisting of citations and summaries of 2,217 books, but I read it cover to cover. One of the things I discovered in doing so was that this cheerful autobiographical subgenre I have been describing was by and large the province of women. (Male writers—including Alexander King, Robert Paul Smith, and Jack Douglas—participated as well, but were decidedly in the minority.) Addis lists autobiographies by the Eleanor Roosevelts, Marian Andersons, and Joan Crawfords, to be sure— as well as by a stunning number of nuns—but to judge from her descriptions, the prevailing model of women's autobiography, at least through the mid-1960s, was MacDonald's and/or Bard's. The MacDonald template was an account of removing oneself to a remote location, usually in the company of a husband and sometimes children, and managing to survive with one's sense of humor intact, despite big and little obstacles. In many cases the remote location was abroad: Addis lists scores of books about the authors' far-flung marriages to archaeologists (*Throw Me a Bone*, by Eleanor Lothrop, 1948), entomologists, journalists, ambassadors, prospectors, anthropologists, and explorers. The Bard model, meanwhile, treated the ups and downs of middle-class Caucasian family life in the postwar suburbs. I started to mark these books with a penciled "N" in the margin, to stand for "normative," but stopped about a hundred pages or so in: there were just too many.

Addis lists hundreds of such books. They were put out by reputable publishing houses, but with one or two exceptions—like Jean Kerr's *Please Don't Eat the Daisies* (1957), about family life in Larchmont, New York, which spent fifty weeks on the *New York Times* bestseller list, including thirteen weeks at number one, and was made into a movie (with Doris Day and David Niven) and a television series—they are completely forgotten today. Her summaries, however, a striking number of which include the word "delightful," leave you feeling you have learned all you need to. Here are just a few:

Virginia Pearson, *Everything but Elephants*, 1947. "The wife of a medical doctor, she spends the first two years of her married life in an oil camp in the jungles of Colombia; her consuming interest in new people and places eases her adjustment to tropical, rather basic housekeeping; she enjoys traveling and being of assistance to her husband, learning cultural tolerance and understanding."

Valentine Teal, *It Was Not What I Expected*, 1948. "Having followed her grandmother's and Teddy Roosevelt's exhortations on motherhood, she presents an entertaining account of rearing a large family with zest and by instinct; she describes the inevitable collection of pets, her children's eccentric eating habits, her work as a Cub Scout leader, and her relaxed housekeeping."

Dorothy Graffe Van Doren, *The Country Wife*, 1950. "A writer and prominent professor's wife, she tells of her summers on the family's Connecticut farm, from spring packing rituals to gardening, to traditional July Fourth celebrations, to the enjoyment of weekend guests; during sabbaticals, they remain in the country, savoring New England winters; she emphasizes the warm moments of close family life."

Olive Barber, *The Lady and the Lumberjack*, 1952. "A schoolteacher on vacation, she succumbs to the 'concentrated wooing' of an Oregon logger;

married life broadens her respect for differing kinds of knowledge and of people; at home on a 'floathouse,' she learns logging slang and develops a deep affection for loggers."

Martha Ruth Rebentisch, *The Healing Woods*, 1952. "After three years in a tuberculosis sanatorium, she seeks a cure by living 'a simple life' in the open in the Adirondacks accompanied by an old guide; her first return to the village reveals profound alterations in her perspective and behavior; the wilderness teaches her the joy of nature, fortitude, and self-reliance, while improving her health." (Rebentisch later wrote two sequels.)

Shirley Jackson (yes, the author of the dark short story "The Lottery"— this template was apparently irresistible even to the otherwise gloomy and pessimistic), *Life Among the Savages*, 1953. "In a delightfully wry examination of family life, the noted writer describes the eccentricities of her ramshackle Vermont home, the inevitable fraying caused by living 'in the society of small children,' the saga of household helpers; her renditions of family conversations are marvelously disjointed, comprehensible only to the participants."

Barbara C. Hooton, "as indiscreetly confided to Patrick Dennis," *Guestward Ho!*, 1956. "A New Yorker, she is transplanted to New Mexico in 1953 when her husband buys a dude ranch; her gloomy predictions based on their inexperience and her lack of enthusiasm give way to a reality of learning through trial and error; she presents humorous anecdotes about 'the servant problem' and various guests; she later rejects an opportunity to return to New York in order to remain in New Mexico."

Guestward Ho! is a fitting place to stop, because of its coauthor, whose real name was Edward Everett Tanner III, who truly and completely absorbed the ethos of mid-century autobiography, and who was certainly the greatest faux-memoirist of all time. In 1952, he ghostwrote *My Ringside Seat in Moscow*, the autobiography of Nicholas Nyaradi, a former Hungarian minister of finance. But he was just getting started. Three years later (after publishing a couple of novels under the name "Virginia Rowans"), he wrote a novel in the form of light autobiography—a man reminiscing about his thirty-year relationship with an eccentric but life-affirming aunt. Seemingly unable or unwilling ever to affix his own name to anything he wrote—a habit of secrecy or double-mindedness that probably was connected with his for-the-most-part-hidden bisexuality—Tanner chose "Patrick Dennis": Patrick being the full form of his own longtime nickname, Pat, and Dennis being (he would later claim, according to his biographer, Eric Myers) a surname he chose from the phone book. He gave the narrator/main character the same name as well, leading most casual readers to assume that the book actually *was* an autobiography. *Auntie Mame* was a huge hit, spending 112 weeks on the *New York Times* bestseller list and becoming a play and then a movie with Rosalind Russell, and a decade later a Broadway musical, *Mame*, with Angela Lansbury. (For her performance in *Mame*, as well as in the films *My Sister Eileen*, *Wonderful Town*, and *Roughly Speaking*, Russell would have to be considered the queen of stage and screen autobiography.)

After collaborating with his friend Barbara Hooton on *Guestward Ho!* (which became a TV series in 1960), Tanner continued to publish novels as Virginia Rowans and Patrick Dennis, but he couldn't leave memoir alone. *Little Me: The Intimate Memoirs of That Great Star of Stage, Screen and Television, Belle Poitrine*, as told to Patrick Dennis, was published in 1961; Tanner succinctly described it to a friend as the "phony autobiography of a rotten movie star." *Little Me* became a camp classic (as well as a

Broadway musical with Sid Caesar); it was followed three years later by *First Lady*, by Martha Dinwiddie Butterfield, as told to Patrick Dennis, the fictional autobiography of the fictional wife of a fictional president.

As for his own autobiography, Edward Tanner never wrote it.

THE EVIDENCE OF THESE BOOKS NOTWITHSTANDING, some Americans continued to lead unhappy, frustrated, or even tragic lives. But that was not reflected in published autobiographies. The vibrant tradition of African-American memoir, which had been kicked off by the slave narrative, dwindled in the early to middle twentieth century. Louis Kaplan offers a shockingly small list of thirty-four autobiographies by "Negroes" in the period 1900–1945 (an almost 40 percent decrease from the number published in 1850–1899). The majority of such books in this period told the stories of black leaders, prominent writers, athletes, and (female) entertainers: James Weldon Johnson, Langston Hughes, Jackie Robinson, Zora Neale Hurston, Ethel Waters, Marian Anderson, Billie Holiday. A book that deserves special mention is Richard Wright's *Black Boy*. It was a great commercial and critical success when it was published in 1945. But it was not the autobiography Wright intended. The book, as published, ends with nineteen-year-old Richard leaving the Jim Crow South for Chicago, "with a hazy notion that life could be lived with dignity, that the personalities of others should not be violated, that men should be able to confront men without fear or shame, that if men were lucky in their living on earth they might win some redeeming meaning for their having struggled and suffered here beneath the stars." In fact, Wright composed those hopeful words only after the Book-of-the-Month Club had put forth as a condition for accepting the book the elimination of the final six chapters, which showed that northern and southern racism differed only in certain particulars, not in force or in the devastating effects on victims. The complete book was not published until 1977, under its original title, *American Hunger*.

A very different sort of memoir, one in which the Book-of-the-Month Club would have had to make zero changes, was Ruby Berkley Goodwin's *It's Good to Be Black* (1953), about growing up in the 1920s in De Quoin, Illinois. Goodwin, described by contemporary press reports as working in the public relations field, starts the book this way:

> Until I once argued with a psychology teacher, I didn't know that all Negro children grow up with a sense of frustration and insecurity. Moreover, I still feel that this statement, along with such kindred observations as "all colored people can sing and dance," must be taken with the proverbial grain of salt.
>
> The philosophy behind this remark, however, I have since found implied in most books about Negroes. Whether the authors are black or white, they are equally guilty of representing us either as objects of pity or objects of contempt, and I have learned to resent this implication much as I earlier resented the flat remark of the psychology teacher.
>
> As a result I have felt impelled to write of life as I have lived it. I sincerely believe the lives of many Negro children follow the same pattern as did mine. We have probably been overlooked by writers because it is much easier to dramatize the brutal and the sordid than the commonplace.

One can hardly begrudge Goodwin her belief that her contented childhood was as normal as anyone else's. And some of the things her strong and wise father (whose pet name for her is "Reuben") tells her in the last pages of the book, when the specter of racial prejudice, violence, and hatred appears for the first time, are prescient, as is his language: "I look at some of our folks. They want to be white so bad they can taste it.

They think 'cause they're light brown or yellow, they're better than dark people. They ain't. They ain't as good. We're the only people I know who are proud of being black—well, someday when you're a little bigger you'll understand. We ought to be proud of being black, Reuben. Black is powerful."

Yet it is surely significant that of the few memoirs by an "ordinary" African-American to be published in that period, it was overwhelmingly sanguine, not least in its title. The few reviewers who took note of the book seemed relieved. *The New York Times* called it "a fine, warm-hearted memoir," and *Kirkus Reviews*, "a personal narrative which substitutes dignity for sensationalism, a quiet strength for the more embittered and embattled attack against discrimination." I am still searching for the sensationalistic, embittered, and embattled memoirs against which Goodwin's book is contrasted.*

Autobiographies by the poor or working class, such a well-populated genre in Victorian Britain and America, had carried on through the 1920s and 1930s, but almost exclusively in narratives by tramps and hoboes, which provided an opportunity for picaresque adventures and sometimes lurid revelations. Examples from the 1920s include *You Can't Win*, by Jack Black (later named by William Burroughs as a strong influence); *Poorhouse Sweeney: Life in a County Poorhouse*, by Ed Sweeney; and *The Main Stem*, by William Edge. George Orwell's first published book, *Down and Out in Paris and London* (1933), was a half-autobiographical, half-journalistic account of his time as a *plongeur* in a Paris restaurant and a tramp in England.

---

*In 1955, Goodwin embarked on an acting career. The Internet Movie Database lists sixteen films and television episodes in which she appeared between then and her death in 1961. Some of her roles, according to IMDb, were: "Sarah (Irene's maid)"; "Dr. Byrne's Maid"; "Louann, the maid"; "Maid"; "Annie, Alice's Maid"; and "Housekeeper."

Sister of the Road (1935) was presented as the autobiography of a female hobo known as Box-Car Bertha Thompson, but in fact Bertha sprang from the imagination of Dr. Ben Reitman, well known as an anarchist, Emma Goldman's lover, and a vociferous advocate for hoboes' rights. (In 1972, Martin Scorsese adapted the book into one of his first films, *Boxcar Bertha*.) Tom Kromer's *Waiting for Nothing* (1935), a first-person, present-tense account of life on the margins, was published as a novel, but its selling point was its air of authenticity; *The Saturday Review* felt that "there can be no question but that the author is telling a true tale." And in the preface to the English edition, Kromer said as much: "Save for four or five incidents, it is strictly autobiographical."

Two years later came John Worby's *The Other Half: The Autobiography of a Tramp* and Mark Benney's *Angels in Undress*, about the author's upbringing in the London demimonde, career as a burglar, and incarceration. Benney's book got excellent reviews both in England, where it had the title *Low Company*, and the United States. But some American critics, still stinging from the Joan Lowell affair and struck by the high literary quality of the book, were skeptical about its provenance. *The New York Times* commented, "The question of authenticity arises because 'Angels in Undress' seems too good to be true," and the *Herald Tribune*, "One must turn continually to the publisher's assurance that it is not a literary hoax." The opportunity for publicity was not lost. The London publisher, Peter Davies, wired his American counterpart, Bennett Cerf: BENNEY IS 100 PERCENT AUTHOR OF LOW COMPANY WELLS SQUIRE HUXLEY BERTRAND RUSSELL ETC HAVE MET HIM I AM POSTING PARTS OF ORIGINAL MSS WRITTEN IN PRISON BACONIAN THEORY IS ALL BUNK. Cerf reproduced the telegram in advertisements for the book. Benney, whose real name was subsequently revealed to be Henry Ernest Degras, went on to publish six more books, including a 1966 memoir, *Almost a Gentleman*.

World War II terminated the flow of low-life autobiographies; in the six and a half decades since, it has not resumed. However, in the period from the war through the early 1960s, a few noncheerful memoirs did manage to see their way into print. Allow me to present a few more summaries from Patricia Addis's book *Through a Woman's I.*

Eunice Walterman, *Don't Call Me Dad*, 1950. "Married and the mother of twins, she is shocked to discover in 1943 that she was an adopted child; obsessed by the search for her biological parents, she has an emotional reunion with her mother but is rebuffed by her wealthy, powerful father, Roosevelt's envoy to the Vatican; she suffers threats and intimidation but does achieve grim satisfaction in a melodramatic confrontation with him; her suit to establish his paternity is unsuccessful in what she argues is a miscarriage of justice."

Mary Payne, *I Cured My Cancer*, 1954. "She tells of her overwhelming fear when a tumor is diagnosed as cancer in 1941; her firm determination to be cured carries her through years of treatment and leads to her equally firm determination to become an X-ray technician to help others like herself."

Eloise Davenport, *I Can't Forget*, 1960. "Reluctant, but persuaded to enter a mental health clinic, she gradually reveals the marital stress and personality traits leading to her breakdown; engaging in mutually supportive discussions with other patients, she tries to heed doctors' advice to express her feelings more freely, but she is indignant when psychiatrists ignore her physical pain and illness; ultimately she finds she must recover from the negative effects of poor clinic treatment."

Janice Fielding, *The Bitter Truth of It*, 1963. "This is a highly emotional, bitter account of the years following a hysterectomy, performed on her without medical necessity and without her informed consent; she feels that the physical mutilation leads to her mental unbalance and resents the attitudes of doctors."

No question, they sound like memoirs that would fit right in today. But there was no place for them in the established publishing industry at the time, and they appeared in print only because their authors paid all costs. Walterman's book was self-published, and those of Payne, Davenport, and Fielding (a pseudonym) were put out by Carlton Press, Exposition Press, and Vantage Press: so-called vanity, or subsidy, publishers. However, there were limits to the kinds of authors whose money even these outfits would take. The president and founder of Exposition, Edward Uhlan, commented in his 1956 memoir, *The Rogue of Publishers Row*, "One type of book comes to my office with unfailing regularity, that of the homosexual trying to explain why he is what he is and seeking approval as a member of society." Even a vanity publisher has to draw the line somewhere, says Uhlan: "He must learn that vice taints him as much as it taints the author—more, perhaps, for while the poor wretch of a writer may be writing under psychopathic compulsion, the publisher is furthering his ends for one purpose—to make money." Reading that, one understands why Edward Tanner/Patrick Dennis never chronicled his own life.

Another outlet for stories that fell outside the consensus could be found on the newsstand rather than in the bookstore. Bernarr Macfadden, a famous and eccentric health nut and the founder, editor, and publisher of *Physical Culture* magazine, started *True Story* magazine in 1919. Under the credo "Truth Is Stranger Than Fiction," the cover of the first issue featured such titles as "A Wife Who Awoke in Time," "My Battle with John Barleycorn," "An Ex-Convict's Climb to Millions," and "How I Learned to Hate My Parents." The magazine was a huge success. By the mid-twenties it had a circulation of two million and had spawned the first of many imitators, which bore the Rousseauesque and slightly redundant title *True Confessions*. The *True Story* formula consisted of first-person accounts, written in an untutored but clear style, of sin and redemption. The sin, usually carnal, was described in some detail; but the actual consummation nearly always seemed to take place between paragraphs, and it was invariably dressed up in a moral lesson. One typical narrator warned, "Let nobody be stirred up by the glamor of a certain part of my experience to attempt a similar adventure. What I went through of mental anguish can be neither described nor imagined."

Moreover, none of the protagonists was really evil; they were usually lower-class girls who were bewitched by some socialite's irresistible charms. Most of them could say, as one did, "In reviewing my life I cannot detect a single instance in which my misfortune was the result of my own misdoing." The confession magazines offered no-fault thrills; their pathos was sentimental in the sense of being wholly unearned.

Macfadden manipulated the formula masterfully. He knew the illusion of authenticity was essential, so instead of hiring what he called "art artists" to illustrate the stories, he used staged photographs—featuring such models as the then-unknown Fredric March, Jean Arthur, and Norma Shearer—and he made every contributor sign an affidavit stating that his or her story was indeed true. But there were some doubters. Oswald Garrison Villard wrote in *The Atlantic* in 1926, "Veracious personal experiences are written by small groups of industrious workers who are paid from two to six cents or more a word. Hence most of the sad wives and disillusioned flappers whose touching narratives appear every month are in reality mature gentlemen residing in Harlem or Greenwich Village." In 1927, after a piece called "The Revealing Kiss" used the names of eight actual residents of Scranton, Pennsylvania, and they sued Macfadden for half a million dollars, he found himself somewhat sheepishly allowing that maybe every story wasn't all that true.

A group of magazines that emerged after World War II—*Argosy, True, Male, Stag, True Action*, and others—offered a men's counterpart to the confession magazine, mixing dubious exposés and soft-core porn with first-person narratives of derring-do. The novelist Bruce Jay Friedman, who worked at several of these publications in the 1950s and 1960s, described their staples as "stories about people who had been nibbled half to death by ferocious little animals. The titles were terrifying cries of anguish. 'A Grysbok Sucked My Bones'; 'Give Me Back My Leg'; they seemed to have even more power when couched in the present continuous tense. 'A Boar Is Grabbing My Brain.'" The most popular tales were about World War II:

> Our staple became the verifiably true story of some fellow who had survived a Japanese "rat cage," made a record-breaking Death Trek through Borneo, raided Schveinfurt, or helped to storm the Remagen Bridge. . . . There were, however, just so many Borneo death trekkers to be gotten hold of. . . . It was at this point that there arose the notion of simply making up "true" stories and providing them with full documentation. . . . Once we had made our little "adjustment," we began with great verve to make up entirely new bombing raids, indeed, to create new World War II battles, ones that had turned the tide against the Axis and brought Hitler to his knees.

If one looked in certain quite specific niches of mainstream publishers' lists, unhappy memoirs were visible: for example, the inspirational account of the illness or death of the author's child. John Gunther's *Death Be Not Proud*, recounting his son's death from a brain tumor at the age of seventeen, was a bestseller when it was published in 1949 and continues to be read and assigned today. Marie Killilea's *Karen* (1952) was about her daughter's cerebral palsy; Harriet Hentz Houser's *Hentz* (1955), about her son, whom an accident rendered quadriplegic; and Katherine Fryer's prescient *Kathy* (1956), about her daughter's struggles with what initially was misdiagnosed as anorexia nervosa but turned out to be a thyroid condition. The comic novelist Peter De Vries's one sober book was a fictional version of his daughter's death from leukemia, *The Blood of the Lamb* (1961).

Two staples of today's memoirs are mental illness and addiction. In the postwar decades, such tales could be published only under strict conditions. One was fictionalization, as in *The Snake Pit*, by Mary Jane Ward, about her own experience of being institutionalized in an asylum, which was a bestseller in 1946 and a film with Olivia de Havilland two years later. Another was the use of a pseudonym, as in *The Final Face of Eve*, published in 1958 by the woman whose experiences inspired the previous year's film about multiple personality, *The Three Faces of Eve* (in subsequent decades she wrote two more books under her own name, Chris Costner-Sizemore), and *The Fantastic Lodge: The Autobiography of a Girl Drug Addict* (1961), by "Janet Clark." Sylvia Plath's *The Bell Jar* (1963) and Joanne Greenberg's *I Never Promised You a Rose Garden* (1964) met both criteria: slightly fictionalized accounts of the authors' experiences of mental illness, they were credited, respectively, to "Victoria Lucas" and "Hannah Green." (After Plath's suicide, *The Bell Jar* was issued under her own name.)

There was one other way such stories could be published: if they were written by celebrities. Not big-time celebrities: a tarnished image would cost them too much. No, these were tales of excess, debasement, and sometimes redemption by B-listers who were just barely on the public radar. These authors revived the tradition of Laetitia Pilkington and Charlotte Clarke—the "scandalous memoirists" of the eighteenth century—and laid the groundwork for the misery memoirs of today. Kicking things off was a minor Chicago jazz musician, born Milton Mesirow, who had adopted a new name—Mezz Mezzrow—and had become such an enthusiastic user and purveyor of marijuana that for a time "mezz" was street slang for the drug. Mezzrow's other claim to fame was his embrace of African-American culture, so fervent that he decided, as he explained in his drug-infused and jive-inflected 1946 autobiography, *Really the Blues*, to "turn myself black." He was to a striking extent successful. His ghostwriter, Bernard Wolfe, subsequently wrote: "Mezzrow, after his long years in and under Harlem, did truly think his lips had developed fuller contours, his hair had thickened and burred, his skin had darkened. It was not, as he saw it, a case of trans-culturation. He felt he had scrubbed himself clean, inside and out, of every last trace of his origins in the Jewish slums of Chicago, pulped himself back to raw human material, deposited that nameless jelly in the pure Negro mold, and pressed himself into the opposite of his birthright, a pure Black." Mezzrow convinced other people as well: when he was arrested for posses-sion of marijuana with intent to distribute, he was sent to the black cell block of the segregated prison, and when he was drafted in 1942, his draft card listed his race as "Negro."

One of the most talked-about books of 1953 was *A House Is Not a Home*, by the longtime New York City madam Polly Adler. In *I'll Cry Tomorrow* (1954), coauthored with Gerold Frank and Mike Connolly, Lil-lian Roth, a former Ziegfeld Follies girl and early-talkies Hollywood in-génue, told the story of her descent into alcoholism and her redemption via Alcoholics Anonymous and conversion to Catholicism.* Adler and

---

*Frank was the master of this category, subsequently collaborating on the tell-all memoirs of Diana Barrymore, the alcoholic and drug-addicted daughter of John; Sheilah Graham, the final mistress of F. Scott Fitzgerald; and Zsa Zsa Gabor, who was and is famously famous for being famous.

Roth had several commonalities: Jewish heritage, movie adaptations (Adler was played by Shelley Winters, Roth by Susan Hayward, who was nominated for an Academy Award), and book sales of well over two million copies, almost all of them in the relatively new format of mass-market paperback. In *Fear Strikes Out* (1954), an unextraordinary baseball player named Jim Piersall (Anthony Perkins in the film) told the story of what was then called a nervous breakdown and would now be diagnosed as bipolar disorder. The one A-lister in this group was the singer Billie Holiday, whose *Lady Sings the Blues* (1956)—embarked on, its ghost-writer, William Dufty, told the writer Julia Blackburn, "to cash in on the confessional book vogue"—tells of the many hard things she had packed into forty-one years: her out-of-wedlock birth, rapes at a young age, time working as a prostitute, alcoholism and heroin addiction, and relationships with many abusive men. The following year came *Gypsy: A Memoir*, by the stripper Gypsy Rose Lee, which told the story of her borderline abusive stage mother. The book inspired the 1959 Broadway musical, which was made into a film in 1962 starring, of course, Rosalind Russell.

Chapter 10

SONGS OF MYSELF

What everyone has in them, these days, is not a novel but a memoir.

—MARTIN AMIS, *Experience: A Memoir,* 2000

No event is too small or too insignificant to write about.

—MAUREEN MURDOCK, *Unreliable Truth:*
Of Memoir and Memory, 2003

LIKE MANY OTHER THINGS IN AMERICAN LIFE, autobiography broke loose in the middle and late 1960s. Leading the way, as it had a little over a century before, was African-American memoir. This time the authors weren't writing narratives of their experiences as slaves, but rather of their experiences as unequal members of society. It was a powerful theme, and these authors' energy, and sometimes rage, breathed new life into the genre.

I would submit that the trailblazer, in 1964, was comedian-activist Dick Gregory's *Nigger*, which began with a searing description of the beatings his father administered to his mother and to him, and which took the 1950s subgenre of scandalous celebrity memoir in an outspoken new direction. (Gregory explained his provocative title in the dedication: "Dear Momma—Wherever you are, if you ever hear the word 'nigger' again, remember they are advertising my book.") This was followed a year later by *The Autobiography of Malcolm X*, about and by the Black Muslim leader who had been assassinated just months earlier, and written "with the assistance of" Alex Haley (later to gain fame as the author of *Roots*). The opening line was: "When my mother was pregnant with me, she told me later, a party of hooded Ku Klux Klan riders galloped up to our home in Omaha, Nebraska, one night." That sentence introduced a character and a voice who would stand with Benjamin Franklin and Henry Adams, with Helen Keller and Mary Antin, in the annals of classic American autobiography. Indeed, Malcolm X—who was born Malcolm Little—hailed back even farther to John Bunyan and the tradition of spiritual autobiography. At thirteen, he lost his father to a suspicious accident and his mother to mental illness, and he eventually found himself lost in the wilderness: known as "Detroit Red," after his hair color, he drifted from city to city, dealing drugs, pimping, gambling, and stealing. As in many such books, the documentation of wickedness is more compelling and ultimately more memorable than his salvation in the Muslim faith, and his subsequent break with the leader of the Nation of Islam. However, the final pages of the book have an almost chilling power as well, as Malcolm X seems to be speaking to us from the grave. He writes:

Anyway, now, each day I live as if I am already dead, and I tell you what I would like for you to do. When I *am* dead—I say it that way because from the things I *know*, I do not expect to live long enough to read this book in its finished form—I want you to just watch and see if I'm not right in what I say: that the white man, in his press, is going to identify me with "hate."

Dick Gregory was a comedian and Malcolm X was a world-historical figure. But possibly more influential, in literary terms, was a quartet of books by "ordinary" people that appeared in succession in the following years: *Manchild in the Promised Land*, by Claude Brown (1965); *Down These Mean Streets*, by Piri Thomas (1967); *Coming of Age in Mississippi* (1968), by Anne Moody; and *I Know Why the Caged Bird Sings*, by Maya Angelou (1969).* Growing up in Harlem in the 1940s and 1950s, Claude Brown was involved in gang life and petty crimes. With the encouragement of a mentor he grew close to at reform school, Dr. Ernst Papanek, he enrolled in Howard University and eventually wrote an article about Harlem for the political magazine *Dissent.* That attracted the attention of an editor at Collier Books, who gave Brown $2,000 to write his autobiography. Unfortunately, soon afterward, Collier was absorbed by Macmillan and the assigning editor departed. In 1964, Macmillan hired a young editor named Alan Rinzler. "I was given a tiny office which had a cardboard grocery box under the desk," Rinzler recalls today. In it was Brown's 1,500-page manuscript. Rinzler says, "I realized it was ground-breaking, electrifying, and totally original from the very first pages I kept turning." He worked with Brown to cut the manuscript down to size and came up with a compelling title. The book made an immediate splash, for its realism and its supercharged language, and for the notion it introduced: that

---

*Another much-talked-about book of the period was *Soul on Ice* (1968), by the Black Panther leader Eldridge Cleaver. It had pieces of autobiography, but was more in the nature of a political statement than a memoir.

a young man's story of growing up on the streets of Harlem was the stuff of autobiography. Among many raves, journalist Tom Wolfe wrote in the *New York Herald Tribune*, "Claude Brown makes James Baldwin and all that old Rock of Ages rhetoric sound like some kind of Moral Rearmament tourist from Toronto come to visit the poor." *Manchild* quickly reached the bestseller lists and ended up selling more copies than any other book Macmillan has published, with the exception of *Gone With the Wind*.

Brown's success paved the way for Thomas (a black Puerto Rican who told a similar tale of his own Harlem childhood and youth), Moody (who grew up in the rural South and was active in the civil rights movement in the early 1960s), and Angelou, a dancer, actress, teacher, journalist, and activist, who had lived the kind of life one would have expected to find in a Toni Morrison novel. She came to write a memoir (according to a *New York Times* account) because of one day in 1968 when she and some other people were at the home of cartoonist Jules Feiffer, telling stories about their childhoods. The next day, Feiffer's wife, Judy, phoned Random House editor Robert Loomis and told him that he had to get this woman to write a book. Loomis asked; Angelou said no. But in a subsequent conversation, the editor told her, "It's just as well, because to write an autobiography as literature is just about impossible." And then Angelou agreed to give it a try. *I Know Why the Caged Bird Sings*, which tells such a dramatic story and is written in such a fresh, compelling manner that it has been continuously in print since its publication, begins when Angelou is three. Her parents' marriage ends, and she and her brother are sent to live with their grandmother, a storekeeper in Stamps, Arkansas. A few years later, after the children are returned to their mother in St. Louis, Angelou is raped by her mother's boyfriend. She becomes mute: "I thought if I spoke, my mouth would just issue out something that would kill people, randomly, so it was better not to talk." She didn't speak again for another five years. By the end of the book, she has moved to San Francisco, worked as the city's first black female streetcar conductor, and given birth, out of wedlock, to a son. And she's only seventeen—meaning that she had plenty of material for her many subsequent memoirs.

These works were actually combining two separate autobiographical traditions into a soon-to-be inordinately popular new one. The first tradition, heretofore largely confined to the British Isles and the Continent, consisted of books that followed the example of Edmund Gosse's 1907 *Father and Son*: literary figures, including Maxim Gorky, Edwin Muir, André Gide, and W. H. Hudson, writing memoirs of their childhood and youth, usually in a novelistic style, with scenes, dialogue, and character development. In his book about the genre, *When the Grass Was Taller*, critic Richard N. Coe gave it a name—the "childhood." The 1960s American black writers took the concept—in the words of Thomas's title—to the mean streets.* In 1967, the young American white writers Willie Morris and Frank Conroy were following their example (consciously or not) when they composed their first books, *North Toward Home* and *Stop-Time*, respectively, as autobiography rather than fiction. The critic Paul Fussell commented in 1970: "Twenty years ago, Frank Conroy's *Stop-Time* would have been costumed as a first novel. Today it appears openly as a memoir."

Back in the 1960s, Brown, Thomas, Moody, and Angelou—and Mal-

---

*The phrase was taken from Raymond Chandler, metaphorically referring to his detective hero Philip Marlowe: "Down these mean streets a knight must go." *Mean Streets* later became the title of Martin Scorsese's breakthrough 1973 film.

colm X, Dick Gregory, and Eldridge Cleaver as well—were also mining a specific sort of material: the trauma of their pasts. That suggests the second tradition they were reinvigorating, and it was not a heavily populated one. The most notable precedent was the slave narrative itself. The most recent one was four decades old: the World War I memoir. Since the time of Caesar, retrospective accounts of battle had been the exclusive province of generals. But the Great War—shocking in its death and destruction, and fought to a greater extent than ever before by a literate battle force— yielded, for the first time, unflinching personal accounts by soldiers on the ground. Even so, this idea took several years to gain acceptance. In 1919, the English writer Herbert Read wrote a short, unvarnished memoir of battle but could not sell it: publishers, he later reported, were not interested in "anything bleak." For some years, the only place to find non-whitewashed first-person accounts was in the verse of Wilfred Owen, Rupert Brooke, Isaac Rosenberg, Siegfried Sassoon, and Robert Graves. By 1925, the world was apparently ready for Read's book, *Retreat*, and it was followed by an influential set of memoirs that focused on the costs, the ironies, and the horrors of war: Edmund Blunden's *Undertones of War* (1928), Graves's *Good-Bye to All That* (1929), Sassoon's *Memoirs of an Infantry Officer* (published in 1930 as a novel but changed little from Sassoon's actual experience), A. M. Burrage's *War Is War* (published in 1931 under the pseudonym "Ex-Private X"), Guy Chapman's *A Passionate Prodigality* (1932), and *Testament of Youth* (1933), by Vera Brittain, who had served as a Voluntary Aid Detachment nurse in London, Malta, and France. A comparable memoir from the German side was Ernst Jünger's *Storm of Steel*.

Interestingly, World War II yielded a smaller group of noteworthy memoirs, though much memorable fiction. The autobiographical accounts tended to be by British writers and to focus on the dramatic, exotic, and often horrific Pacific War. It included Richard Hillary's account of his service as a pilot, *The Last Enemy*; George MacDonald Fraser's and John Masters's memoirs of Burma, *Quartered Safe Out Here* and *The Road Past Mandalay*, respectively; and the American Eugene B. Sledge's memoir of Okinawa, *With the Old Breed*.

The most horrific aspect of World War II—probably the most horrific event in the history of Western civilization—was the Nazi Holocaust. A number of memoirs by survivors appeared in the years immediately following the war. In her book *Writing the Holocaust*, Zoë Waxman reports that Yad Vashem, the Israeli archive, library, and museum of Holocaust studies, has counted seventy-five of them published between 1945 and 1949 in a range of languages, notably Yiddish (fifteen books), Hebrew (thirteen), and Polish (twelve). The list included two books that would be translated into English and gain global acclaim years later. Viktor Frankl was a Viennese psychiatrist who, beginning in 1942, was confined in four different concentration camps. Soon after his liberation in 1945, Frankl composed in just nine days a manuscript chronicling his experience in the camps. He had "the firm conviction that the book should be published anonymously," but at the last minute he was convinced by some friends to put his name on the title page—that version of the book was called (in translation from the German) *Saying Yes to Life in Spite of Everything: A Psychologist Experiences the Concentration Camp*. (It is one of history's sad ironies that the profound truth of the title should have become one of the late twentieth century's most vapid clichés.) Still, Frankl never sought glory or to present himself as a "witness"; rather, he wrote years later, "I wanted to convey to the reader by way of a concrete example that life holds a potential meaning under any conditions, even the most miserable ones." The English edition, published in 1959 and supplemented by an outline of Frankl's theory of "logotherapy," was called *Man's Search for Meaning*. According to the afterword of a 2006 edition, to that point the various editions of the book had sold more than twelve million copies in twenty-one different languages.

Primo Levi was a Jewish Italian chemist who was captured by the Fascist militia in December 1943. He was transported to Auschwitz shortly afterward and spent eleven months there before liberation. Like Frankl, he felt compelled to tell his story and completed a book quickly: for Levi it took "a few months." At that point, he recounted late in his life, "the manuscript was turned down by a number of important publishers; it was accepted in 1948 by a small publisher who printed only 2,500 copies [under the title *If This Is a Man*] and then folded. So this first book of mine fell into oblivion for many years: perhaps also because in all of Europe those were difficult times of mourning and reconstruction and the public did not want to return in memory to the painful years of the war that had just ended." Republished in Italy in 1958 and, under the title *Survival in Auschwitz*, in English in 1959, the book was recognized as a classic and Levi as a major writer. In 1963, he wrote a second memoir, *The Truce*, about his journey from Auschwitz back to Italy. And until his death in 1987, in essays, poems, stories, and his book *The Periodic Table*—a tour de force that combined memoir, meditation, and a sense of language and form equal to the finest fiction—he kept returning to his experience in the camps.

A handful of first-person accounts were indeed published in New York or London in the immediate postwar period, and they deserve mention: Mary Berg's *Warsaw Ghetto: A Diary* and Leon Szalet's *Experiment "E": A Report from an Extermination Laboratory* (both 1945); Albert Menasche's *Birkenau (Auschwitz II): How 72,000 Greek Jews Perished* and

Seweryna Szmaglewska's *Smoke over Birkenau* (both 1947); Ella Lingens-Reiner's *Prisoners of Fear* and Gisella Perl's *I Was a Doctor in Auschwitz* (both 1948). But the books did not penetrate the American public's consciousness. Of them, only Berg's, a teenage girl's record of Warsaw life under Nazi cruelty and deprivations, was reviewed (favorably) in *The New York Times*. *Experiment "E,"* a firsthand account of Szalet's eight months in the Sachsenhausen concentration camp at the beginning of the war, was listed in an article about forthcoming titles; none of the other books was mentioned in the *Times*'s pages even once.*

The relatively small number of such memoirs in the immediate postwar period is not surprising. Elie Wiesel, a native of Romania who endured a horrific experience in the camps as a teenager, and who would eventually become the most widely read memoirist of the Holocaust, subsequently explained (in his book *A Jew Today*):

> I knew the role of the survivor was to testify. Only I did not know how. I lacked experience. I lacked a framework. I mistrusted the tools, the procedures. Should one say it all or hold it all back? Should one shout or whisper? Place the emphasis on those who were gone or on their heirs? How does one describe the indescribable? How does one use restraint in recreating the fall of mankind and the eclipse of the Gods? And then, how can one be sure that the words, once uttered, will not betray, distort the message they bear? So heavy was my anguish that I made a vow: not to speak, not to touch upon the essential for at least ten years.

---

*In 1983, the Showtime television network aired *Out of the Ashes*, based on Perl's memoir of being forced to assist Josef Mengele, and her subsequent struggle to be granted permanent residence in the United States.

When that ten years had passed, Wiesel started to speak, and he has not stopped. He began his first book on board a ship to Brazil, where he had an assignment as a freelance journalist. He wrote "feverishly, breathlessly," and ended the journey (according to his account in his later memoir *All Rivers Run to the Sea*) with an 862-page manuscript that he called *Un di Velt Hot Geshvign* (*And the World Remained Silent*). On board that same ship, he met a Brazilian publisher, who brought the book out in Buenos Aires. In 1958, a significantly shortened French version was published in Paris under the title *La nuit*, with an introduction by the Nobel laureate François Mauriac, who had become a friend of Wiesel's and encouraged him to write and publish his memories.

Wiesel's American literary agent, Georges Borchardt, began sending the French manuscript to New York publishers. Fifteen turned it down. "Nobody really wanted to talk about the Holocaust in those days," Borchardt told *The New York Times* in 2008. A typical comment came from an editor at Scribner's, who wrote him, "It is, as you say, a horrifying and extremely moving document, and I wish I could say this was something for Scribner's. However, we have certain misgivings as to the size of the American market for what remains, despite Mauriac's brilliant introduction, a document." Finally, in 1960, Arthur Wang of Hill & Wang bought it for $1,000. Spare, poetic, and riveting in its unflinching description of the horrors Wiesel experienced, *Night* got favorable reviews but sold just 1,046 copies over the next eighteen months. The book had legs, however. Passed from one admirer to another, eventually included in many middle school, high school, and college and university reading lists, and given a further boost when Wiesel was awarded the Nobel Peace Prize in 1986, *Night* had, by early 2006, sold some six million copies in the United States and been translated into thirty languages. In January of that year, Oprah Winfrey selected *Night* for her television book club, and one million paperback and 150,000 hardcover copies were printed in a new translation by Wiesel's wife, Marion, and carrying an "Oprah's Book Club" logo on the cover. Within a month, *Night* was number one on the *New York Times* paperback nonfiction bestseller list. It spent the next eighty weeks on the list, selling three million more copies.

The most famous and widely read Holocaust memoir was neither a memoir nor, strictly speaking, about the Holocaust. It is sort of a companion piece to *Night*, written by a Dutch girl just a year Wiesel's junior. In 1942, when Anne Frank was thirteen, the Nazis occupied Amsterdam, and shortly afterward Anne and her family were forced to hide in the top floor of an office building. She began keeping a diary and continued it for the next twenty-five months, until the family was apprehended in 1944 and deported to concentration camps. Anne herself died of typhus in Bergen-Belsen in 1945. The only member of the family to survive was Anne's father, Otto Frank. After the war, he was presented with the diaries by a friend who had preserved them. They were published in Dutch in 1947, and then in England and the United States in 1952 (with an introduction by Eleanor Roosevelt), under the title *Anne Frank: The Diary of a Young Girl*. It was a bestseller and inspired a 1955 play and a 1959 film, both great successes; to date, the book, published in dozens of languages, has sold millions upon millions of copies. In retrospect, it appears as an almost necessary transitional step in the world's dissemination of the Holocaust. Within the confines of the book, nobody is brutalized or torn from her family, and only in the last line of a brief epilogue is Anne's fate (dispassionately) revealed: "In March 1945, two months before the liberation of Holland, Anne died in the concentration camp at Bergen-Belsen." In 1952 and for years afterward readers could not handle anything more than that. Yet the book is neither a whitewash nor an extended euphemism: in and of itself, it is a powerful document that flinches from nothing.* Much of its power comes from presenting the most remarkable case of dramatic irony—a situation in which an audience or readers know important information that a character does not—in the history of the printed word. Anne is very bright and sensitive and eloquent but also a normal teenage girl, with normal worries and concerns, including her crush on the boy who is in hiding with her; her innocence about the happenings in the world outside, and her ultimate fate, lend an overwhelming poignancy to the happenings in the attic.

The African-American autobiography of the late 1960s and the Holocaust memoir were both "documents" (to borrow a word from the clueless editor who turned down *Night*): testaments to the wrongs suffered by a people coming from the pen of a survivor. Given the prominence and success of both genres, it was probably inevitable that the victims of individual, as opposed to social, travail would replicate their stance. Traumatic tales that had hitherto been consigned to vanity publishers, published under pseudonyms, or turned into fiction now were exhibited in the sunlight as memoirs, signed by the authors who wrote them. Such books—many of them, it so happened, by people who were one step removed from celebrity, or who were prominent but not quite famous—streamed

---

*Some critics, including Bruno Bettelheim, Lawrence Langer, and Cynthia Ozick, have disagreed, charging that, as presented and understood, the Anne Frank story is a sanitized and sentimental tale that deflects attention from the truth and magnitude of the Holocaust. The view has some justice when it comes to the play and movie, which at several points endeavored to make the story less "Jewish" and more "universal." Thus Anne wrote: "Who has inflicted this upon us? Who has made us Jews different from all other people? Who has allowed us to suffer so terribly up till now?" In the play, she says, "We're not the only people that've had to suffer. . . . There've always been people that've had to. . . . Sometimes one race . . . sometimes another . . . and yet . . ." The playwrights (and later screenwriters) Albert Hackett and Frances Goodrich end the work with a scene in which Otto Frank is reading the diaries for the first time and comes across one of Anne's least perceptive and least supportable comments (the audience hears her offstage voice): "I still believe, in spite of everything, that people are really good at heart." The curtain line is Otto's: "She puts me to shame." But no one can deny that the story in all its iterations brought truths about the Holocaust to tens of millions of people.

---

forth in the middle and late 1970s. Some notable examples: *Conundrum* (1974), by Jan Morris, who had originally been James Morris, a noted journalist, and whose book chronicled her sex change; Mark Vonnegut's *The Eden Express* (1975), an account of schizophrenia by the novelist Kurt Vonnegut's son; Percy Knauth's *Season in Hell* (1975), a veteran journalist's recounting of his battle with suicidal depression; *First, You Cry* (1976), by Betty Rollin, a television news correspondent, about dealing with breast cancer; and *Haywire* (1977), by Brooke Hayward, the daughter of the film star Margaret Sullavan and the agent Leland Hayward, who quotes herself, at the age of twenty-three, summing up her life story to a friend: "I'm the daughter of a father who's been married five times. Mother killed herself. My sister killed herself. My brother has been in a mental institution. I'm twenty-three and divorced with two kids." *Haywire*, published by the prestigious house Knopf, was a critical and popular success, spending sixteen weeks on the *Times* bestseller list. In *The Times of My Life* (1978), former First Lady Betty Ford described her addiction to alcohol and painkillers. Child abuse entered the memoir via *Mommie Dearest* (1978), by Joan Crawford's daughter Christina, and *Going My Own Way* (1983), by Bing Crosby's son Gary, both of whom describe being beaten up by their famous (and deceased) parent.

The mid-century normative memoir—the genre of *The Egg and I*; *See Here, Private Hargrove*; and *Please Don't Eat the Daisies*—was kaput. It soon had a successor, whose parameters were established by a series of books that came out in a period lasting less than a decade. Most of these titles still resonate in the zeitgeist:

1989: *This Boy's Life: A Memoir*, Tobias Wolff
1990: *Darkness Visible: A Memoir of Madness*, William Styron;
    A Hole in the World: An American Boyhood, Richard Rhodes

1991: *Cures: A Gay Man's Odyssey*, Martin Duberman; *Patrimony: A True Story*, Philip Roth

1992: *Becoming a Man: Half a Life Story*, Paul Monette; *Making Love: An Erotic Odyssey*, Richard Rhodes

1993: *Girl, Interrupted*, Susanna Kaysen; *A Child Called "It": One Child's Courage to Survive*, Dave Pelzer

1994: *Autobiography of a Face*, Lucy Grealy; *Prozac Nation: Young and Depressed in America: A Memoir*, Elizabeth Wurtzel; *Shot in the Heart*, Mikal Gilmore

1995: *The Liars' Club: A Memoir*, Mary Karr; *Secret Life: An Autobiography*, Michael Ryan; *An Unquiet Mind: A Memoir of Moods and Madness*, Kay Redfield Jamison

1996: *Angela's Ashes*, Frank McCourt

1997: *The Kiss: A Memoir*, Kathryn Harrison

Not much happy talk here: these books chronicled dysfunction, abuse, poverty, addiction, mental illness, and/or bodily ruin. And there was none of the coyness or veiling strategies of earlier works on such subjects. Thus *Girl, Interrupted* tells exactly the same kind of story of female adolescent mental illness as had the novelized *The Bell Jar* and *I Never Promised You a Rose Garden* some thirty years before. The difference of three decades is that Susanna Kaysen leads off her book with a facsimile of the first page of her own case record folder at McLean Hospital (where Sylvia Plath herself had been committed and to which she had given a pseudonym in her novel), complete with her name, her parents' names and address, her date of birth, and her diagnosis of "borderline personality." These authors faced the camera straight on and told the truth—the more unsettling, shocking, or horrifying the truth, it sometimes seemed, the better.

The first memoir on the above list was in some ways uncharacteristic of the flood that followed, but it did much to establish a template for the genre. Picking up *This Boy's Life* today, one encounters several key conventions even before starting to read it. The first is on the cover: the subtitle, *A Memoir*. As was noted on page 2 of this book, the singular form (as opposed to the plural "memoirs," a venerable, slightly pretentious equivalent of "autobiography") had previously been a designation for an author's extended reminiscences of *another* person.* I credit Tobias Wolff with inaugurating the current usage. Also immediately apparent is the book's *lack* of photographs and an index: subtle signs that it is more literary than literal. (Books of history and biographies almost always have this apparatus; novels, never.) Still, before the text proper comes a list of Wolff's previous works—two short story collections and one novel. Thus he was countering the tradition among literary folk in which your autobiography was the last, or nearly the last, book you wrote, the tradition followed by Gibbon and Trollope and Henry James and William Dean Howells and H. G. Wells and W. Somerset Maugham and nearly every other author of the past two centuries. Finally, between the dedication and the epigraphs comes an author's note, where Wolff thanks some friends and colleagues, and notes:

I have been corrected on some points, mostly of chronology. Also my mother thinks that a dog I describe as ugly was actually quite handsome. I've allowed some of the points to stand, because this is a book of memory, and memory has its own story to tell. But I have done my best to make this a truthful story.

---

*My admittedly unscientific investigations have unearthed just one use, pre-Wolff, of *A Memoir* as the subtitle of an autobiography: *Gypsy*, published in 1957, by the stripper Gypsy Rose Lee.

The manifesto is brief but remarkable. It begins with the suggestion that any factual discrepancies in the narrative to come—Did an event occur in February or March? How good-looking was the dog?—are trivial. But then, with a misleading stylistic affability that masks his will, Wolff asserts his power as a storyteller. He writes, "I've allowed some of the points to stand," but what he means is, "I'm going to tell this the way I want to." Memory is an impression, not a transcript. Doing one's "best" to tell "a truthful story" involves not conducting interviews or reading dusty clippings but consulting one's heart. That is the baseline position of the modern memoir. Surprisingly, Wolff neglects to say that he has changed the names of all characters in the book except for himself and his mother. Subsequently, it would become standard practice to have a small-type statement on the copyright page. I quote semi-randomly: "This is a true story. To protect the privacy of the participants, the names of most of the characters have been changed, as have some details about them and the events recounted here." (This one—the inevitable reaction to which is "What part of 'true' don't you understand?"—comes from Paul Monette's *Becoming a Man*.)

But I mentioned that *This Boy's Life* was to some extent atypical of the many books that followed it. *This* is clear once you read the opening sentences, which are:

Our car boiled over again just after my mother and I crossed the Continental Divide. While we were waiting for it to cool we heard, from somewhere above us, the bawling of an airhorn. The sound got louder and then a big truck came around the corner and shot past us into the next curve, its trailer shimmying wildly. We stared after it. "Oh, Toby," my mother said, "he's lost his brakes." The sound of the horn grew distant, then faded in the wind that sighed in the trees all around us.

By the time we got there, quite a few people were standing along the cliff where the truck went over. It had smashed through the guardrails and fallen hundreds of feet through empty space to the river below, where it lay on its back among the boulders. It looked pitifully small. A stream of thick black smoke rose from the cab, feathering out in the wind. My mother asked whether anyone had gone to report the accident. Someone had. We stood with the others at the cliff's edge. Nobody spoke. My mother put her arm around my shoulder.

For the rest of the day she kept looking over at me, touching me, brushing back my hair. I saw that the time was right to make a play for souvenirs. I knew she had no money for them, and I had tried not to ask, but now that her guard was down I couldn't help myself. When we pulled out of Grand Junction I owned a beaded Indian belt, beaded moccasins, and a bronze horse with a removable, tooled-leather saddle.

The quality of the writing—simple, assured, specific, and vivid—is unusual enough. But the key to the brilliance of *This Boy's Life* is the second sentence of the final paragraph quoted, which, in the adult Wolff's unsparing rendering of his younger self, is about as good as a sentence can be. A one-line précis of the memoir would probably cast it as being about young Toby's abuse (mostly verbal) at the hands of the man his mother eventually marries, Dwight. But in its characters, its perspective, its insight, and its wit, the book transcends the trauma it recounts.

Probably not coincidentally, Mary Karr was a student of Wolff's at Syracuse University, and *The Liars' Club*, though its writing was demotically lush where *This Boy's Life*'s was spare, was a worthy literary successor. So was *Angela's Ashes*, about Frank McCourt's miserable Irish boyhood, also stylistically a world apart. Both Karr's and McCourt's memoirs were also fabulously successful, taking residence on the *New York Times* bestseller list for a year or so each and ringing in a period in which publishers opened up their checkbooks and paid big (usually too big) bucks to ordinary people with troubled youths. Many of these memoirs, from the early 1990s through the present day, revolved around, were defined and branded by, a particular ailment or condition. Their value tended to be less literary than social or journalistic in putting a human face on the problem; this value sometimes was lessened by the authors' self-pity or self-aggrandizement and/or a not wholly convincing happy and redemptive ending.

The most commercially successful of all these books was Dave Pelzer's *A Child Called "It."* In prose that occasionally descends to melodramatic cliché but is usually simple and straightforward, it tells the story of the abuse Pelzer received at the hands of his alcoholic mother, who systematically beat him, burned him, starved him, humiliated and verbally abused him, and on one occasion stabbed him in the stomach. The book takes him to the age of twelve, when concerned teachers alerted authorities and he was placed in a foster home. Originally published in 1993 by a small Nebraska press, it was picked up in 1995 by Health Communications, a self-help publisher known for the Chicken Soup for the Soul series. Spurred by Pelzer's appearance on Montel Williams's talk show and his never-ending lecture tour, the book cracked the *New York Times* paperback bestseller list in 1997 and stayed there for an astonishing 333 weeks—almost six and a half years. Pelzer continued his story with *The Lost Boy*, about his years in foster care, which spent 228 weeks on the *Times* list, and *A Man Named Dave*, about his adult life, which in 2000 checked in for a stay of "only" 82 weeks.*

---

*Pelzer has been charged with pumping up those numbers by buying mass quantities of his works from amazon.com and other booksellers that report sales to the *Times* list, then peddling them at his talks. It is a slightly sketchy practice, but it doesn't change the fact that people bought all those books. Doubts have also been raised about the truth of his accounts of the events of his early childhood—which are extremely detailed—though not about the fact that he *was* abused. Since the only two characters in most of the scenes are Pelzer and his mother, and she died in 1992, a year before the publication of *A Child Called "It,"* these doubts will never be resolved. (Pelzer's father, depicted as a weak and helpless bystander, died in 1980.)

As popular as Pelzer's books were in the United States, they had an even greater impact in Britain, where they not only sold brilliantly but, in concert with more literary efforts like *Angela's Ashes*, Blake Morrison's *And When Did You Last See Your Father?* and Lorna Sage's *Bad Blood*, ushered in a new genre: the "misery memoir." By roughly 2000, these tales of extreme woe had established themselves as a major player in publishing, with their nearly interchangeable titles and pastel covers with a photograph of a plaintive child. Marketed mostly in supermarkets and to women, the genre reached its peak in 2006: according to *The Bookseller*, 1.9 million misery memoirs were sold that year, accounting for eleven of the one hundred top-selling paperback titles.

The extreme misery memoir is a particularly and somewhat alarming British taste, like Marmite or mushy peas. (BBC Online columnist Carol Sarler suggested that the phenomenon shows that "as a nation, we seem utterly in thrall to paedophilia. We are obsessed with it. And now, with these books, we are wallowing in the muck of it. It's all rather disgusting.") But though the American version has been milder, it started earlier, is more wide-ranging, and has provoked more harrumphing.

Starting in the early 1990s, the flood of memoirs was met with criticism, regret, and annoyance—often expressed in arguments and tropes that had been first used as far back as the 1830s. The most satisfyingly bilious early volley came from the critic William Gass in a 1994 screed in *Harper's* magazine. Gass had a few choice words for celebrity autobiographers— "celluloid whores and boorish noisemakers whose tabloid lives are presented for our titillation by ghosts still undeservedly alive." He saved the bulk of his scorn for the genre itself:

The fact that Pelzer's website continues to describe him as a "Pulitzer Prize nominee" even though numerous journalists have pointed out that that is a meaningless designation does not instill trust.

Are there any motives for the enterprise that aren't tainted with conceit or a desire for revenge or a wish for justification? To halo a sinner's head? To puff an ego already inflated past safety? . . . To have written an autobiography is already to have made yourself a monster. . . . Why is it so exciting to say, now that everyone knows it anyway, "I was born . . . I was born . . . I was born"? "I pooped in my pants, I was betrayed, I made straight A's."

To the familiar charge of narcissism came a new accusation: extreme unseemliness. Michael Ryan's *Secret Life*, a well-known poet's story of sex addiction brought on by childhood abuse, includes an oft-cited scene of the author having sex with his dog. (This was actually not a first: the British writer J. R. Ackerley also had some man-on-dog carnality in his posthumous 1968 autobiography, *My Father and Myself.*) In *Making Love*—a follow-up to *A Hole in the World*, in which he recounts his childhood physical abuse at the hands of his stepmother—Richard Rhodes describes every aspect of his sexual history, including a chapter on his formidable masturbation regimen. Paul Monette's *Becoming a Man* describes, in (literally) painful detail, his own loss of virginity to a stranger in a London bed-sit. He recognizes this will unsettle some readers, and he doesn't care. He quotes a friend, now dead from AIDS:

> *Is this more than you want to know?* as Stevie used to say, listing the weirdo side effects of chemo, the propulsive diarrhea. . . . When I'd talk about this book before he died, balking at the details of my first fuck . . . Stevie would wag his finger at me and say, *Rub their faces in it, Paulie. Nobody told us anything. You tell them.*

It's one thing to sacrifice your own privacy or dignity. But a memoir necessarily involves at least some members of the rest of the world, and recent memoirists have frequently been chastised for their alleged betrayal of family and so-called friends. Traditionally, the characters who had come off worst in memoirs were dead at the time of publication, which makes sense, since the dead can't sue the author for libel or invasion of privacy, punch the author in the nose, or air the author's dirty laundry in a memoir of their own.* The classic modern case is Ernest Hemingway's brutal treatment of his long-deceased friend F. Scott Fitzgerald in *A Moveable Feast,* which he completed in 1960, just before his own suicide. He starts with their initial meeting, in which he was struck by nothing so much as Fitzgerald's feminine looks: "He had very fair wavy hair, a high forehead, excited and friendly eyes and a delicate long-lipped Irish mouth that, on a girl, would have been the mouth of a beauty." That leads to a series of chapters in which Hemingway appears determined to chip away at the reputation of a rival. The final set piece is almost predictable: Fitzgerald confides to Hemingway (of course, no one else is present) that he is insecure about the size of his penis.

That Fitzgerald could not sue or protest is a pragmatic matter. What about doing the right thing? Can other people, alive *or* dead, be honorably sacrificed to the betterment of someone else's commercial enterprise, i.e., his or her book? The better memoir writers had always been aware of the moral ambiguity of the enterprise, and implicated themselves as much as or more than anyone else. Maxine Hong Kingston began her classic and unclassifiable *The Woman Warrior: Memoirs of a Girlhood Among Ghosts*

---

*The libel suit against Betty MacDonald described in the previous chapter was one of the few such actions against a memoir author, which is puzzling, given how frequently journalists have been sued. A suit against Marjorie Kinnan Rawlings, author of *Cross Creek* (1942), is the only one I am aware of for invasion of privacy. Even though the Rawlings suit ended with the Florida Supreme Court ruling (somewhat halfheartedly) in favor of the plaintiff, it's not surprising that few have followed her lead: a lawsuit from a person who felt violated by the airing of his or her dirty laundry would entail public proceedings, drawing even more unwanted attention.

(1977) with this unforgettable self-indicting sentence: "'You must not tell anyone,' my mother said, 'what I am about to tell you.'" In his 1991 *Patrimony: A True Story*, Philip Roth describes cleaning up his elderly father's shit. Mr. Roth says, "Don't tell Claire," referring to Roth's companion (and later wife), Claire Bloom. The writer replies, "Nobody."*

As the 1990s progressed, those nuances and complexities were cast aside, a process crystallized in three memoirs that appeared at the end of the decade. In the much-publicized *The Kiss: A Memoir* (1997), Kathryn Harrison details a longtime incestuous relationship with her living father. Joyce Maynard's *At Home in the World: A Memoir* (1998) describes her creepy and, in her account, borderline-abusive sexual relationship with a man old enough to be her father, the exorbitantly reclusive (and alive) J. D. Salinger. Published the same year, Lillian Ross's *Here But Not Here: A Love Story* recounts her decades-long affair with Salinger's buddy and editor, the almost-as-private William Shawn. True, Shawn wasn't living at the time of publication, but his widow was. And no one who knew the longtime *New Yorker* editor could possibly think he would have been happy with passages such as this one:

> Bill was attracted physically to all kinds of women. He lusted for beautiful models pictured in magazines; for wild American movie stars, such as Louise Brooks; for French movie stars, such as Simone Signoret or Annie Girardot or Françoise Rosay or Jeanne Moreau; for English movie stars, such as Julie Christie; for Italian movie stars, such as Anna Magnani or Sophia

---

*Roth and Bloom married in 1991 and divorced in 1995. The following year, she published a memoir, *Leaving a Doll's House*, that accused Roth of being a self-absorbed misogynist who forced her to make her own daughter move out of the house. Roth's 1998 novel *I Married a Communist*, which features a neurotic, vengeful ex-wife, Eve Frame, seemed refreshingly old-fashioned—fiction being the traditional way of settling scores.

Loren; for Swedish movie stars, such as Liv Ullmann or Bibi Andersson; for big brains, such as Susan Sontag or Hannah Arendt; for singers who phrased like Mabel Mercer or Rosemary Clooney; for women with little-girl looks; for women with Alice-in-Wonderland hair or gamin haircuts; for strange women he had noticed for an instant, days or months or years earlier, getting into a taxi or buying a newspaper; for fat women (the fatter the better); for elderly women who resembled his mother (full-bosomed); for athletic women, as long as they resembled the tennis star Evonne Goolagong; for women wearing aprons or silk-print dresses or sleek suits or nothing. In later years, he was attracted to Whoopi Goldberg, Vanessa Redgrave, and Madonna.

If an illustration of the concept "too much information" is ever required, there is no need to look any further.

In 2000, Dave Eggers made an impressive attempt to kill the memoir, or at least to deconstruct it until it was unrecognizable. Eggers was an exorbitantly talented young writer who had had an eminently memoir-worthy experience: when he was twenty-one, both his parents died of cancer, and he became largely responsible for raising his seven-year-old brother. He wrote a sprawling manuscript about what happened, called it *A Heartbreaking Work of Staggering Genius*, and adamantly refused to use the subtitle *A Memoir*, choosing instead *Based on a True Story* (this was dropped for the paperback edition). He included sections where characters acknowledge their existence in the book, scenes of pure fantasy, and various prefaces, footnotes, and addenda in which he comments on the text, or on anything that happens to cross his mind.

The book was an impressive tour de force, a critical hit, and a big bestseller, all of which may have been why it did nothing to slow, much less stop, the parade of memoirs. Even the doubters and haters had to admit defeat. Back in 1996, at the peak of the memoir backlash, the critic James Atlas put in his two cents on the deficiencies of the genre. "We live in a time when the very notion of privacy, of a zone beyond the reach of public probing, has become an alien concept," he lamented.

Nine years later, a memoir called *My Life in the Middle Ages: A Survivor's Tale* appeared in stores. Its author was James Atlas.

THE CRITICS WERE RIGHT about some long-term trends that contributed to the memoir boom: more narcissism overall, less concern for privacy, a strong interest in victimhood, and a therapeutic culture. As long ago as 1956, the critic V. S. Pritchett noted a "tremendous expansion in autobiographical writing" and ascribed it, in part, to the "dominant influence of psychological theory." The understanding that it's not only an acceptable but a good thing to lie on a couch in public, as it were, and disgorge personal stories has only grown since then. Carolyn See, author of the 1994 memoir *Dreaming: Hard Luck and Good Times in America*, shrewdly pointed to the growth of Alcoholics Anonymous and the recovery movement as another key forebear: "Those people in AA in the late 40's and early 50's can be said to have reinvented American narrative style. All the terrible, terrible things that had ever happened to them just made for a great pitch."

These trends came together in the empathetic 1990s, the era of Bill Clinton's feel for pain, of Oprah Winfrey's furrowed brow and concerned nod. Oprah and her many fellow TV and radio talkers were crucial not merely in setting the mood but also in selling the units. In the publishing environment of the time, promotion was seen as the key to commercial success; the key to promotion was getting on talk shows; and the best way to get on a talk show was with a dramatic or unusual personal story. Once a novelist answered the "Is it autobiographical?" question, the only thing left to discuss was No. 2 pencils versus Microsoft Word. But Elizabeth Wurtzel could talk about how Prozac helped her manic depression, and Mikal Gilmore could talk about what it was like to be Gary Gilmore's brother! Julie Grau, the editor of *Girl, Interrupted*, explained to *Vanity Fair* in 1997 why memoir trumped fiction in the marketplace: "You can send the 'I' out on tour."

There were other factors as well. Dictating his own memoirs, *At Random*, in the late 1960s, Bennett Cerf, the cofounder of Random House, commented that when he started in the publishing business, in the 1920s, "fiction outsold nonfiction four-to-one. Now that ratio is absolutely reversed, and nonfiction outsells fiction four-to-one." The reversal reflects the craving we have developed for the literal. Fiction has become a bit like painting in the age of photography—a novelty item that has its place in the Booker Prize/Whitney Museum high culture and in the genre-fiction/black-velvet-Elvis low but is oddly absent in the middle range. Certainly, when it comes to proving points and making cases, fiction's day is done. Referring to her novel *Uncle Tom's Cabin*, Abraham Lincoln called Harriet Beecher Stowe "the little lady who started this Great War." But that was then. The most recent novels to have had a social impact, or that were even paid attention to in any national debate, were the muckraking works of Frank Norris and Upton Sinclair in the first decade of the twentieth century. Today, for a didactic text to be taken seriously or even attended to, it requires a certification of documentary truth.*

On the other hand, the memoir—defined and determined by its

---

*The last painting to have had a significant effect on public opinion may have been Norman Rockwell's 1964 *The Problem We All Live With*, a depiction (photographic in style) of a little black girl on her way to integrate a New Orleans school, surrounded by a quartet of safety officers.

subjectivity—dovetailed with a doubt or denial of "objective truth" that gathered force throughout the twentieth century. In the 1980s, an unfamiliar pronoun began to appear in works of academic philosophy, history, literary criticism, anthropology, and other fields: "I." An especially popular formulation was "I want to argue that," introducing a clause that, twenty years earlier, would have been the entire sentence. (A 2009 search on "Google Scholar" for the phrase "I want to argue that" turned up 9,060 hits.) The natural culmination of this trend was for scholars to eschew scholarship in favor of actual memoirs; and sure enough, this was done in the 1980s and 1990s by professors Frank Lentricchia, Jane Tomkins, Cathy Davidson, Alice Kaplan, Alvin Kernan, Paul Fussell, and Henry Louis Gates, Jr., among others.

Memoir is to fiction as photography is to painting, also, in being easier to do fairly well. Only a master can create a convincing and compelling fictional world. Anyone with a moderate level of discipline, insight, intelligence, and editorial skill—plus a more than moderately interesting life—can write a decent memoir. The classroom cliché "Write about what you know" is a cliché for a reason: intimate familiarity with the material is the most important factor leading to strong prose. Thus while only a handful of recent memoirs, such as *This Boy's Life* and *The Liars' Club*, can take their place with literature of the first order, the boom has spawned hundreds—if not thousands—of worthwhile books. Many have shed light on an impressive variety of social, ethnic, medical, psychological, regional, and personal situations. And many are just plain good. The memoir boom, for all its sins, has been a net plus for the cause of writing. Under its auspices, voices and stories have emerged that, otherwise, would have been dull impersonal nonfiction tomes or forgettable autobiographical novels, or wouldn't have been expressed at all.

The ascendance of memoir as a boffo category made it easy for publishers to spot prospective authors; the equation was: Compelling personal story equals potentially lucrative memoir. Some of these deals led to crummy and/or self-indulgent books. But a lot of them led to memorable and creditable ones, and that seems the important thing. In the early 1990s, a biracial man from Hawaii was elected the first African-American editor of the *Harvard Law Review*. Naturally, a publishing house signed him up to write his memoirs, and *Dreams from My Father* was published in 1995. It didn't turn up on the *Times* bestseller list until 2004, a few weeks after its author, Barack Obama, delivered the keynote speech at the Democratic National Convention.

Another biracial man, a journalist and musician named James McBride, confirmed only as an adult that his mother, who had always claimed she was "light-skinned," was in fact Jewish and white, and had passed for black for years. In 1996, McBride published the story as a memoir, *The Color of Water*. The book, like many other memoirs, confirmed the wisdom of the writing-class bromide "Write about what you know." It is compelling and authoritative and close-to-the-bone honest. In another era, the story would have been told in a magazine article, or a not especially believable first novel. Thanks to the memoir boom, it is a fine book.

Chapter II

TRUTH AND CONSEQUENCES

SWIFTLY AND DRAMATICALLY, the memoir had opened up: authorship had been democratized, subject matter had been set free, expectations had been established for a high level of frankness. Along with the changes came a new set of expectations for the form. More than at any time since the heyday of the slave narrative, an autobiography was expected to be a testament, containing an account that shined a light on suffering, exposed wrongdoing, or, more broadly, advanced a cause. A tale of one's own experience—whether surviving a historical conflagration, enduring racial discrimination, or confronting personal or family demons—was the coin of the realm.

In any society where a particular currency has high value and is fairly easily fashioned, counterfeiters will quickly and inevitably emerge. And so it has been with memoir. Make no mistake: for anyone with a minimal conscience, plus reasonable imagination and literary and research skills, writing an autobiography that's substantially or even totally fake is elementary. Once the writing is complete, given an only slightly higher level of cunning and guile, the marketing of such a work is easier still. Absent any cause for suspicion, humans by nature are trustful. Perceptive people and confidence men have always known this; science confirms it. A recent review of more than one hundred psychological studies found that when subjects are presented with examples of lying and truth-telling, they could identify the liars only 54 percent of the time—nearly the results you would get by flipping a coin. That credulousness is on the whole a good thing, probably, but it leaves us vulnerable.

Newspapers and some magazines have internal mechanisms that guard against all but the craftiest fabricators (and even they are usually found out eventually). For newspapers, the guard is job security: the industry operates on an understanding that if reporters are found to be making stuff up, they will be fired. In the 1920s and 1930s, *Time* and *The New Yorker* introduced "fact-checking": a process in which staff members hired for that purpose attempt to verify every statement in every article to be published. Subsequently, most major magazines have adopted the practice, more or less. Verification is a much more casual matter in book publishing. Editors and others in the industry see themselves as working in the interest of the author and his or her story; it is the author's name that goes on the book, the author who goes on tour to promote it, and the author who is judged in reviews. Today, authors customarily sign an agreement certifying that the work is their own, that it is not libelous, and more and more commonly, that it is true. Well, not exactly "true." The author of a nonfiction work is usually required to affirm something to the effect that (the quotations are from actual recent contracts) (a) "all statements in the Work asserted as facts are true or based on reasonable research for accuracy," or (b) "all statements asserted as facts are based on the Author's careful investigation and research for accuracy." Memoirists, of course, *remember*; no one truly expects them to engage in "careful investigation and research." These clauses are about nothing other than publishers' protecting themselves in anticipation of defamation lawsuits, which often hinge on negligence in gathering and checking facts.

In the editing process, egregiously dubious assertions may raise suspicions that the author is a liar and/or a wingnut; defamatory statements about identifiable individuals send up libel red flags and bring in the lawyers; and easily lookupable facts, like the spelling of "Medvedev" or the number of feet in a mile, are checked by a copy editor, usually freelance. That's about it. Publishers have not, nor will they ever, put in a more systematic mechanism, because this would cost a lot of money, money they have no economic, legal, or institutional motivation to spend.

Whatever amount of skepticism may greet a manuscript at the outset, it dissolves to near nothing if it comes to be perceived as a potential big or even healthy seller. At that point the project is overwhelmed by a posse of cheerleaders: editors, publicists, a sales force, booksellers, and readers who enthusiastically want a given good story to be a true story. Reviewers don't have a dog in the fight, but in the absence of any internal discrepancies or strong fishy odors, they have no reason to doubt a memoir's veracity; nor is it seen as part of their job to investigate it.

The pendulum swings once a memoir experiences success in the marketplace. The more it sells, the more parties emerge with an interest in exposing inaccuracies: journalists; bloggers; injured parties; political, personal, or business enemies or rivals. The higher the stakes—if the book's "facts" are in support of charged political issues (as with slave narratives or Holocaust memoirs), if it makes unlikely or melodramatic representations (as with Joan Lowell or James Frey), if it hurls slurs at some

BEN YAGODA

recognizable individuals, or if it starts *really* selling (ditto)—the quicker the faker will be outed. To the extent a fake book is innocuous and/or obscure, it may go unchallenged forever.

Whenever a scandal erupts, one particular response is guaranteed to be uttered. It is a rhetorical question to this effect: "It's such a good story—why didn't he [or she] just call it fiction?" A short answer is that James Frey tried just that with *A Million Little Pieces* and found no buyers until he changed the label to memoir. A longer answer was well expressed by a Holocaust survivor named Ruth Klüger, who observed that *Fragments* seemed like a modern masterpiece when it was presented, on its 1995 publication, as a memoir by a Holocaust survivor named Binjamin Wilkomirski, but suddenly became mediocre when it later emerged that Wilkomirski was in fact a Swiss Gentile named Bruno Grosjean and the book a complete fabrication. "A passage is shocking perhaps precisely because of its naïve directness when read as the expression of naïve suffering; but when it is revealed as a lie, as a presentation of invented suffering, it deteriorates to kitsch," Klüger wrote. "It is indeed a hallmark of kitsch that it is plausible, all too plausible, and that one rejects it only if one recognizes its pseudoplausibility. . . . However valid it may be that much of this may have happened to other children, with the falling away of the authentic autobiographical aspect and without the guarantee of a living first-person narrator identical with the author, it merely becomes a dramatization that offers no illumination."

The past four decades will probably be remembered as the golden age of autobiographical fraud. There has been about a scandal a year, and sometimes more than that. Looking at these books in retrospect, with the knowledge that they are fakes, one is continually reminded of Ruth Klüger's perception: as soon as it's exposed as fraudulent, a text that had seemed powerful and original is reduced to schlock.

The run kicked off with a doozy. In 1969, Clifford Irving, a novelist who had always gotten respectful reviews but mediocre sales, put out his first nonfiction book, *Fake!*, which was, in the words of the subtitle, "The Story of Elmyr De Hory, the Greatest Art Forger of Our Time." It did somewhat better commercially than his novels and got Irving to thinking about *literary* forgery. With a buddy, Richard Suskind, he concocted a plot to produce an authorized biography of the reclusive billionaire Howard Hughes. Over time the conspirators became so enthusiastic about the venture that they changed the form to straight autobiography, produced a manuscript, and received an advance of $750,000.

This was an act of rather breathtaking chutzpah. De Hory and other forgers of all kinds had always specialized in faking the work of dead people, who were not around to dispute them. Hughes may have been cuckoo but he was very much alive. Irving presumably was counting on the millionaire's reclusiveness being so distended as to deter him from publicly objecting to this theft of his name and life. The other thing Irving had going for him, as he knew, was people's willingness to be fooled in the absence of any obvious cause for suspicion. He and Suskind did an assiduous job of research, and of forging supposedly handwritten correspondence from Hughes. When doubts first began to be raised, Irving's publisher, McGraw-Hill, had the letters examined by handwriting experts Osborn Associates, who were quoted in *Time* magazine as saying: "The evidence that all of the writing submitted was done by the one individual is, in our opinion, irresistible, unanswerable and overwhelming." But inevitably, Howard Hughes himself emerged, via a conference telephone call with reporters, to assert that not only was the manuscript a fake, he had never met or even corresponded with Clifford Irving. Irving ultimately served seventeen months in federal prison—making him the only autobiographical faker, as far as I have been able to determine, to do time for the offense. After his release, he resumed his writing career, which continues. In 1976 he teamed with Suskind on a memoir of the Hughes episode, *Project Octavio*. In 2006, to coincide with the release of a film about the incident, starring Richard Gere as Irving, *Project Octavio* was rereleased under the same title as the film: *The Hoax*. Suskind had died some years earlier, and apparently feeling that it violated no standards of law, honesty, or decency to leave his collaborator's name off the cover, the title page, and the copyright notice, Irving did just that. The film's producers had hired him as a technical adviser, but after reading the final script, he reports on his website, he asked that his name be removed from the project. He felt that the movie took too many liberties with the truth.

It doesn't take a genius to see that it would be easier to get away with faking the words of an unnamed fifteen-year-old girl than those of a world-famous tycoon. The 1971 *Go Ask Alice*, by "Anonymous," ostensibly the journal of a teenager whose accidental sip of LSD-laced punch leads her on the road to addiction and ultimately death by drug overdose, proved the point. In the original edition, a note from "The Editors" states: "*Go Ask Alice* is based on the actual diary of a fifteen-year-old drug user. . . . Names, dates, places and certain events have been changed in accordance with the wishes of those concerned." The book created a sensation among adolescents in the early 1970s and has been continuously in print since then, with, according to the publisher, more than five million copies sold; the American Library Association ranked it number 23 on the list of the most "challenged books" of the decade 1990–2000. People have challenged it because it graphically describes drug use and sex, not because it is a fake. But a fake it is.

This fact emerged slowly, and has still not been completely absorbed into the general consciousness. In a 1979 interview in *School Library Journal*, a Mormon youth counselor named Beatrice Sparks stated that *Go Ask Alice* had been based on the diary of one of her clients, and that she had compiled the book by combining it with some experiences of other teens she had worked with. She also said that she could not produce the original diary: she had destroyed part of it and the rest was locked away in the publisher's vault. That portion has never been produced, and in any case, Sparks (who is the sole copyright holder for *Go Ask Alice*, according to the U.S. Copyright Office) didn't persist in this absurd claim. In future editions, the following message was added to the copyright page: "This book is a work of fiction. Any references to historical events, real people, or real locales are used fictitiously. Other names, characters, places, and incidents are the product of the author's imagination, and any resemblance to actual events or locales or persons, living or dead, is entirely coincidental." But this is small print; the editors' note about "the actual diary of a fifteen-year-old drug user" is still featured—more prominently—and Sparks's name does not appear anywhere. Thus, to this day, the presentation of the book suggests it is true. "Justine," the author of one of the more recent of the more than 1,250 comments about *Go Ask Alice* posted at amazon.com, writes:

> this is the diary of an anonymous girl and her struggle with drugs and addiction. as chance would have it i read it sometime after i watched that movie thirteen, which is supposedly also true, and that was kind of similar so i guess the book had less of an impact on me than it would have if i'd read it without any preparation. it was still a good read though. as you would expect from reading a diary, it did a good job making the story realistic, though i suppose knowing this is based on an actual diary helped with that, though how much of this diary is fact is up for debate . . .

The reason Sparks talked to *School Library Journal* in 1979 was to publicize *Jay's Journal*, her second book, which was described as having been "edited" by her and which was published by Times Books, then a division of The New York Times Company. It was supposedly the diary of a boy who committed suicide after becoming involved with satanic practices and the occult. In this case there *was* an actual diary, given to Sparks by the mother of Alden Barrett, a boy who had indeed killed himself. However, according to Ben Dieterle, a Utah journalist who interviewed Alden's mother twenty-five years after the book's publication, Mrs. Barrett maintained that Sparks invented the majority of the text, including the entire occult angle. Dieterle also talked to Alden's brother, who calculated that of the 212 entries in *Jay's Journal*, only twenty-one—less than 10 percent—came directly from Alden's diary. Sparks told Dieterle that she got the occult material from friends of Alden's whom she had interviewed; she could not name any of them and the reporter could find no evidence of any satanic activity in Alden's past. Sparks bids fair to be the Daniel Defoe of young adult literature. She has gone on to produce many other cautionary diaries, including *Treacherous Love: The Diary of an Anonymous Teenager*; *Almost Lost: The True Story of an Anonymous Teenager's Life on the Streets*; *Annie's Baby: The Diary of Anonymous, a Pregnant Teenager*; and *It Happened to Nancy: By an Anonymous Teenager*. These works are all pointedly ambiguous on the question of authenticity. They are presented as the words of, you got it, anonymous teenagers as "Edited by Beatrice Sparks, Ph.D." Yet they are shelved in the Young Adult fiction section of bookstores and catalogued as fiction in the Library of Congress.

Sparks has a sharp eye for the main chance, so it is no surprise that she should have jumped on the Satan angle back in 1979. Something was in the air. The following year saw the publication of a memoir titled *Michelle Remembers*, jointly authored by a Canadian woman named Michelle Smith and her psychiatrist (and later husband), Lawrence Pazder. The book recounts that Smith went to see Pazder for treatment of depression and, while under hypnosis (to quote psychologist Elizabeth Loftus), "she began to have 'memories' of being imprisoned at age five by her mother and a fiendish assemblage of satanists. Michelle remembered bloody rituals led by a man called 'Malachi,' a sadistic nurse dressed in black, and dozens of chanting and dancing adults who tore live kittens apart with their teeth, cut fetuses in half and then rubbed the dismembered bodies on her stomach, penetrated her with a crucifix, and then forced her to urinate and defecate on the Bible." The book was composed of that and many more such incidents, all recalled by Smith in the course of her therapy. Same old same old, you might think: but at the time, this was new ground, and *Michelle Remembers* made headlines, was uncritically featured in *People* magazine and on ABC's *20/20*, sold many copies, and spawned such imitators as Eileen Franklin's *Sins of the Father*, Betsy Peterson's *Dancing with Daddy*, and Lauren Stratford's *Satan's Underground: The Extraordinary Story of One Woman's Escape*.

It was nonsense, of course. In the early 1990s, authors Debbie Nathan and Michael Snedeker investigated the claims made in *Michelle Remembers*. They found no corroboration. On the contrary, they interviewed neighbors of the family, who reported they witnessed nothing remarkable during the period described by Smith and Pazder. They interviewed a former teacher of Michelle's, who recalled that, during the time she was supposedly locked in a basement for months, she was attending first grade and was even photographed for the yearbook. And they combed local newspapers, which "gave detailed coverage to even the most minor mishaps," and found no reference to a major car accident described in the book. Unfortunately, this came too late to prevent the damage done by *Michelle Remembers*, which was taken seriously for years in academic, medical, and legal circles. In 1981, Lawrence Pazder presented a paper at the annual meeting of the American Psychiatric Association, where he coined the term "ritual abuse." In 1984, he and Michelle Smith went to Los Angeles to meet with parents whose children attended the McMartin Pre-school, staff members of which had been accused of child abuse. According to Los Angeles County District Attorney's Office notes seen and summarized by Nathan and Snedeker, Pazder presented "a theory that the children had been molested as part of an international satanic cult conspiracy. Pazder held that anyone could be involved in this plot, including teachers, doctors, movie stars, merchants, even—as some parents came to believe—members of the Anaheim Angels baseball team." The McMartin investigation and subsequent trial, which ended in 1990 with no convictions, represented a low point in the history of American law and journalism but at least did much to end the satanic-abuse panic.

Vying with that panic in the 1980s tall-tales sweepstakes was alien abduction. Its memoirist emerged in 1987 with the publication of Whitley Strieber's *Communion*. Strieber was a journeyman thriller writer who, as he recounted in the book, was abducted from his cabin in upstate New York by nonhuman beings. The book included a forensic apparatus reminiscent of the affidavits and facsimile signatures on slave narratives: a transcript of a lie-detector session Strieber undertook and a statement by a psychiatrist who hypnotized him, both of which suggested that he actually believed the malarkey he was committing to paper. A twentieth-anniversary edition of *Communion* was recently published; one can find it in the Metaphysical Speculation section at Borders.

It is notoriously difficult to prove a negative. Consequently, the controversy over a discredited memoir often ends in a hung jury: evidence and facts suggesting guilt, but no conclusive evidence and therefore no conviction. Such is the case with "Julia," a chapter in Lillian Hellman's *Pentimento: A Book of Portraits* (1973) that was the basis for the 1977 film with Jane Fonda and Vanessa Redgrave. Hellman described Julia (not, of course, her real name) as a wealthy American who attended Oxford University, then went to a medical school in Vienna, became a patient-pupil of Freud and a socialist, and, as an underground fighter against the Nazis, got involved in various escapades with her great friend Hellman. According to the book, she died in May 1938, apparently after having been tortured by the Nazis. In 1981, a woman named Muriel Gardiner published her memoirs. She describes herself as being a wealthy American who attended Oxford University, then went to a medical school in Vienna and became a patient-pupil of Freud, a socialist, and an underground fighter against the Nazis. Unlike Julia, Gardiner did not die, but rather sailed to the United States in 1939 and lived a happy life. Also unlike Julia, she never met Lillian Hellman—although she and Hellman did have a mutual close friend and attorney. No evidence or indication of a non-Gardiner "Julia" has ever emerged; Hellman, until her death in 1984, continued to insist that she existed.

Then there was Lorenzo Carcaterra's 1995 *Sleepers*, ostensibly a memoir about four friends from New York's Hell's Kitchen neighborhood and their violent exploits. Even before the book was published, journalists raised doubts about its assertions, notably the account of two of the friends' trial for murder. *The New York Times* reported, "The Manhattan District Attorney's office said that the circumstances of the trial, as reported in the book, were unbelievable and, further, that no one in the office remembered a case even vaguely like the one described by Mr. Carcaterra." Speaking to a reporter for *Time*, Carcaterra explained why no one had been able to verify a single occurrence represented in the book: "You have to change dates, names, places, people. The way they looked; you have to make them look a different way. If it happened here, you have to make it happen there. . . . The what, where and when these things happened were not as important to me as the fact that they did happen." Thus, a stalemate, but one in which Carcaterra seemed to have the last laugh. *Sleepers* was sold to Hollywood for a reported $2.1 million; Barry Levinson directed the film, which starred Kevin Bacon and Robert De Niro. And the book spent a total of forty-seven weeks on the *Times* nonfiction bestseller list (albeit with a blurb beginning "The true story, the narrator claims, of four boys . . ."). Still in print, the book is classified as nonfiction by amazon.com and in the Library of Congress, which catalogues it under the subject heading "Gangs—New York (State)—New York—Case studies."

An even odder case was that of a book called *A Rock and a Hard Place: One Boy's Triumphant Story*, which appeared in 1993 and was credited to Anthony Godby Johnson and included a foreword by poet and memoirist Paul Monette and an afterword by Fred "Mister" Rogers. "Anthony," supposedly a fifteen-year-old, describes in great detail the beatings and sexual abuse he experienced at the hands of his parents and their friends. At the age of eleven, he runs away and is eventually adopted by a kind couple. But then he discovers that he has AIDS. As with *Sleepers*, doubts were raised about the book at its initial publication, and none of its assertions could be verified. The difference is that Lorenzo Carcaterra exists. Monette, Rogers, the author Armistead Maupin (who later wrote a novel based on the affair), the editor of the book, and dozens of other people developed intimate telephone relationships with someone they thought was "Anthony" but in fact appears to have been the woman who supposedly was his adoptive mother and who is probably the true author of *A Rock and a Hard Place*. No one but this woman has ever reported seeing "Anthony" in the flesh. But she continues to insist he is real and to threaten legal action against anyone who claims otherwise—most recently in 2006, when ABC's *20/20* produced yet another report on the story.

Except for Clifford Irving, Lillian Hellman, and Whitley Strieber (who emerged from his encounter unscathed), the main characters in the

fake memoirs described above have one thing in common: they are victims. One particular type of victim appears in a clear plurality of modern
fake memoirs: a member of an oppressed minority group. Such masquer-
ades of course have had a long tradition, as seen in Long Lance, James
Beckwourth, and others, but as identity politics and memoir both hit their
stride in the late twentieth century, they exploded. As the recent cases of
"Nasdijj," Mischa Defonseca, "Margaret B. Jones," and Herman Rosenblat suggest, the trend shows no sign of slowing down.

The first entry in the recent run was *The Education of Little Tree*, published in 1976 as (in the words of *Kirkus Reviews*) "a Cherokee boyhood
of the 1930s remembered in generous, loving detail." The author, Forrest
Carter, describes how, after his widowed mother died, he was sent to live
with his Cherokee grandparents in the hills of Oklahoma and learned
much about nature, people, and the world. In fact "Forrest Carter" was an
invention of the author, who was born Asa Carter and had been a notorious Alabama segregationist who broke with George Wallace because Wallace had supposedly abandoned the principles of white supremacy. The
masquerade had been exposed in a 1976 *New York Times* article, published
before the book came out; it further suggested that Carter had adopted the
pen name "Forrest" in honor of Nathan Bedford Forrest, the first grand
wizard of the Ku Klux Klan. But no one paid attention. Published in
paperback by the University of New Mexico Press in 1985, the book
became first a cult favorite, and then an improbable commercial success.
In 1991, reporting *Little Tree*'s selection by the American Booksellers
Association as best book of the year, the *Times* referred to it as "an autobiographical account of the author's boyhood." The award propelled it to
the *Times* paperback nonfiction bestseller list, where it reached the number-
one spot and spent nineteen weeks. In October, a history professor at
work on a biography of George Wallace wrote an op-ed column in the

Times that provided further details of Carter's racist past and discredited the book for good. But it kept right on selling. Reclassified as fiction, the book stayed on the bestseller list for another eleven weeks.

Looking at *The Education of Little Tree* today, one can't help thinking, How could anyone have been fooled? Consider a passage that takes place soon after Little Tree comes to live with his grandparents:

> It had broke day and I hadn't even noticed. Me and Granpa moved down to the creek bank clearing and et our sour biscuits and meat. The dogs was baying back around and coming along the ridge in front of us. The sun topped the mountain, sparkling the trees across the street and brought out brush wrens and a red cardinal. Granpa slid his knife under the bark of a cedar tree and made a dipper by twisting one end of the bark. We dipped water from the creek, cold, where you could see the pebbles on the bottom. The water had a cedary taste that made me hungrier, but we had et all the biscuits.

Remember—these were supposedly not the words of a child but of the grown-up author Forrest Carter, who had previously published a novel called *Gone to Texas* (made into the Clint Eastwood film *The Outlaw Josey Wales*). So he is saying "It had broke day" and remarking that he "et"? Unlikely. As fiction, the book is a passable and occasionally effective Twain/Hemingway pastiche. As autobiography, it is ludicrous.

For the first time in history, it seemed, being a member of a put-upon minority had value in the marketplace of ideas, and in the commercial marketplace as well. It followed that ethnic impersonation became an alluring prospect. In 1983, Simon & Schuster published *Famous All Over Town*, a first-person novel about Mexican-American life in the Los Angeles barrio. The author, Danny Santiago, was described on the dust jacket as a first novelist who had grown up in Los Angeles; there was no photograph. The novel got excellent reviews, most of which assumed it was thinly veiled autobiography; David Quammen, writing in *The New York Times Book Review*, called the book a "minor classic." It received the $5,000 Rosenthal Foundation Award for fiction, which is given annually to "a young novelist for a book published during the previous year, which, though not necessarily a commercial success, is a considerable literary achievement," and which previously had gone to John Updike, Bernard Malamud, Thomas Pynchon, and Joyce Carol Oates at early stages in their careers. Santiago did not appear at the ceremony to collect his award, and it later emerged that his editor, Bob Bender, had never met with him or even spoken to him by phone. "We figured there was something strange going on, having to write him in care of a post office box and his saying he did not have a telephone," Bender told the *Times*. "But we figured he was probably in prison and didn't want anybody to know." Santiago wasn't in prison. He wasn't a young novelist. He wasn't even Danny Santiago. In reality, *Famous All Over Town* was the work of Daniel James, a seventy-three-year-old onetime blacklisted screenwriter who grew up in Kansas City and graduated from Yale in 1933. He based the novel on his twenty years as a volunteer worker in the Eastside neighborhood depicted in the book. He told the *Times*—which revealed that Santiago was James in 1984—that he wrote under a pen name because, after the enforced anonymity of the blacklist years, he had lost confidence in his own voice. He didn't mention the presumed difficulty of marketing a novel about the Chicano experience written by a white septuagenarian from Kansas City.

For reasons probably having to do with its rich and troubled racial mix, Australia has proven particularly susceptible to all manner of ethnic fraud. Consider:

257

- In the 1980s, B. Wongar, the supposedly Aboriginal author of the novels *Walg* and *Karan*, turned out to be a Serbian immigrant named Sreten Božić.

- In 1992, an autobiographical novel by an Aborigine, Wanda Koolmatrie, won a $5,000 award for the best first novel by an Australian. When Koolmatrie offered the publishers a sequel, they insisted on meeting her for the first time. That demand induced Leon Carman, a forty-seven-year-old white former cabdriver from Sydney, to confess that he was Wanda Koolmatrie.

- In 1995, *The Hand That Signed the Paper*, a novel set in World War II Ukraine, won the prestigious Miles Franklin Award; the citation praised the book for bringing to light "a hitherto unspeakable portion of the Australian migrant experience." The author was Helen Demidenko, who presented herself as the daughter of a poor Irish mother and an illiterate Ukrainian taxi driver on whose family's experiences she said she had based the book. In truth, the author was the daughter of prosperous parents who had emigrated from Great Britain.

- In 1997, an elderly white artist named Elizabeth Durack revealed that for years she had been creating paintings attributed to "Eddie Burrup," who had been presented as an ex-convict born in Western Australia's Pibara region.

Forbidden Love, a hugely popular 2003 Australian memoir by a woman named Norma Khouri, told of how, when she was living in her native Jordan, her best friend, a Muslim, fell in love with a Christian soldier and then was stabbed to death by her own father. In 2004, a Sydney journalist discovered that Khouri had indeed been born in Jordan, but had immigrated to the

United States at the age of three, and had stayed there until moving to Australia in 1999. Her memoir, in other words, was fiction.

The case of Rigoberta Menchú played out for higher stakes. Menchú is a Guatemalan Indian activist whose father, mother, and two brothers all died at the hands of government security forces between 1979 and 1983. Her autobiography, *I, Rigoberta Menchú,* was published in 1983 and rapidly became a canonical text among students and scholars of multiculturalism, eventually selling more than 150,000 copies. In 1992, Menchú was awarded the Nobel Peace Prize. But in 1998, a Middlebury College anthropologist named David Stoll published a book, based on several years of research and more than one hundred interviews, which documented many inaccuracies in Menchú's account. A *New York Times* reporter, Larry Rohter, undertook an investigation of his own and confirmed Stoll's allegations, including (he wrote) that "a younger brother whom Ms. Menchú says she saw die of starvation never existed, while a second, whose suffering she says she and her parents were forced to watch as he was being burned alive by army troops, was killed in entirely different circumstances when the family was not present." Stoll has always acknowledged that incidents similar to those described by Menchú did indeed happen to other Guatemalans, and has never accused her of lying. "That would be to dismiss her morally, and that is definitely not my view," he told the *Times.* "You can understand and defend her narrative strategy, of folding others' experience into her own, making herself into a kind of all-purpose Maya." Menchú herself has for the most part declined to address the specific allegations of inaccuracy, citing the "larger truth" of killings and atrocities directed at her family and the Guatemalan people. She has had many defenders in academia, some of whom have placed her book (which was based on tape-recorded interviews with a Venezuelan-born sociologist) in the Latin American tradition of *testimonio,* which dates from the 1970s and has been described by John Beverley, a scholar of the form, as a first-person narrative that "may include, but is not subsumed under, any of the following textual categories, some of which are conventionally considered literature, others not: autobiography, autobiographical novel, oral history, memoir, confession, diary, interview, eyewitness report, life history, *novela-testimonio*, nonfiction novel, or 'factographic literature.'" That seems reasonable. Yet in a legal setting, testimony is valuable only insofar as it is true: and true on the level of small details, not merely large patterns. The world of public opinion is not a courtroom, but in that world as well, it can't be good for your cause when large parts of what you say are shown never to have happened. And certainly Menchú has not been helped by some of her defenders, such as a Wellesley College professor of Spanish who was quoted in *The Chronicle of Higher Education* as saying, "I think that Rigoberta Menchú has been used by the right to negate the very important space that multiculturalism is providing in academia. Whether her book is true or not, I don't care."

Autobiographical impersonation insinuated its way into perhaps the most important, or at least highly charged, rhetorical space of the twentieth century in the person of Jerzy Kosinski, a Jewish native of Poland, born in 1933, who was able to survive World War II because his family assumed false identities and were sheltered in Polish villages. He emigrated to the United States in 1957, embarked on a career as a writer, and little by little created a new past for himself: he told friends and acquaintances that during the war, he had survived on his own, wandering in the Polish countryside and encountering all manner of human behavior, most of it brutal. (Some of these episodes were borrowed from the actual childhood experiences of Kosinski's friend Roman Polanski.) One such listener was an editor with the Houghton Mifflin publishing house, which in 1965 brought out Kosinski's narrative recounting the tales. The book—*The*

Painted Bird—was labeled as fiction, in keeping with the custom of the time, but the editor assumed it was based largely on Kosinski's own life, and he pointedly did nothing to disabuse her of this notion. None other than Elie Wiesel was assigned to review the book for *The New York Times Book Review*; he, too, had thought the book was pure fiction, but Kosinski informed him it was autobiography. At that point, Wiesel later told Kosinski's biographer James Park Sloan, "I tore up my review and wrote one a thousand times better." In that review he wrote, "It is as a chronicle that *The Painted Bird* . . . achieves its unusual power."

Perhaps the saddest case, for both personal and political reasons, is that of the book published in Switzerland in 1995 under the title *Fragments: Memories of a Wartime Childhood 1939–1948.* The author, a Swiss clarinet maker named Binjamin Wilkomirski, begins:

I have no mother tongue, nor a father tongue either. My language has its roots in the Yiddish of my eldest brother, Mordechai, overlaid with the Babel-babble of an assortment of children's barracks in the Nazis' death camps in Poland. . . . At some point during this time, speech left me altogether and it was a long time before I found it again.

My early childhood memories are planted, first and foremost, in exact snapshots of my photographic memory and in the feelings imprinted in them, and the physical sensations. Then comes memory of being able to hear, and things I heard, then things I thought, and last of all, memory of things I said. . . .

My earliest memories are a rubble field of isolated images and events. Shards of memory with hard knife-sharp edges, which still cut flesh if touched today. Mostly a chaotic jumble, with very little chronological fit; shards that keep surfacing against the orderly grain of grown-up life and escaping the laws of logic.

If I'm going to write about it, I have to give up on the ordering logic of grown-ups; it would only distort what happened.

Consequently, the book is composed of a series of impressionistic scenes and images, some more fragmentary than others. On the third page, Wilkomirski describes his earliest specific memory: how, in Riga, Latvia, a man—maybe his father—was crushed by uniformed soldiers against the wall of a house. Binjamin and his brothers flee and hide out in a farmhouse in Poland. Then he is arrested and brought to two separate Nazi concentration camps, in one of which he encounters his dying mother for the last time. After the war, he is brought to an orphanage in Kraków and, finally, to Switzerland, where he is encouraged by foster parents to forget everything. But, decades later, after watching a documentary film about concentration camps, he is finally able to begin reconstructing his fragmented past.

The book was translated into nine languages (including English, in 1996) to general praise, and it won three major awards: the National Jewish Book Award in the United States, the Prix Mémoire de la Shoah in France, and the *Jewish Quarterly* literary prize in Britain. Wilkomirski himself was interviewed and videotaped by Holocaust archives and, in some quarters at least, was accorded the same witness status as Anne Frank, Elie Wiesel, and Primo Levi. But then, in 1998, a Swiss journalist, Daniel Ganzfried, published an article claiming that "Wilkomirski" was actually Bruno Grosjean, not a Latvian Jew but rather the son of an unmarried (Gentile) woman from Biel, Switzerland. When the article appeared, Wilkomirski insisted he was indeed an authentic Holocaust survivor, maintaining that he had been secretly switched with Bruno Grosjean upon his arrival in Switzerland. In addition, he criticized his critics for treating the book as a "historical and factual report of an expert adult witness," whereas the true issue was of images "that remained in a child's memory, without the critical and ordering logic of adults." Wilkomirski/Grosjean stuck to his guns, even as subsequent researchers and journalists confirmed and expanded on Ganzfried's findings. It is hard to condemn him for that; it seems to be the case that he sincerely believes his story. As with the Menchú case, harder to defend are some who support him in the face of these revelations, including the woman who wrote to him: "No one has the rights and powers to steal your memories! You are who you remember that you are. I hope you will be strong and keep your memories like a precious treasure."

One of his supporters was a Holocaust survivor named Laura Grabowski, who said on several occasions that she remembered him from Birkenau and from a Kraków orphanage. The two were reunited in Los Angeles in 1998 and together gave a musical performance for the Children of Holocaust Survivors Group. But she turned out not to be the most sterling character witness. An investigation by Bob Passantino, Gretchen Passantino, and Jon Trott, writing in *Cornerstone* magazine, revealed that "Laura Grabowski" was not a Holocaust survivor at all. She was in fact "Lauren Stratford," the author of the satanic-ritual-abuse memoir *Satan's Underground*. A previous *Cornerstone* article had identified "Stratford" as a mentally troubled woman who had been born Laurel Willson, had fabricated elaborate tales of abuse, and had published them in a memoir.

A SCENE IN THE OPENING CHAPTER of *Breaking Clean*, a 2002 memoir by Judy Blunt about her unhappy life as a housewife on a Montana ranch, recounts how her father-in-law picked up her typewriter, brought it outside, and "killed it with a sledgehammer." After the father-in-law disputed the account, Blunt acknowledged to a *New York Times* reporter that the machine's death by sledgehammer was "symbolic." In reality, she said, "the old man pulled the plug on the typewriter and shouted and screamed, but the typewriter survived."

In his 1992 memoir, *Goat Brothers*, Larry Colton describes a minor-league road trip in which his baseball team walks into an Alabama diner. A waitress says that the black players won't be served, and manager Andy Seminick orders his players back on the bus. "As I rose from my stool," Colton writes, "I poured the water out of my plastic glass onto the counter, then fired a riser over the cash register, scoring a bull's-eye into the middle of a pyramid of plastic glasses, sending them flying in all directions. The waitress ducked." In an interview with *The Oregonian*, Colton maintained that he did indeed pour the water on the counter, but acknowledged that he never threw a baseball at the glasses. He manufactured the scene, he said, because he was thinking "cinematically. How would this look in the mind of the reader?"

It's easy to condemn the likes of Clifford Irving, Forrest Carter, and Laurel Willson/Lauren Stratford/Laura Grabowski. But the more difficult question has to do with typewriters that never were sledgehammered, fastballs that never were hurled. As memoirs have proliferated, such "small" deceptions or fabrications have repeatedly been found and publicized, then endlessly debated in op-ed essays, blog posts, bulletin-board exchanges, and scholarly articles. Almost always, one of two positions is taken:

1. *J'accuse.* It is shocking, shocking, that a book labeled as "memoir" and sold in the nonfiction section of the store should include untruths. Not only is that false advertising, but even one deception—whether deliberate or unwitting—undermines every other statement in the book. If newspapers and magazines can fact-check everything they publish, why can't

book publishers? (The people expressing this opinion are often journalists themselves.) All in all, this is just one more example of the epidemic of deceit in modern life.

2. Get a life, people. Human memory is flawed, and everybody knows it. And memoir, as a genre, is universally understood to offer subjective, impressionistic testimony. It doesn't pretend to offer *the* truth, just the *author's* truth. That is the value of memoir. The people who spend their time scouring these works for mistakes, and then proudly trumpet their findings, are hypocritical scandalmongers.

The flaws in position number 1 are a bit more readily apparent, as it presupposes an unrealistic and naive moral absolutism. A very small number of a life's components can even *be* fact-checked: place and date of birth, names of relatives, job titles, a few other details in the space-time continuum. Everything else is a matter of impression. Now, in order to create a book that anyone would possibly care to read, a writer must express these impressions in the form of narrative. It's ludicrous to expect any of this narrative to conform to what a hypothetical video camera would have recorded had it been on the scene at the time. Needless to say, video cameras or tape recorders are rarely on the scene as we live our lives, and as a result all memoirs that contain dialogue—which is to say all recent and current memoirs—are inaccurate. Think of the most recent conversation you had. Can you remember the exact words said by you and the other participant(s)? Of course not. And that conversation took place at most a couple of hours ago. Memoirs offer ostensibly verbatim exchanges from ten, twenty, thirty years before. The dialogue in a memoir is the author's best-faith representation of what the people who were present could have/would have/might have said. Every other description of a past event in a memoir works on the same principle. Hence if one accepts dialogue in a work of memoir or autobiography (and I haven't heard any calls for its abolition), then it's inconsistent to complain about the rest.*

But position number 2 has significant holes as well. Nonfactual assertions in a "nonfiction" book matter. People respond to such books precisely because they are supposed to be true; it may be the biggest part of their appeal. James Frey could not sell *A Million Little Pieces* as fiction. He took exactly the same book and changed the label to memoir and immediately it was snapped up. When Herman Rosenblat's Holocaust love story was exposed as a fairy tale, a publisher announced tentative plans to publish his book as a novel. Inevitably, the plans fizzled. It wasn't true, so his story no longer had allure. To the extent a memoir is shown to be false, it loses its identity, its authority, and its power.

But there are untruths and untruths. The key to a more nuanced view on this question is putting them into a hierarchy. Or maybe into a formula, as follows: inaccuracy is a problem to the extent a memoir depicts identifiable people, depicts those people in a negative light, (demonstrably) gets gists as well as details wrong, is poorly written, is self-serving, or otherwise wears its agenda on its sleeve. The more of these things it does and the more egregiously it does them, the bigger the problem is.

Consider these passages from two hugely successful recent books. On page 42 of *The Glass Castle: A Memoir* (2005), Jeannette Walls describes how, about thirty-five years before, on a drive between two Texas towns, her parents had a fight after her mother insisted she was ten months pregnant.

---

*I will share, in passing, my rule of thumb on this: The less dialogue a memoir contains, the better it is. In Frank McCourt's books, dialogue is given without quotation marks. I like the technique, which is also used by such novelists as Samuel Beckett and Cormac McCarthy; it emphasizes that these could not be and are not supposed to be the exact words said at the time. But it makes the books a little less readable, and I would not be surprised if McCourt had to fight for it with his publisher.

"I always carry children longer than most women," Mom said. "Lori was in my womb for fourteen months."

"Bullshit!" Dad said. "Unless Lori's part elephant."

"Don't you make fun of me or my children!" Mom yelled. "Some babies are premature. Mine were all postmature. That's why they're so smart. Their brains had longer to develop."

On page 45 of his 2002 *Running with Scissors: A Memoir*, Augusten Burroughs describes the first day he spent (at the age of twelve) at the house of his mother's psychiatrist, called Dr. Finch in the book. He and two of the doctor's daughters, Natalie and Vickie, are playing with an old electroshock therapy machine. Natalie says that she will pretend to be "paranoid schizophrenic."

She fluttered her eyelashes. "Just like Dottie Schmitt."

Vickie made a face. "Oh, God. She's disgusting. Did you know she's so filthy that Agnes [their mother] has to peel her bra off her?"

Natalie gasped. "Where did you hear that?"

"It's true, Agnes told me so herself."

"Who's Dottie?" I said.

"And then Agnes has to scrub under her tits with a sponge to get rid of all the scum." Vickie shrieked, grossing herself out.

Both authors were lying. The people in the passages did not say those exact words all those years ago. But the two memoirs are very different in the way they present their material. Reading Burroughs's book, I found myself continually shaking my head. He gave the psychiatrist's family (with whom he eventually moved in) fake names but not a fake town;

anybody who knew or knew of them could identify them. As soon as he showed them doing lunatic and/or unappealing things, then the standard of truth got higher. That became clear to Burroughs when members of the family sued him for defamation and reached an out-of-court settlement. Walls portrays her parents as lunatics, too. But despite the great success of her book, neither her mother nor any of her siblings, nor anyone else, raised public objections to her characterizations. (Her father had died long before she started writing.) That is in part because she is a better writer and a more sympathetic and insightful observer of human beings than Burroughs. Her dialogue is relatively sparing and it rings true; his is overused (well over half the book's words are between quotation marks) and it often does not. His characters are cartoons, sometimes funny and sometimes scary but never flesh-and-blood. Walls's characters are funny and scary, too, but also poignant and on some level mysterious: real people.

Memoirs have all kinds of agendas. Some are narrow (settling scores) and some large (glorifying God); some have to do with craft (telling a good story), some with commerce (selling a lot of copies), and some with politics (bringing about the end of slavery). When an action or quote or detail in a memoir is an obvious servant to its agenda, the standard of truth rises again, along with the reader's eyebrows. And if the "fact" turns out to be false, the book is deservedly discredited. Judy Blunt felt her family stifled her artistic ambitions and she expressed that in her memoir. Fair enough. But when she made up the part about the sledgehammer, she ran the risk of squandering her credibility and authority.

A couple of months before *A Million Little Pieces* was published, James Frey gave an interview to *The New York Observer*. Talking about some of his fellow authors, he said, "I don't give a fuck what Jonathan Safran whatever-his-name does or what David Foster Wallace does. I don't give a fuck what any of those people do. I don't hang out with them, I'm not friends with them, I'm not part of the literati." Asked about Dave Eggers and *A Heartbreaking Work of Staggering Genius*, he said, "A book that I thought was mediocre was being hailed as the best book written by the best writer of my generation. Fuck that. And fuck him and fuck anybody who says that." He said his wife called him a savage "because I eat with my hands. Because my best friends are my dogs. And I like pit bulls. And N.W.A. And I love boxing. Writers aren't like that anymore. They're all these guys who have fucking master's degrees and are so 'sophisticated' and 'educated.'"

After his book had come out to striking success, Frey spoke to *Entertainment Weekly.* "When I walk into Random House, they treat me like a rock star," he said. "People are breathless. They can't believe I'm alive. They're like 'Oh! Oh! Oh!'"

Is it any surprise that such a self-absorbed poseur should, in his book, have pumped up his life to make it seem more violent, painful, melodramatic, and extreme than it was? Of course not. Nor was it a surprise to see Frey talking again, post-scandal, in the summer of 2008, to *Vanity Fair,* in what he claimed would be his last interview ever. The author of the article, Evgenia Peretz, observed:

> At the age of 38, he still makes crank calls. Sometimes he'll call from the street corner and put on a high-pitched, crazy-old-person voice, drawing out every syllable of your name. Sometimes he pretends to be in an emergency, as he did the other day when he phoned his editor's assistant:
>
> "Allison, fuck, Allison, I need your help now! I'm on the corner of 56th and Fifth Avenue and a fucking bus just drove by and drenched me! I have

two more meetings and I need you to go buy me some underwear and buy me some pants."

AFTER SPENDING SEVERAL YEARS thinking and reading about the standard of truth in memoir, I am pleased to reproduce the wisest statement about it that I've ever come across. It was written in 1960 by a *New York Times* reporter named Raymond Walters, Jr. He observed:

> The reader who picks up an autobiography merely for several hours' entertainment is not likely to be troubled about its truthfulness as long as it tells a good yarn. But what of the reader who hopes to learn something about the ways of the world and how one individual responded to them? He may follow a method discerning critics have used for centuries: when you start reading an autobiography, think of it as a person to whom you have just been introduced. Size up as best you can the personality of the man or woman who is talking and take it constantly into consideration as you judge the truthfulness of what he has to say.

The people we encounter as we go about our lives are always telling us "true" stories. (I think the last time I listened to a made-up tale presented as such, I was sitting around a fire at Camp Brant Lake.) We read memoirs just as we listen to these people: always poised to judge their intelligence, their insight, their credibility. Sometimes we encounter a puffed-up braggart who is the hero of every story, or else the victim; we doubt his every other word. An aggrieved tone, or a low talker who invades our personal space, or someone who gets too intimate too soon? We're looking for the nearest exit. Someone who seems to remember too many details from too long ago is dubious, too. Once in a while the person talking is just plain funny; the wink in her eye and the tone of her voice tells us we shouldn't take anything she says too literally. Then there are the prodigious storytellers. They look us straight in the eye, and they have us from the first word. There may be—there probably are—hidden deceptions in these people's tales. But we never find them out.

ACKNOWLEDGMENTS

It's my pleasure to offer my thanks to the following people for different kinds of assistance and support: Shalom Auslander, Bruce Beans, Jerry Beasley, Steven Bernhardt, Peter Canby, John Caskey, Cynthia Crossen, Wes Davis, Carl Dawson, Jim Dean, Bruce Dorsey, Dave Eggers, Ann Fabian, David Friedman, Tad Friend, Henry Louis Gates, Jr., Marianne Green, Steven Helmling, Martha Hodes, McKay Jenkins, Erik Leefeldt, Donald Mell, Randall Miller, Elizabeth Mosier, Alan Rinzler, Charles Robinson, David Rosenthal, Al Silverman, Rachel Simon, Paul Slovak, Bill Stempel, Rick Valelly, and Tobias Wolff. As always, I am grateful to librarians, specifically Susan Brynteson and Linda Stein, of the University of Delaware Library, and Alison Masterpasqua, Chris Gebert, Linda Hunt, and Mary Ann Wood of Swarthmore College. Thanks to Tye Comer, Brianna Buckley, and Jim King of the Nielsen Company for giving me access to proprietary information. Certainly deserving of a separate sentence are my crack research assistants—Jocelyn Terranova did the most work, but also providing valuable service were Maura Brady,

Kirsten Cotton, Stefanie Gordon, Jordan Mebane, Kathryn Pellegrini, Dane Secor, Sue Wiker, Lizy Yagoda, and Maria Yagoda (who translated Simone Signoret from the French). This book was dreamed up by Geoffrey Kloske of Riverhead Books; I hope he still thinks it's a good idea. I certainly always appreciated his smart reactions on the other end of the line. Thanks also to his efficient associate, Laura Perciasepe. Stuart Krichevsky of the eponymous literary agency, so ably assisted by Shana Cohen and Kathryne Wick, is the man. If I ever were to write my own memoir, it would start and end with Gigi Simeone, Lizy Yagoda, and Maria Yagoda. There would be some good stuff in the middle as well.

A NOTE ON SOURCES

I made significant use of the following bibliographies: Patricia K. Addis, *Through a Woman's "I": An Annotated Bibliography of American Women's Autobiographical Writings, 1946–1976* (Metuchen, New Jersey: Scarecrow Press, 1983); Mary Louise Briscoe, *American Autobiography, 1945–1980: A Bibliography* (Madison: University of Wisconsin Press, 1982); Louis Kaplan, *A Bibliography of American Autobiographies* (Madison: University of Wisconsin Press, 1961); and William Matthews, *British Autobiographies: An Annotated Bibliography of British Autobiographies Published or Written Before 1951* (Berkeley: University of California Press, 1955). A great deal of information about sales and bestseller status can be found in Alice Payne Hackett and James Henry Burke, *80 Years of Best Sellers 1895–1975* (New York: R. R. Bowker, 1977); Keith L. Justice, *Bestseller Index: All Books, Publishers Weekly and The New York Times Through 1990*; and Michael Korda, *Making the List: A Cultural History of the American Bestseller, 1900–1999* (New York: Barnes & Noble, 1999). *American National Biography* and the *Dictionary of National Biography* were useful reference works. I am grateful to the proprietors of *The New York Times, The New Yorker, Time, The Times* of London, *Publishers Weekly*, and *The Bookseller* for making all or part of their archives available online. NewspaperArchive.com, a commercial service, was helpful for digging up old articles in small-town newspapers.

ADDITIONAL SECONDARY WORKS CITED

Adams, Timothy Dow. *Telling Lies in Modern American Autobiography*. Chapel Hill: University of North Carolina Press, 1990.

Amelang, James. *The Flight of Icarus: Artisan Autobiography in Early Modern Europe*. Stanford, California: Stanford University Press, 1998.

Andrews, William. *To Tell a Free Story: The First Century of Afro-American Autobiography, 1760–1865*. Urbana: University of Illinois Press, 1986.

"Are Literary Hoaxes Harmful?" *The Bookman* 69 (1929).

Barclay, C. R. "Accuracies and Inaccuracies in Autobiographical Memories." *Journal of Memory and Language* 25 (1986).

Bartlett, Frederic C. *Remembering: A Study in Experimental and Social Psychology*. Cambridge, England: The University Press, 1932.

Beverley, John. "The Margins at the Center." In Paul John Eakin, ed., *The Ethics of Life Writing*. Ithaca, New York: Cornell University Press, 2001.

Billington, Ray Allen. *The Protestant Crusade, 1800–1860: A Study of the Origins of American Nativism*. New York: Rinehart, 1938.

Bissinger, Buzz. "Ruthless with Scissors." *Vanity Fair*, January 2007.

Bjorklund, Diane. *Interpreting the Self: Two Hundred Years of American Autobiography*. Chicago: University of Chicago Press, 1998.

Blackburn, Julia. *With Billie*. New York: Pantheon, 2005.

Browder, Laura. *Slippery Characters: Ethnic Impersonators and American Identities*. Chapel Hill: University of North Carolina Press, 2000.

Campbell, Jeremy. *The Liar's Tale: A History of Falsehood*. New York: W. W. Norton, 2001.

Cockshut, A. O. J. *The Art of Autobiography in 18th and 19th Century England*. New Haven: Yale University Press, 1984.

Coe, Richard. *When the Grass Was Taller: Autobiography and the Experience of Childhood*. New Haven: Yale University Press, 1984.

Couzens, Tim. *Tramp Royal: The True Story of Trader Horn with Such of His Philosophy As Is the Gift of Age and Experience Learned in His Quest from Joss House to Doss House*. Johannesburg, South Africa: Ravan Press and Witwatersrand University Press, 1992.

Delany, Paul. *British Autobiography in the Seventeenth Century*. London: Routledge & Kegan Paul, 1969.

Dieterle, Ben. "Teen Death Diary." *SL Weekly*, June 3, 2004.

Fabian, Ann. *The Unvarnished Truth: Personal Narration in Nineteenth-Century America*. Berkeley: University of California Press, 2000.

Fleischner, Jennifer. *Mrs. Lincoln and Mrs. Keckly: The Remarkable Story of the Friendship Between a First Lady and a Former Slave*. New York: Broadway Books, 2003.

Friedman, Bruce Jay. Foreword to Adam Parfrey, *It's a Man's World: Men's Adventure Magazines—The Postwar Pulps*. Los Angeles: Feral House, 2003.

Gates, Henry Louis, Jr., ed. *The Classic Slave Narratives*. New York: New American Library, 1987.

Gibson, Ian. *The Erotomaniac: The Secret Life of Henry Spencer Ashbee*. New York: Da Capo, 2001.

Grosskurth, Phyllis. Introduction to *The Memoirs of John Addington Symonds*. New York: Random House, 1984.

Halttunen, Karen. *Confidence Men and Painted Women: A Study of Middle-Class Culture in America, 1830–1870*. New Haven: Yale University Press, 1982.

Hindmarsh, D. Bruce. *The Evangelical Conversion Narrative: Spiritual Autobiography in Early Modern England*. Oxford and New York: Oxford University Press, 2005.

Lejeune, Philippe. *On Autobiography*. Ed. Paul John Eakin; trans. Katherine Leary. Minneapolis: University of Minnesota Press, 1989.

Loftus, Elizabeth, and Katherine Ketcham. *The Myth of Repressed Memory: False Memories and Allegations of Sexual Abuse*. New York: St. Martin's Press, 1994.

Mächler, Stefan. *The Wilkomirski Affair: A Study in Biographical Truth*. Trans. John E. Woods. New York: Schocken Books, 2001.

Maurois, André. *Aspects of Biography*. Trans. Sydney Castle Roberts. New York: D. Appleton, 1929.

McFeely, William. *Grant: A Biography*. New York: W. W. Norton, 1981.

Mott, Frank Luther. *Golden Multitudes: The Story of Best Sellers in the United States*. New York: Macmillan, 1947.

Myers, Eric. *Uncle Mame: The Life of Patrick Dennis.* New York: St. Martin's Press, 2000.

Nathan, Debbie, and Michael Snedeker. *Satan's Silence: Ritual Abuse and the Making of a Modern American Witch Hunt.* New York: Basic Books, 1995.

Neisser, Ulric. "John Dean's Memory: A Case Study." *Cognition* 9 (1981).

Neisser, Ulric, and Nicole Harsch. "Phantom Flashbulbs: False Recollections of Hearing the News About *Challenger.*" In Eugene Winograd and Ulric Neisser, eds., *Affect and Accuracy in Recall: Studies of "Flashbulb" Memories.* New York: Cambridge University Press, 1992.

Pascal, Roy, *Design and Truth in Autobiography.* Cambridge, Massachusetts: Harvard University Press, 1960.

Passantino, Bob, Gretchen Passantino, and Jon Trott. "Satan's Sideshow: The True Lauren Stratford Story." *Cornerstone* 18 (1990).

Peretz, Evgenia. "James Frey's Morning After." *Vanity Fair,* June 2008.

Rohter, Larry. "Tarnished Laureate." *The New York Times,* December 15, 1998.

Saxon, A. H. *P. T. Barnum: The Legend and the Man.* New York: Columbia University Press, 1989.

Schacter, Daniel L. *The Seven Sins of Memory: How the Mind Forgets and Remembers.* Boston: Houghton Mifflin, 2001.

Shumaker, Wayne. *English Autobiography: Its Emergence, Materials, and Form.* Berkeley: University of California Press, 1954.

Sloan, James Park. *Jerzy Kosinski: A Biography.* New York: Dutton, 1996.

Smith, Donald B. *Chief Buffalo Child Long Lance: The Glorious Imposter.* Calgary, Canada: Red Deer Press, 1999.

Stoll, David. *Rigoberta Menchú and the Story of All Poor Guatemalans.* Boulder, Colorado: Westview Press, 1999.

Thwaite, Ann. *Edmund Gosse: A Literary Landscape, 1849–1928.* Chicago: University of Chicago Press, 1984.

Treadwell, James. *Autobiographical Writing and British Literature, 1783–1834.* New York: Oxford University Press, 2005.

Umansky, Ellen. "Representations of Jewish Women in the Works and Life of Elizabeth Stern." *Modern Judaism* 113 (1993).

Van de Water, Frederic. "The Ghost Writers." *Scribner's Magazine* 85 (1929).

VanDerBeets, Richard. *The Indian Captivity Narrative: An American Genre.* Lanham, Maryland: University Press of America, 1984.

Walters, Raymond, Jr. "The Confessions of Practically Everybody." *The New York Times*, September 11, 1960.

Waxman, Zoë. *Writing the Holocaust: Identity, Testimony.* New York: Oxford University Press, 2006.

Wilson, Robin. "Anthropologist Challenges Veracity of Multicultural Icon." *The Chronicle of Higher Education* 15 (January 1999).

Wiseman, T. P., "The Publication of *De Bello Gallico*." In Kathryn Welch and Anton Powell, eds., *Julius Caesar as Artful Reporter: The War Commentaries as Political Instruments.* Swansea: The Classical Press of Wales, 1998.

INDEX OF MEMOIRISTS AND
AUTOBIOGRAPHERS

ABOUT THE AUTHOR

Ben Yagoda is a journalism professor in the English Department at the University of Delaware. He is the author of *Will Rogers: A Biography*; *When You Catch an Adjective, Kill It: The Parts of Speech, for Better and/or Worse*; *The Sound on the Page: Style and Voice in Writing*; *The Art of Fact: A Historical Anthology of Literary Journalism* (coedited with Kevin Kerrane); *About Town: The New Yorker and the World It Made*, and *All in a Lifetime: An Autobiography* (with Dr. Ruth Westheimer). He has written for *Slate*, *The Chronicle of Higher Education*, *The New York Times Book Review*, *Stop Smiling*, and many other publications. Yagoda lives in Swarthmore, Pennsylvania, with his wife and two daughters.